THE DANGEROUS
EDGE

GAVIN LAMBERT
THE DANGEROUS EDGE

BARRIE & JENKINS
COMMUNICA - EUROPA

First published in 1975 by
Barrie & Jenkins Limited
24 Highbury Crescent, London N5 IRX

ISBN 0 214 20076 0

Printed in Great Britain by The Anchor Press Ltd
and bound by Wm Brendon & Son Ltd
both of Tiptree, Essex

To Paul Bowles

CONTENTS

Prologue

Our interest's on the dangerous edge of things.
The honest thief, the tender murderer,
The superstitious atheist . . .

Robert Browning,
Bishop Blougram's Apology

In his autobiography, *A Sort of Life*, Graham Greene writes that he would choose Browning's lines as an epigraph for all his novels. When he first read them as a student, they promised and warned of a particular world – violent, mysterious, conflicted. Today they sum up an obsession that he shares with the other subjects of this book, all of them driven to interpret life in terms of melodrama. Raymond Chandler has most accurately defined melodrama as 'an exaggeration of violence and fear beyond what one normally experiences in life'. Yet all art exaggerates some kind of experience. The mystery of the crime-artist – a generic term for this group of novelists and a film-maker – is why he chooses this distinctive method and what it means to us and to him.

It begins with the discovery of a country in which the dominant reality is criminal. To reach the dangerous edge is to find a point of no return. The same obsession grips the atheist as well as the Roman Catholic, the public figure and the recluse. It becomes a protest against defying the will of society or the will of God. It uncovers impulses at war within the self. It betrays fear of social change and fear of the existing order. Whatever the protest or the fear, a dark cloud is always moving nearer. External mystery of plot – flight and pursuit, riddle and warning – creates a metaphor for the deeper mystery of the threat itself.

The first map of the country was made halfway through the nineteenth century by Wilkie Collins. Although he didn't invent the detective or the mystery novel, he was the first to grasp its expressive possibilities. The genre became personal with *The Woman in White* and mechanical soon afterwards.

ix

But a few genuine explorers persisted, of whom Greene, Simenon, Eric Ambler, and Hitchcock in films, still survive. It seems likely that they will be the last. *In Cold Blood* signalled the end of one direction and the beginning of another. For this reason the moment is apt for a summing up.

To trace the separate lives of crime-artists is like trying to find the vital but submerged link between the different travellers who passed each other on *The Bridge of San Luis Rey*. Relating the biographical material to the work and looking for figures in both carpets, I decided to follow one of Sherlock Holmes's favourite principles of detection: Truth is usually a matter of seizing the correct improbability.

To be seduced by fear and to convey it so fanatically, one must have felt its power some time before the end of childhood. Adolescents are not quite vulnerable enough. Uncertainty is one of the hardest things for a child to bear – and suspense, as the adult imagination conceives it, is still based on that vivid apprehensive need to know what's going to happen next. Most children have moments of paranoia when the world seems in monstrous conspiracy against them. Everyone then becomes potentially murderer, pursuer, enemy, and life a struggle between hunters and hunted. So many childhood games project that situation. For the adult unable to shake off early influences, the division of hunter and hunted remains and the pattern of identification with victim or killer grows set. Then curiosity and dread interact. The quarry must finally be cornered and the antagonist's motive unlocked. The climax of most crime stories is ritualistic, almost dreamlike – Holmes face to face with Moriarty at the Reichenbach falls, Buchan's Richard Hannay transfixed by his own prey across the precipice in Scotland, the Hitchcock hero lured to confrontation on Mount Rushmore or the isolated bell-tower, Chandler's Marlowe in the empty room as he waits for the last door to open.

We are not led gradually in this world to a point of no return, but begin on the edge. The cold sweat is a condition of daily life and Buchan's 'How thin is the protection of civilization' the warning that hangs in the air. This appeal to an immediate sense-response of panic and excitement creates a wrinkle in the fastidious nose. But doesn't the nose fail to see further than itself? The record contradicts all the familiar charges of sensationalism, lack of depth, escape from reality. When asked why he so often chose to write thrillers, Greene pointed out that subjects choose writers. 'It sometimes seems as though our whole planet has swung into the fog belt of melodrama . . .' His answer echoes the most compelling crime stories since 1850, which are touched with prophecy, not evasion. The charge of sensationalism becomes the escape from reality. A glance at the newspaper refutes it.

Only one recent crime story is the imaginative equal of Chandler's last novel, and it re-creates an actual happening and 'invents' nothing at all. To illuminate the facts of *In Cold Blood*, Truman Capote chooses the crime novelist's basic apparatus of suspense, betrayal and pursuit. On one level he recognizes today's fact through yesterday's fiction. On another he detects a link with his own early life in the deprived and wretched childhood of a young murderer. The shared experience produces both a creative and a destructive person, and leads one to become obsessed with the other. It provides a clue to the mystery that haunts all the subjects of this book.

An increasingly regulated society not only arouses in many people the desire to escape, but makes escape more difficult. Until the First World War dissatisfaction could be relaxed by drugs, since laudanum was freely available in many countries. The occult offered the stimulus of ghosts and mediums, a trip to the irrational. Travel books provided transportation to exotic and primitive ways of life, dime novels and penny dreadfuls released fantasies of sex and aggression. A privileged few could even live like outlaws, rejecting established conventions without ending up in jail. They could even end up as heroes. Explorers like Burton, creative adventurers as different as Gauguin, Rimbaud and Isadora Duncan, even gunfighters like Wyatt Earp, confronted danger, loneliness, ridicule – but they freed themselves from the pressure of the human crack. Their lives might be cut short and yet they remained somehow complete, faithful to the idea of a private destiny. Some died unhappy, but perhaps this was the least unconventional thing about them.

When exits begin to close, the possibilities of release are narrowed. T. E. Lawrence typifies the new dilemma, driven to escape from himself but uncertain where to go. A private freedom slips away when almost everywhere is on the map. The next explorers of a totally untouched region, the astronauts, are no longer individual agents but uniformed servants of the state. Other mysteries are pre-empted by the middle class, mediums employed for assurance that the next world is friendly and respectable, astrologers contacting the silent planets for tips on investments. All kinds of vicarious escape – books, movies, the new mass availability of travel – inevitably confront the law of diminishing returns.

One route has remained open. For the double man interned with his obsessions, the criminal life has always been the most democratic choice, accessible in some form to all. In the end it offers only a new set of pressures, but so intense and fantastic that they can be glamourized by the name of risk. The successful criminal aims for freedom by celebrating the death of conscience, which means defining 'right' and 'good' as whatever he wants. But after this act of self-assertion he must settle for a masked and anonymous life. To get away literally with murder he has to abandon any hope of recognition and satisfy his vanity in secret. He will be safer if not too intellectual or gifted with a sense of theatre, for here again the temptation to show off is strong. (Vanity and carelessness, a by-product of vanity, are the flaws that most often lead to capture.) Most important of all, he commits himself to the situation of the hunted man, in which any close human involvement is an invitation to betrayal. The prescription for secrecy, mistrust and remoteness is not far from Joyce's motto for survival as an artist: 'Silence, exile, cunning.' An implicit point of departure for this book is the criminal act as a gesture of the imagination, equally appealing to criminal and artist.

When Wilkie Collins developed the idea of writing novels 'with a secret', he was thinking not only of the puzzle element in detective stories but of something traumatically buried and seeking release. The ideal mystery, Chandler has written, is 'one you would read if the end was missing'. The crime-artist, as opposed to the technician of the genre, uses the devices of melodrama to discover 'the strange coincidences, the plannings, the cross purposes, the wonderful chain of events . . . leading to the most *outré* results', as Conan Doyle expressed it through Holmes. Shock, with its threat of the alien and inexplicable, is his basic weapon. 'There was no *because*,' one of Simenon's murderers insists, 'it was a word for fools.'

'Those extraordinary accidents and events which happen to few men' seemed to Wilkie Collins 'legitimate materials for fiction to work with', just as much as 'the ordinary accidents and events which may, and do, happen to us all'. When an extraordinary accident happens to someone he becomes, instantly, an outsider. He is placed in a situation where he either rejects everyday beliefs and assumptions or they cease to be helpful. The whole ordinary world is a long cry away. The accident transforms him into an archetypal character – murderer, victim, spy, hunted man – whose predicament is a metaphor of isolation. In Collins's best novels, and those of his successors, crimes lead like underground passages to a discovery about the foundations of the world above.

The idea of a story 'with a secret' leads back, by way of Poe, to the autobiography of a French detective, Eugène Vidocq was a criminal who became a successful police spy and then the first chief of the Paris Sûreté in 1811. Later he returned to crime and ended where he began, in obscure respectability. His *Mémoires* were probably dramatized with the aid of a ghost-writer, like those of Mafia figures today, but Collins and Conan Doyle, as well as Poe, found them a rich source of mythology and fact. Vidocq had an unquestioned genius for disguise which enabled him to give the first insider's account of both the detective and the criminal world. Hunter and hunted, working for both sides, he proved that established authority and crime could be opposite faces of the same coin. Here his shadow reaches forward as far as Chandler, whose novels are dedicated to this proposition. The most spectacular anecdote in the *Mémoires* comes from Vidocq's period as a police spy. Assigned (in disguise) to track down and liquidate an elusive criminal, only Vidocq knows that the quarry is himself.

It seems likely that the situation inspired Poe's *William Wilson*. '*In me thou didst exist*,' says the dying man to his assailant, '*and, in my death, see by this image, which is thine own, how utterly thou hast murdered thyself*.' Certainly Vidocq's methods sparked Poe's creation of the puzzle story with a fictional detective. Dupin, though on the side of the law, is 'perhaps of a diseased intelligence'. *The Murders in the*

Rue Morgue (1841) is the first and most ingenious of these stories, none of which shows Poe's imagination at its freest. Thinly characterized essays in deductive logic, they contain puzzles too laboured to be dramatic. Poe's symbolic pieces are much more arresting, and one of them, influenced by the persona rather than the techniques of Vidocq, projects a powerful vision of the criminal as hunted man. The Man of the Crowd is old and decrepit, but something in his appearance suggests ideas of 'vast mental power, of caution, of penurious-ness, of avarice, of coolness, of malice, of blood-thirstiness, of triumph, of merriments, of excessive terror . . .'. Following him as he wanders through a city, the narrator discovers someone who cannot bear to be alone. Perpetually on the run, he is unable to make contact with the crowd and yet terrified of not being part of it. In this estrangement from himself and alienation from the world Poe senses 'the type and genius of deep crime'.

At this point the narrator gives up the chase. Face to face for a moment with his quarry, he has his intuition and delib-erately turns away. Some secrets, he feels, never reveal them-selves. The essence of all crime remains 'undivulged'. The hunted creature is allowed to escape and disappear again into the vast unknowing crowd.

The detection of crime, Poe implies, lies beyond the crimi-nologist's grasp and has nothing to do with the technical solution of a problem. The Man of the Crowd symbolizes everything that Dupin will never decode. Having invented the puzzle story, Poe defines its limitations. Chandler echoes him when he describes the ideal mystery as a story without an end. Most crime-artists are haunted by the idea that solving a puzzle involves dishonesty or anticlimax. To fool the reader is to cheat him. In fact the only detective novels that go beyond a mechanical puzzle to the creative puzzle of life are *The Moon-stone* and some of Simenon's Maigret series: the only detective stories, the Sherlock Holmes cycle and a few of Father Brown's adventures. In each case the writer is concerned with raising questions, not answering them. The crime-artist's solution is a stimulant, the technician's a sedative.

The history and ingenuity of the detective novel has been well studied by its devotees, but their approach is inevitably the opposite of mine. They look at Collins, Conan Doyle, Simenon and others as superior exponents of a fixed genre. They subdivide Greene, Chandler and the rest into writers of spy stories and thrillers. But to fix a genre is to make it academic. The creative approach starts from scratch. Collins switches from the labyrinth of the puzzle to the stretched-out line of pursuit and suspense. Conan Doyle and Simenon find innumerable variations within a precisely structured world. Chandler is impatient with structure. The profiles in this book are of individual artists whose only fixed element is the mystery of the criminal himself.

For Greene he is one of the damned. For Eric Ambler he is beyond normal feeling and 'emotionally *un*disturbed'. For Simenon he is his own victim and for Chandler he embodies 'the simplest and yet most complete pattern of the tensions on which we live'. In every case he emerges as a private fear made public. A crime may or may not be detected, as Collins wrote, but its *raison d'être* lies in the fact that it was committed.

ONE
Enemy Country

There is probably no better proof of the accuracy of that definition of man which describes him as an imitative animal, than is to be found in the fact that the verdict of humanity is always against any individual member of the species who presumes to differ from the rest.

Wilkie Collins,
The Dead Secret

London, 1855: a warm, still, late night in late summer, with a full moon. The young pre-Raphaelite painter J. E. Millais (already famous), the young writer Wilkie Collins (not yet famous) and his brother (a painter and writer never to be famous), are taking a stroll near Regent's Park after a dinner party. The streets are empty and silent. Passing the garden of a villa with a high wall and an iron gate, the three men are stunned by the sound of a loud and desperate scream.

What happened next was told many years later in the biography of Millais by his son:

. . . the iron gate leading to the garden was dashed open, and from it came the figure of a young and very beautiful woman dressed in flowing white robes that shone in the moonlight. She seemed to float rather than run in their direction, and, on coming up to the three young men, she paused for a moment in an attitude of supplication and terror. Then, suddenly seeming to recollect herself, she suddenly moved on and vanished in the shadows cast upon the road.

The painter could only remark, 'What a lovely woman!' But the writer said at once, 'I must see who she is, and what is the matter,' and ran after her. The others waited a few minutes, then continued their walk when he didn't return. Next day they all met again and found Collins mysteriously reluctant to talk. Under pressure he admitted that he'd caught up with the woman and found out what was the matter.

For several months she'd been kept prisoner by the owner of the villa, and because of his threats and 'mesmeric influence' never dared to try and escape. Finally, on the night that the three of them happened to be walking past, she could bear it

1

no longer and fled from the house. The man came after her with a poker, yelling that he'd beat her brains out. At the sudden arrival of witnesses he gave up and went back inside.

This was all that Collins would tell, maybe all that he knew. The woman said her name was Caroline Graves. She had a baby daughter who was somehow rescued later from the villa. The sinister jailer was called Graves, but it's not certain that he was Caroline's husband. She may simply have taken his name for the sake of respectability. How she met him and why he kept her prisoner remains unknown. Within a few days Collins and Caroline began living together. They remained lovers (with one interruption) until he died, and were eventually buried side by side. Her rescue provided the starting point for Collins's first widely successful novel, *The Woman in White*, published five years later.

'Those extraordinary accidents and events which happen to few men . . .' Collins had published his manifesto as the preface to an early novel, *Basil*, three years before the scream and the apparition in the moonlight. In a sense the pattern of his life had already been set. By going to live with him, Caroline only confirmed his position as a complete outsider in Victorian society.

The isolation began with his appearance. The rescuer was a far from romantic figure, just over five feet tall, with an abnormally large and almost hydrocephalous head, abnormally weak eyes behind thin steel-rimmed spectacles, tiny feet that could fit snugly into the smallest size of women's shoes. Although thirty-one, he still lived at home with his mother.

Wilkie's childhood and adolescence had been shaped by a prolonged duel with his father. A successful academic painter of landscapes, William Collins was one of those genuinely affectionate tyrants, loving and unjust at the same time. Believing in the value of 'aristocratic connections', he sent his son to a fashionable private school. There Wilkie first discovered, like many writers, the existence of hell on earth. His physical appearance made him a natural victim and he quickly sensed that the best way to deal with torturers is to distract them. The pressures of fear released his talents as a story-teller. Not always inventive enough to postpone the game of whipping and beating, he could quite often gain remission and a piece of candy. Years later he made a laconic comment on the advantages of an expensive education: 'I learnt to be amusing at a short notice.'

While still at school he knew that he wanted to write. His father opposed the idea and apprenticed him as clerk to a firm of London tea-brokers. He began writing a novel about ancient Rome in his spare time. 'Tact and taste' was the tyrant's verdict after reading the first half, but he remained unsympathetic to Wilkie becoming a professional writer. With no apparent logic or predictability he offered his son the chance of leaving the tea business to study law. Wilkie chose what seemed the lesser of two evils.

But the old man had unintentionally steered him to an important creative experience. Attending a few trials, Wilkie became fascinated by the rituals of prosecution, defence and conflicting evidence. An image occurred: he saw an arena in which games of truth were played out. The image dropped back somewhere into his subconscious, to be rediscovered later and have a detonating effect on his work.

In the meantime, less than a year after Wilkie began his law studies, his father died. His will exacted a last act of obedience from beyond the grave, demanding that Wilkie write his biography. The duty was performed and Wilkie's first work published at the family's expense in 1848. Returning to his story of ancient Rome, the young writer began his career as a novelist. By staying on with his mother at the old man's house he could live very comfortably and uneventfully (until he met Caroline Graves) on the income his father left him.

Accused of murdering ten woman and the seventeen-year-old son of one of them, convicted on circumstantial evidence, Landru was asked on his way to the guillotine, 'What is the truth?' His answer, like his life, was a model of imaginative self-effacement. 'My secret is my piece of hand-luggage,' he said, before moving on like Poe's Man of the Crowd with his mystery undivulged.

Wilkie Collins's hand-luggage is full of secrets. The old master of the detective and mystery story presented a witty, genial and reserved surface. At school he had discovered a good deal about human cruelty and from his father he learned the pain of humiliation. While several of his early novels note its scars, his persona from the first was cool and ironic. As a

3

young man he ruled out established society and never changed his mind. It struck him as dominated by injustice and hypocrisy and he was never interested in being accepted by the great world. Although his pride demanded professional success, he despised its social rewards. The fixtures of family and church left him indifferent. The feared and powerful father had been notably pious; the son embraced atheism. His strongest emotional attachment was to his mother, and he never married. Before Caroline Graves there had been no personal involvement with women. Their relationship led to the writing of one mystery story and the living of another.

After they'd been together for a few years Caroline claimed to have news that Graves was dead. She insisted that Collins marry her and threatened, if he refused, to accept the proposal of a local plumber. Collins not only refused but promptly arranged a wedding with the plumber and attended it as a witness. Shortly afterwards he met another woman, obscure and derelict, and set her up as his mistress. The arrangement with Martha Rudd had lasted over two years when Caroline, disillusioned with her plumber, asked Wilkie to take her back. They resumed living together, but Collins still supported and visited Martha in a separate establishment, and had three children by her. Impossible to guess what he really felt about either of the women, but reasonable to suppose that in his private life he was sardonically determined to break all the rules. Social disapproval only confirmed his opinion of society.

The historical novel, *Antonina*, had been a false start and one of Collins's few homages to convention. Afterwards he began his own journey. It led him to the underground of his time, a world of criminals, victims, grotesques and drop-outs that appealed to his sense of isolation. From his father, whose correct but accomplished landscapes he admired, he had inherited a strong visual intelligence. As a law student he had learned the value of documentation. Setting out to explore London on foot and by bus, he collected evidence of what was already in his mind – a city (and by extension a society) that concealed half its face. A few blocks away from the Strand, at that time the most elegant street in Europe, he could step into alleys with appalling tenement slums that stank of excrement and uncollected corpses. Even by day many of them were

4

unsafe for strangers. At night the nineteenth-century equivalent of mugging, known as coshing, haunted a multitude of underlit streets. In the slums of the East End, like an image from a bad dream, dead cats and dogs floated on black stagnant lakes. Respectable districts also had their enclaves of mystery: blood-stained abortionist and squalid private mental home on the quiet residential avenue, and of course handsome villas with terrified prisoners.

Whatever his personal feelings about her, Collins was fascinated by Caroline as a symbolic figure. She signalled the presence of the irrational hidden below the rational surface, like the month-old bodies in their coffins in the back street below the fashionable hotel. In a novel by Collins the submerged element will always force its way up with an explosion – violence, psychosis, drugs, suicide. The effect is enthusiastically crude in the early *Basil* and *Hide and Seek*. But in *The Dead Secret* (1857), which appeared two years after the encounter with Caroline, her impact is conveyed in a character who seems like a first sketch for the strange and disturbed Woman in White. Apart from the secret itself, this novel develops another favourite device, the idea of substitution. A girl brought up as the heir to an important estate turns out to be the illegitimate daughter of a maidservant and a miner. Collins has not yet mastered the explanation scene, that usually fatal curse of the detective story, but until it arrives the suspense has a personal tone, at once ominous and sarcastic. Technically the novel makes a sharp departure from its time, its structure dense and compact, dispensing with the usual three-volume baggage. It also contains two darkly original characters, disturbers of the ordered world who reflect Collins's ironic-sinister vision.

The secret of the girl's birth is contained in a letter. Her real mother, bowing to her false mother's deathbed instructions, hides it in a closed-up wing of the house. Collins describes the maidservant as already traumatized by the original lie and act of substitution. Her eyes betray a perpetual contraction of anxiety, her face is still pale from remembered shock, but the colour of her hair reveals the most 'unnatural change' of all:

She looked, from the eyes downward, a woman who had barely reached thirty years of age. From the eyes upwards, the effect of her

5

abundant grey hair, seen in connection with her face, was simply incongruous – it was absolutely startling: so startling as to make it no paradox to say that she would have looked most natural, most like herself, if her hair had been dyed. In her case, Art would have seemed to be the truth, because Nature looked like falsehood.

Essentially gentle, able for much of the time to deal with everyday realities and even hold down a job, Sarah Leeson reacts with violent paranoia to anything that threatens discovery of the letter. Anxiety makes her so unnaturally polite and deferential that the frightened creature herself provokes fear. Such a person *is*, of course, potentially dangerous, and we see it when Collins describes her behaviour through the eyes of someone who knows nothing about her. The first of several female characters in his novels who live in a state of repressed hysteria, she walks the borderline of sanity, unable to find release. Dostoyevsky was not the only novelist who anticipated Freud.

The drop-out from the privileged family is an equally original creation. Immuring himself in a house in London, he rejects all contact with the outside world. Treverton's isolation began when he was attracted to a student at college and discovered the boy was only interested in his money. He turns into 'Timon of London' and forms a two-man commune with his servant. They grow their own vegetables, grind their own corn, brew their own beer and wear beards at a time when the habit is considered 'proof of unsoundness of intellect'. To his family and former friends Treverton is a lost man, to himself someone who refuses ever to suffer again for his belief in other people. The character is clearly an ironic projection of Collins the outsider with his subterranean life and chosen estrangement from society.

For the rest, *The Dead Secret* shows Collins getting the feel of a new genre and learning how to sustain an atmospheric undercurrent of danger. A night-time prologue set in a Cornish estate describes the death of the false mother. Her husband is away at sea, servants gossip in the basement. The ex-actress lies in a huge shadowy bed in a remote wing of the house, all her play scripts scattered around her, surf pounding outside the windows. She plays a last scene, threatening to haunt her maid from beyond the grave if the secret is not kept. Sarah Leeson hides the letter as instructed, then disappears without trace.

6

With an abruptness like a quick cut in a movie Collins takes up the story fifteen years later. The substituted child has grown up into a young woman with all the charming arrogance of the class to which she thinks she belongs. She marries a blind man and seems to enjoy dominating him. Collins's fascination with physical abnormality leads to some absorbing detection passages. Leonard's hyper-acute other senses help his wife to discover the letter:

'What are the walls like?' asked Leonard, placing his hand on the wall behind him while he spoke.
'They are covered with paper, are they not?'
'Yes, with faded red paper, except on one side, where strips have been torn off and thrown on the floor. There is wainscoting around the walls. It is cracked in many places, and has ragged holes in it, which seem to have been made by the rats and mice.'
'Are there any pictures on the walls?'
'No. There is an empty frame above the fireplace. And, opposite – I mean just above where I am standing now – there is a small mirror cracked in the centre . . . But no pictures anywhere. Now you know everything about the walls. What is the next thing? The floor?'
'I think, Rosamond, my feet have told me already what the floor is like.'

The blind detective (some seventy years before Ernest Bramah's popular creation, Max Carrados) is only one of several original elements here. There is the imaginative setting of a disused room with its emblematic family junk, the final secret buried somewhere among it. A subtle cruelty underscores the tension. Spurred only by curiosity, Rosamond is unconsciously searching for her own humiliation. She has no idea of the contents of the letter that will expose her as lowborn and illegitimate, and since her husband is blind she has to read it aloud.

The Dead Secret collapses only in the last chapter. After the flawed explanation scene Collins has to struggle with a period convention: the happy ending. Long before it confronted Hollywood movie-makers, it acted as a powerful curb on some of the greatest Victorian novelists.

Early in his career Collins had met one of these novelists, and Charles Dickens was to become his only important connection with the literary establishment. The friendship lasted

7

twenty years and went through several phases. At first Collins was the protégé. Dickens published some of his stories in *Household Words*, the magazine he edited. Later he serialized both *The Woman in White* and *The Moonstone* in its successor, *All The Year Round*. The older (and greater) writer was a more conventional person, and a delicate balance always existed in the relations between insider and outsider. In his life, Dickens wanted and achieved social acceptance. In his work, for all its poetic muckraking and ferocious comedy, he found himself essentially on the side of things as they were. Disturbed by Collins's private life – too influenced by 'French novels', he thought – he worried about the alienating effect it might have on the public. (There seems an echo here of Wilkie's father with his insistence on 'aristocratic connections'.) After the enormous popular success of *The Woman in White*, Dickens even became critically wary of his friend's talent. At first he greeted *The Moonstone* with cautious praise, then decided he disliked it. Yet at the end he was imitating his protégé in the unfinished *Mystery of Edwin Drood*.

Dickens and Collins shared two passions, for amateur theatricals and for that new phenomenon, the detective. Together and separately they wrote a number of melodramas and acted in them, usually at charity performances for which the name of Dickens ensured fashionable support. The climax of these was Collins's *The Frozen Deep*, in which the two writers appeared for an audience that included Queen Victoria. They played rival lovers in a story of attempted murder set at the North Pole. Each writer also 'discovered' his own detective. Inspector Field belonged to Dickens, who occasionally accompanied him on police raids and used him as the model for Inspector Bucket in *Bleak House*. Collins appropriated Inspector Whicher and followed his investigation of the Road Murder, a famous case of the time. Sergeant Cuff in *The Moonstone* will reflect Whicher's character and methods.

The writers also visited Paris together and saw the latest melodramas by Dumas and others. But for Collins the city held another, more vital fascination: the Morgue. He would join the crowd that watched the bodies brought in and laid out (and would describe this vividly at the end of *The Woman in White*), his sense of mystery aroused by the display of criminals and victims at the end of the road, the puzzle of what had happened to them, their faces, costumes, wounds. To the accumulating theatre of his world he added another element: histories of famous French criminal cases that he found in bookstalls along the banks of the Seine. They excited his appetite for the real thing.

Soon after finishing *The Dead Secret* he attended a long murder trial in London. Like his early explorations of the city, like the bodies beyond the glass screen in the Morgue, like Inspector Whicher tracking a killer through a maze of clues, it resolved itself into spectacle. The buried image from his days as a law student was revived, and he saw how the drama of the courtroom could be adapted to the novel. The theatre he had already defined as 'drama acted' and the novel as 'drama narrated'. The suspense of a trial suggested how the two could be fused:

By the same means employed here, I thought, one could impart to the reader that acceptance, that sense of belief which I saw produced here by the succession of testimonies so varied in form and nevertheless so strictly unified by their march towards the same goal . . .

When the case was over he decided to make the attempt in his next novel. The experiment with form was not to be the only new attempt of *The Woman in White*. Up to this point the 'secret' in Collins's work had created tension on an effective but relatively subdued level. It never led to confrontation with a major criminal, with 'the type and genius of deep crime'. Collins was now to invent a disturbing archetype, a true original who would later be flattered by several imitations.

Although Count Fosco (self-styled 'Count of the Holy Roman Empire, Knight Grand Cross of the Order of the Brazen Crown, Perpetual Arch-Master of the Rosicrucian Masons of Mesopotamia') speaks fluent English with no trace of an accent, he comes from an ancient though obscure Italian family. Sixty years old and immensely fat, he moves like a ballet dancer and has a baby face. He travels with a menagerie of cockatoos, white mice, canaries and a thin, fiercely adoring wife. The birds perch on his fingers and sing, the mice crawl up his arms and receive kisses, the wife rolls his cigarettes. Fosco loves poetry and music, especially Italian opera. He has a remarkable knowledge of medicine and chemistry and is a practising hypnotist. He has even invented a 'means of petrifying the body after death, so as to preserve it, hard as marble, to the end of time'.

This concertina-player and architect of a pagoda for white mice dandifies his enormous bulk with silk blouses, brocaded waistcoats and purple morocco slippers. He gorges on fruit pies and discourses on the beauty of nightfall, the English character, his tenderness of heart and his theory of light. Outrageously grotesque, he is still attractive to women. 'Women can resist a man's love, a man's fame, a man's personal appearance, and a man's money, but they cannot resist a man's tongue when he knows how to talk to them.' Second thoughts occur only when they look into his eyes. Cold and grey, with a beautiful glitter, they reflect the criminal within, his activities as varied as his conversation and his intelligence chillingly sharpened by a Jesuit education. In the confession finally extorted from Fosco, a document of superb but almost insane conceit, the spy, the informer, the swindler, the seeker of 'illimitable power' through chemistry regrets that so much of his genius has been expended on obtaining money by criminal means for himself and his friend Sir Percival Glyde. Even for a man of such protean talent there is no getting away from money. 'Immense necessity! Universal want! Is there a civilized human being who does not feel for us? How insensible that man must be! Or how rich!'

Like the greatest criminals, Fosco is blessed with infinite cunning, nerve and capacity for self-justification. The 'horrible freshness and cheerfulness and vitality of the man' is overwhelming. (Even after death, his body unclaimed in the Paris Morgue, he remains 'sublime' and women in the crowd exclaim how handsome he is.) Most charming at his most dangerous, he approaches a victim with tender fastidious concern, like the raccoon that cleans its prey before eating it. Collins makes this phenomenon doubly exotic and powerful by importing him to insular nineteenth-century England. At the dinner table of a country house he dismisses with marvellous insolence the English illusion that their country is becoming safe from crime:

'It is truly wonderful,' he said, 'how easily Society can console itself for the worst of its shortcomings with a little bit of clap-trap.

The machinery it has set up for the detection of crime is miserably ineffective – and yet only invent a moral epigram, saying that it works well, and you blind everybody to its blunders from that moment. Crimes cause their own detection, do they? And murder will out (another moral epigram) will it? . . . In the few cases that get into the newspapers, are there not instances of slain bodies found and no murderers ever discovered? Multiply the cases that are reported by the cases that are *not* reported, and the bodies that are found by the bodies that are *not* found, and what conclusion do you come to? This! That there are foolish criminals who are discovered, and wise criminals who escape . . . If the police win, you generally hear all about it. If the police lose, you generally hear nothing. And on this tottering foundation you build up your own comfortable moral maxim that Crime causes its own detection. Yes – all the crime *you* know of. And what of the rest?'

Between the lines, of course, Fosco is discussing his own career and celebrating crimes that remain undetected, obviously confident that he's about to increase their number. *The Woman in White* hinges on an elaborate deception carried out in the most correct surroundings and only gradually suspected by a series of astonished narrators. The crime is based on a French court case that Collins had read about, in which a woman was drugged, hidden away and eventually presumed dead so that her brother could inherit her estate. Collins grafts on to it his favourite substitution theme. The penniless Sir Percival Glyde marries Laura Fairlie, heir to a family fortune. Laura bears a marked resemblance to Anne Catherick, the Woman in White who has escaped from a private asylum as the story opens. Since Anne Catherick is weak in the heart as well as the head, Fosco conceives the idea of frightening her to death, then burying her as Lady Glyde. Laura is drugged and delivered back to the asylum as the Woman in White. In due course her estate will be delivered to Sir Percival.

The central crime leads into a maze of other revelations, emerging as each narrator supplies his testimony of events. Sir Percival's past is uncovered, the true identity of Anne Catherick revealed, the spectacular nature of Fosco himself exposed. Points of view shift, contradict each other, finally coincide. The voices – of aristocrats, servants, lawyers, a doctor, a whore turned respectable, an illiterate, an artist – are all distinct parts of a social composition. Their different levels of perception not only deepen the mystery but reflect Collins's own sympathies and antagonisms. Walter Hartright, the young art-teacher who begins and ends the story, is a low-key hero with some points of resemblance to Collins himself. His father was a successful artist, he is devoted to his widowed mother, his visual intelligence responds sharply to the lonely place and the incongruous image. The meeting with the Woman in White establishes a powerful uneasy atmosphere, pushed almost to the frontier of dreams – the walk home late at night through an empty heat-struck city, the solitary road, the silhouetted houses, the touch of a hand laid suddenly on Hartright's shoulder, the troubled apparition with 'her hand pointing to the dark cloud over London'. It reproduces almost exactly the encounter with Caroline Graves:

We set our faces towards London, and walked on together in the first still hour of the new day – I, and this woman, whose name, whose character, whose story, whose objects in life, whose very presence by my side, at that moment, were fathomless mysteries to me . . . Had I really left, little more than an hour since, the quiet, decent, conventionally domestic atmosphere of my mother's cottage?

In a subdued way Hartright appears from the start as an alienated man, prepared for vertigo and dislocations, asking himself 'What shall I see in my dreams tonight?' Arriving at Limmeridge House in the north of England to teach drawing to Laura Fairlie and her half-sister Marian Halcombe, he is immediately drawn to Laura. Fascinated by her resemblance to Anne Catherick, he responds to her gentle, obscurely frightened manner. To him, as to Collins, the victim-type is instantly appealing.

In his later narrative – when he and Marian have rescued Laura from the asylum and all three are hiding out in the East End of London – Hartright becomes both hunter and hunted man. Determined to expose Fosco and Sir Percival, on the run from their agents, discouraged by lawyers who don't believe he has a case, he commits himself to 'the hopeless struggle against Rank and Power'. Here Collins anticipates Buchan and Hitchcock, creating the first doggedly isolated hero who moves in that open country where danger can strike in broad daylight, in the peaceful field or the suburban street. Followed by one of Sir Percival's henchmen, Hartright remembers an escape-experience in the wilds of Central America and comments that

12

he has to run and hide 'with the same purpose and with even greater caution, in the heart of civilised London'. He is also the first private eye in fiction. He unmasks Fosco and Sir Percival with a combination of logic and daring, and in his dedication to 'the long fight with armed deceit' looks forward to the crusading spirit of Chandler's Marlowe. Chandler first thought of calling Marlowe Mallory. A romantic streak appears in Collins's choice of the name Hartright.

Marian Halcombe, the second most important narrator, is again an outsider. A woman of 'masculine' force and intellect, with a strongly latent lesbian attraction to her half-sister, she has a graceful figure, large hands, ugly face and faint moustache. She fails to outwit Fosco but realizes with disgust – one of Collins's most acutely sinister strokes – that the huge bizarre old man is attracted to her. Duelling with a woman whose strength is almost equal to his own, Fosco succumbs to tender admiration and a stirring of ancient lust. When Marian falls ill he dismisses the local doctor and treats her with his private supply of drugs. In spite of his feelings he is tempted to poison her – 'to assist worn-out Nature', as he puts it – but instead he saves her life. 'Deplorable and uncharacteristic fault!' he comments later. 'Behold, in the image of Marian Halcombe, the first and last weakness of Fosco's life!'

While the criminal is drawn to a kind of ambisexual power the artist-hero turns on to neurosis. Laura Fairlie, for whom Hartright risks everything, is on the surface a classically innocent and submissive Victorian heroine. Perhaps taking a sideswipe at Dickens's idealized virgins, Collins goes on to show that Laura's resemblance to Anne Catherick is more than physical. A dominating father has pushed her to the edge of a breakdown. She obeys his deathbed order to marry Sir Percival, a man twenty-five years older than herself. When he turns out more wicked uncle than father, she transfers her complex to Hartright, who in spite of his youth responds with 'fatherly' feelings. Their relationship grows even more complex after Laura's experience in the asylum. She seems almost to *become* the Woman in White, welcoming the limbo of superimposed identity and wanting madness. 'A real and living resemblance,' Hartright notes, 'asserted itself before my own eyes.' Like Collins himself with the girls he rescued, Hartright appears sexually cool, more doctor and healer than lover.

13

By the end of the story Collins has established a link between his afflicted wanderers, Anne Catherick and Sarah Leeson in *The Dead Secret*, and the aristocratic girl driven into a state of private terror by her father. The deprived and the privileged are equally victims of a powerful will. Collins also infers that the only chance for a woman to become independent in Victorian society is to be like Marian, strong but freakish. Even so, she spends the rest of her life as 'companion' to Walter and Laura Hartright in their country house.

Outsiders have offered the only effective opposition to Fosco and Sir Percival. Without the art-teacher and the two-fisted bachelor lady, crime would clearly sweep the board. The police are never called in because Fosco is too skilful to give them a case. The law, as Hartright discovers, is a 'pre-engaged servant of the long purse'. Everyone else is either an accomplice – the illiterate piglike maidservant, the foreign agent masquerading as a trained nurse – or an obtuse hypocrite. The housekeeper at Limmeridge, a clergyman's widow reduced to domestic service and quoting her late husband's sermons, refuses to believe that Fosco is not a perfect gentleman. The only other surviving Fairlie, Laura's uncle, is an absurd hypochondriac from whom nothing can be expected, too preoccupied with imaginary pains to understand that his niece is in real danger. Tracking down Anne Catherick's mother in an ugly expanding industrial town, Hartright finds the former slut seated on a couch in a hideous room, draped in respectable black. A bible stands on a table nearby. Concerned only to obliterate her past, 'I stand high enough in this town to be out of your reach,' she tells him. '*The clergyman bows to me.*' All these are sardonic examples of the society that Fosco dismisses as living off 'clap-trap'. No wonder that Hartright sometimes finds the struggle long and hopeless.

Nemesis arrives as a figure from Fosco's past. Earlier in the story Hartright has come across some puzzling incidental facts about the count. Pieced together, they suggest that his main vocation is that of a spy. This explains why he remains in England after the success of his current enterprise. It is the year of the famous Crystal Palace Exhibition and London is full of foreigners. Hartright deduces that Fosco has been entrusted by his government 'with the organization and management of agents'. But a man like the count is also by nature

14

a double agent. Hartright follows him to the opera, and the scene that follows, an explosion of private intrigue in a public setting, reads like the scenario for a Hitchcock climax.

During the intermission Fosco catches sight of another Italian in the audience. Dissolved by panic, his face goes grey and his bloated figure slumps into a weird paralysis. Then he lurches away, manages to lose himself in the crowd and escapes from the theatre. This is the first and only time when Fosco is shown not in charge of the situation, and it completes his reality. Exactly who or what he betrayed is never known. His pursuer never speaks. But the element of mystery persisting after Fosco's death somehow clarifies his life. Fished out of the Seine, his murdered body lies in the Morgue. Hartright notices that the old dandy is disguised as a French workman. It is more humiliating than if he'd been naked.

Placing the emphasis in *The Woman in White* not just on 'what happens' but on 'what happens next', which is the basic difference between story and plot, Collins masters the art of the logical shock. A wild architecture of suspense rises on very solid foundations. The most improbable events are impeccably documented. Collins immerses himself in background, mapping the north of England as he previously explored London. He checks every legal and criminal detail. This pattern is intensified in the later novels, and at times he seems to be testing reality, seeing how far it can support his most original hallucinations. In *Armadale* (1866) a beautiful young drug addict plans to kill her enemies with a portable contraption that leaks poison gas. To make sure it would work, Collins had the piece of machinery built and sniffed (literally) the result of his invention.

By the time he was writing *Armadale* he had become a drug addict himself. His imagination seems accordingly more extreme. *The Woman in White* contains occasional dreams and premonitions, but they remain on the fringes of the story, muted extra-sensory warning signs. In *Armadale* everything takes place in a sinister paranoid borderland, and is forecast by a dream at the opening. The addict moves with her lethal apparatus through a kind of fantasy-underworld and a plot tissued with murder, suicide, forgery, theft and abortion. The novel is at times haunting in a nightmarish way – the

15

rendezvous on an empty beached ship at night, the confrontation in a shadowy library during a thunderstorm – and at times heavily clouded. Its story becomes almost impossible to follow. The contrast with *The Women in White* suggests that Collins hasn't yet learned to control the drug, although he senses that it can extend his powers.

A few months after publication of *The Woman in White* he began to suffer from rheumatic gout. Taking laudanum to ease periods of extreme pain, he discovered not only relief but a stimulant. Occasionally he smoked opium as well, but his basic addiction was to glassfuls of the liquid tinctured form. The kind of ironic-sinister episode that might have occurred in one of his novels provides a clue to its strength. Noticing a glass in his master's bedroom one day, Collins's manservant decided to try the drug out of curiosity. He drank only half the contents but died within an hour.

Gout can be hereditary, but is also associated with nervous depression. Conrad suffered from it and recorded the pain at its worst when he was having problems with a novel. Depression also preceded the attacks in Collins's case, but its cause – like much of his life – remains unclear. By following the method of logical detection employed in his novels, it's possible to make a guess. No clue exists in his personal life, but it seems worth noting that the attacks began so soon after *The Woman in White* was attacked by nearly all the critics. They not only dismissed the book but made the point that Collins was a cheap entertainer with delusions of being an artist. The literary establishment remained cool to its great popular success. Dickens said privately that the construction was poor, and although Thackeray told friends that he enjoyed the novel he never praised it in public. Collins had to endure this kind of thing throughout his life. Trollope in his *Autobiography* admits that Collins 'has excelled all his contemporaries in a certain most difficult branch of his art', but adds that it gives him no pleasure. Swinburne writes a friendly but guarded obituary tribute. And that is all.

The underlying reasons for the critics' dislike of *The Woman in White* lay in Collins's violation of a code. The Victorians believed that you must not write about crime and other unpleasant subjects without an explicit moral purpose. But Collins insisted that Fosco, while his intentions were

16

criminal, was an engaging figure, more original and better informed than the mass of respectable people. He never rebutted the count's amused celebration of the undetected criminal and his mockery of the idea that 'murder will out'. At a time of official appeals for law and order he showed the equivocal thrill of the enemy. This in itself is enough to lift him out of the nineteenth century into the twentieth.

When Collins started writing, there was no literary precedent for the 'serious' mystery story. It was a low-grade product associated mainly with the penny dreadfuls, adventure serials that appeared in weekly paperback instalments. The new genre began under a critical cloud that has never completely lifted. It placed Collins and his successors in a defensive situation and left a residue of self-doubt and mistrust. Conan Doyle protested that the Holmes stories were only a minor aspect of his work. Greene praised Ambler and Buchan and 'the new imaginative form' but subtitled his own novels in the same form, 'Entertainments'. Chandler grew resigned to being asked why he never wrote a 'serious' novel. The effect on Collins can probably be seen in the various illnesses that began to plague his life after *The Woman in White* appeared, and certainly in the embattled tone of his preface to the second edition. He begins by insisting on the legal research that most critics derided, then pointedly thanks 'a very large circle of readers' for their support. 'The primary object of a work of fiction,' he goes on, 'should be to tell a story; and I have never believed that the novelist who properly formed this first condition of his art was in danger, on that account, of neglecting the delineation of character.' This was evidently an answer to the charge that he cared only about spinning a sensational plot. A story, he writes, depends not only on events but on the human interest connecting them, and he promises his readers to remain faithful to this principle in the future.

And yet the years after *The Woman in White* find him shaky and uncertain. He follows it with *No Name* (1862), another novel about that Victorian obsession, illegitimacy. An exercise in the social realism of Dickens and Charles Reade, who received a much better press than himself, it strikes the free personal note only in some bizarre incidental characters and is weighted with sermonizing. On laudanum while writing it, he progresses to opium smoking by the time of *Armadale*.

All this suggests someone recovering from a private wound, and the tone of the prefaces – 'the Art which has always been the pride and pleasure of my life' – points to its location.

Soon after he started *The Moonstone* (1868), Collins was faced with 'the bitterest affliction of my life and the severest illness from which I have ever suffered'. His mother lay dying and the attacks of gout reached a crippling, agonized stage. But he met all the serialization dates, finishing the novel on schedule by dictating much of it to a parade of secretaries. His shrieks of pain so appalled some of these that they left the room, and the job. Even more intricately designed than *The Woman in White* and using the same multi-narrative technique, *The Moonstone* shows a creative balance restored. Alongside Baudelaire's *Paradis Artificiels* it refutes the idea that drugs invariably confuse the artist's perception or weaken his control. Cool and precise about the practical details of using hashish, Baudelaire explains how to prepare it and how much to take, catalogues its values and limitations and then creates an extraordinary drug-activated poetry. Operating with an addict's intensity in *The Moonstone*, Collins produces something as clear and hard as its title.

When you looked down into the stone, you looked into a yellow deep that drew your eyes into it so that they saw nothing else. It seemed unfathomable; this jewel, that you could hold between your finger and thumb, seemed unfathomable as the heavens themselves. We set it in the sun, and then shut the light out of the room, and it shone awfully out of the depths of its own brightness . . .

Like Fosco in *The Woman in White*, the Moonstone itself is to prove a disturbing foreign element. Most unlike him, it is inanimate. A sacred diamond embedded in the forehead of a statue of the Moon God, it was looted by a British officer during the Indian Mutiny. A legend accompanies it: falling into profane hands, the jewel carries a fatal curse. The officer returns to England, locks the diamond away in a safe at his bank and becomes one of those malicious recluses who populate Collins's novels. Various threats on his life incline him to believe the curse, and after quarrelling with his entire family he hopes for posthumous revenge by willing the diamond to his niece.

18

Made into a brooch, the Moonstone glitters on Rachel Verinder's bosom at her twenty-first birthday party. Next morning it has vanished, presumably stolen. The story takes place in a country house on the Yorkshire moors. There is a closed group of suspects. A detective is called in. A group of mysterious Indians (high-caste Brahmins disguised as travelling jugglers and determined to restore the jewel to its statue) shadow the house. Everyone becomes nervous. The atmosphere of spying, mistrust and guilt leads to further surprises and revelations. Here is the classic detective story formula, but Collins perfects and goes far beyond it.

Built on a remote part of the coast, the house overlooks a bay famous for its quicksand. It provides an underlying symbol as well as playing a part in the story: 'The bared wet surface of the quicksand itself, glittering with a golden brightness, hid the horror of its false brown face under a passing smile.' The theft of the Moonstone is a detonation that exposes the underside of people's lives. The criminal's identity is only one element of a virtuoso suspense, and the most important question is whether anybody is really what he seems. The smooth philanthropist, adored by silly rich ladies who work on charity committees, ends up murdered in disguise in a hotel room in the East End of London. Social façade is stripped away with his beard and make-up. The hunchbacked maid, Rosanna Spearman, has a past as a child thief. Another of Collins's female derelicts, she commits suicide in the quicksand. This is not a confession of guilt but of sexual desperation – passionately loved by 'Limping Lucy', a local farm girl with a club foot, she is destroyed by her infatuation with a charmer who can hardly bear to look at her. The grotesque is resisted here, and Rosanna's fantasies have a rare, sombre, direct pain. In the case of Miss Clack, the sly and pious spinster forever handing out spiritual tracts, Collins treats frustration less kindly. At first merely absurd, she is gradually revealed as a monster. A scene of mean, dark comedy betrays her romantic feeling for the young philanthropist. Hypocrite, Collins implies, naturally falls for hypocrite.

Hero and heroine in a novel by Collins are relative terms. He introduces them here through the sharp though affectionate eyes of an old servant who narrates the first part of the story. Betteredge's reverence for *Robinson Crusoe* gives a taste of his disposition. He is a literate and quirky commentator on the frailties of the rich:

Their lives being, for the most part, passed in looking about them for something to do, it is curious to see – especially when their tastes are of what is called the intellectual sort – how often they drift blindfold into some nasty pursuit . . . You dabbled in nasty mud, and made pies, when you were a child; and you dabble in nasty science, and dissect spiders, and spoil flowers, when you grow up.

At least Franklin Blake and Rachel Verinder refrain from mutilating frogs and newts in the name of natural history, but they are shown as dilettantes, dabbling in art and music to pass the time, no real anchor in life except for the physical attractiveness and social position. Rachel is the stronger of the two, as independent and outspoken as Marian Halcombe, but without her freakishness. All the same, she creates problems. Her lawyer points out that while independence is considered a great virtue in a man, for a woman it has 'the serious drawback of morally separating her from the mass of her sex'. Rachel is often misunderstood and driven 'to shut herself up in her own mind'. She is beautiful and much less abrasive than Marian, but Collins implies that any kind of female non-conformism breaks an unwritten law of the time.

Franklin is a simpler case, an elegant and amiable drifter with a promiscuous past which he abandons when he falls in love with Rachel, but with a habit of running up debts that persists. All these gradations of character are vital to the central mystery. Rachel's violent change of mood after the theft occurs, her refusal to speak to anyone and her unexplained flight, cause suspicion to fall on her as inevitably as Franklin's extravagance makes him a potential thief. Collins brings a cutting insight to the situation of two people with a fairly narrow experience of life pushed beyond their limits.

A series of revelations mark out the novel like surprise witnesses at a trial. Tracking down Rachel in London, Franklin is stunned when she explains her behaviour by accusing him directly: '*I saw you take the Diamond with my own eyes!*' The scene has the clear illogic of a dream and he awakes from it with a confused sense of guilt:

I advanced toward her, hardly conscious of what I was doing . . . From the moment when I knew that the evidence on which I stood condemned in Rachel's mind was the evidence of her own eyes, nothing – not even my conviction of my own innocence – was clear to my mind.

The Woman in White developed the suspense story's first classic situation, the isolated hero determined to expose a crime at the risk of his life. *The Moonstone* introduces the second, the innocent man who must somehow disprove the overwhelming evidence that condemns him.

Two agents help to solve the mystery. The first is Sergeant Cuff, called in on the case by Lady Verinder, Rachel's mother, but later dismissed. (At this time members of the detective branch of Scotland Yard could be hired privately, then paid off if considered unsatisfactory.) Inspector Bucket of *Bleak House* was the first detective to appear in an English novel, but Sergeant Cuff provides the first analytical portrait of a professional at work. Writing out of uncritical admiration for the forces of law and order, Dickens created an effective silhouette – the jovial, modestly heroic flusher-out of criminals, hawk-eyed below the friendly surface. But Dickens makes his operations look rather simple-minded. At once more real and more mysterious, Cuff with his insinuating walk and long clawlike hands strikes Betteredge as a member of a new species:

His face was as sharp as a hatchet, and the skin of it was as yellow and dry and withered as an autumn leaf. His eyes, of a steely light grey, had a very disconcerting trick, when they encountered your eyes, of looking as if they expected something more from you than you were aware yourself . . . He might have been a parson, or an undertaker – or anything else you like, except what he really was.

The Moonstone presents Cuff at the end of his career, burdened and melancholy with years of service, looking forward to a retirement that he will spend cultivating roses. He despises his profession and calls himself 'one of the many people in this miserable world who can't earn their money honestly and easily at the same time'. With no pretence of being a protector of society, he admits only to a talent for a lonely and depressing business. 'Dreary', 'dismal' and 'underground' are the words that Betteredge frequently uses to describe him, and he releases little aphorisms that reflect a soured but not unkind outsider's nature: 'Human life, Mr Betteredge, is a sort of

21

target – misfortune is always firing at it, and always hitting the mark.'

A man who deals in riddles, he also talks in them. At first he bewilders Betteridge by his apparent uninterest in everything except Lady Verinder's rose garden. When the old servant comments that he finds a passion for roses odd in soneone of Cuff's profession, the reply is characteristic:

'If you will look about you (which most people won't do),' says Sergeant Cuff, 'you will see that the nature of a man's tastes is, most times, as opposite as possible to the nature of a man's business. Show me any two things more opposite one from the other than a rose and a thief: and I'll correct my tastes accordingly – if it isn't too late at my time of life.'

Yet the thin, grey, ageing lover of roses is the first to notice a figure approaching in the distance: to pounce upon a minor but vital discrepancy in evidence: to make people reveal themselves in casual conversation without being aware of it. ('He began with the Royal Family, the Primitive Methodists, and the price of fish . . .') He also prefigures Sherlock Holmes in the way he senses, like a clairvoyant reading a palm, a person's motives and character from his dress or habits. An electrifying example of this occurs when he traces Rosanna's footsteps on the beach:

'Very confused footsteps, you will please to observe – purposely confused, I should say. Ah, poor soul, she understands the detective virtues of sand as well as I do! But hasn't she been in rather too great a hurry to tread out the marks thoroughly? I think she has. Here's one footstep going *from* Cobb's Hole; and here is another going back to it. Isn't that the toe of her shoe pointing straight to the water's edge? . . . I don't want to hurt your feelings, but I'm afraid Rosanna is sly. It looks as if she had determined to get to that place you and I have just come from, without leaving any marks on the sand to trace her by. Shall we say that she walked through the water from this point till she got to that ledge of rocks behind us, and came back the same way, and then took to the beach again? . . . Yes, we'll say that. It seems to fit in with my notion that she had something under her cloak when she left the cottage . . . Perhaps, if we go on to the cottage, we may find out what that something is?'

Faced with something he doesn't understand, Cuff seems wrily pleased: 'I am indebted to an entirely new sensation.'

Explaining to Betteredge how a detective looks at landscape, not for its beauty but for its usefulness, he deplores the admired local coastline. 'There isn't a scrap of cover to hide you anywhere.' Initiated into a new world, Betteridge contracts what he calls detective-fever. He becomes a kind of Dr Watson, following his hero's deductions with dogged amazement – until a typical ironic stroke reveals that Cuff has painstakingly misread the case. Lady Verinder fires him and he departs without regret, mildly impatient with Betteredge's fallen hopes and also commenting on other popular fiction of that time: 'It's only in books that the officers of the detective force are superior to the weakness of making a mistake.'

But he recovers face. As he leaves he casually mentions three events that he expects to occur in the near future. The prophecies all come true and Cuff is later summoned back from retirement to help wind up the case. While professional pride has nothing to do with his return – 'I don't care a straw about my reputation' – he feels that he owes Lady Verinder something because she paid him off so handsomely. With a sly sense of theatre, however, he examines the new evidence and writes down a name on a sheet of paper which he seals in an envelope. When the thief is finally unmasked, the envelope is opened and the paper bears his name. 'As dreary and as lean as ever', Cuff goes back to his roses, to a non-criminal but non-human world.

The new evidence comes from a doctor's assistant, Ezra Jennings, the most directly autobiographical character in all of Collins's work. His appearance late in the novel is a signal for its tone to grow more sombre. Visual detail prepares us for someone eerie and haunted:

He was sitting alone in a bare little room, which communicated by a glazed door with a surgery. Hideous coloured diagrams of the ravages of hideous diseases decorated the barren buff-coloured walls. A book-case filled with dingy medical works, and ornamented at the top with a skull, in place of the customary bust; a large table copiously splashed with ink; wooden chairs of the sort that are seen in kitchens and cottages; a threadbare drugget in the middle of the floor; a sink of water, with a basin and waste-pipe roughly let into the wall, horribly suggestive of its connexion with surgical operations – comprised the entire furniture of the room.

Jennings is an opium-addict. At first he took the drug to

relieve the pain of an illness, but now he feels the penalty of abusing rather than using it. By the time Collins had begun dictation of this part of the novel, there are clear repeated signs that he was living in fear of where his own situation might lead him. 'My nervous system is shattered; my nights are nights of horror . . .' Jennings provides much incidental intelligence about the drug, some of it designed to clear up popular misconceptions. It is not, he explains, just a narcotic. Its action stimulates at first, then sedates. Under the stimulating influence the mind and senses become hyper-active. The problem, which may be insoluble, is to control both functions. The addict feels himself at the end of the road when stupefaction begins to erode the dynamic effects.

Nerve-ends exposed, riddled with nightmares, Jennings is additionally handicapped by his appearance. His skin is gipsy-dark and his hair black on top but startlingly white at the sides and back, producing a sinister piebald effect. Again like Collins, he resigns himself to the suspicions created by physical oddity. The few people not repelled by him find something inscrutably sympathetic in his manner, and his most striking quality is described as *'unsought self-possession'*. In today's phrase, he is cool. A student of the unconscious, his theories not only reflect Collins again but provide a final key to the mystery. He has read the work of leading physiologists and is particularly struck by the devious processes of memory:

There seems much ground for the belief, that *every* sensory impression which has once been recognized by the perceptive consciousness, is registered (so to speak) in the brain, and may be reproduced at some subsequent time, although there may be no consciousness of its existence during the whole intermediate period.

Jennings has reasons to believe that, on the night of the theft, someone laced Franklin Blake's glass of brandy with laudanum. His explanation of Rachel's *'I saw you take the Diamond with my own eyes!'* is that Franklin went to sleep in a state of opium-heightened anxiety for the safety of the Moonstone; entered Rachel's bedroom in a trance to take the jewel to a hiding-place; then woke up with no memory of what he'd done. Ignoring what Jennings calls 'only the protest of the world against anything new', they decide to test the theory by restaging Franklin's trance. He is given opium under the same conditions, then goes to bed. After a few hours he gets up and enters Rachel's bedroom, looking for the Moonstone. But when Franklin can't find the jewel, the problem remains of what happened after he originally took it.

At this point Cuff is called back, alights upon the final clue and deduces how the actual thief surprised Franklin back in his bedroom with the diamond still in his hands:

'You looked at him in a dull sleepy way . . . You said to him, "Take it back, Godfrey, to your father's bank. It's safe there – it's not safe here." You turned away unsteadily and put on your dressing-gown . . . You heaved a heavy sigh – and you fell asleep.'

Collins had conceived this climax from the beginning, and all the clues to it are subtly planted. But he may not have foreseen that he would describe a trance in a state of trance. He was certainly unprepared for what happened afterwards. An epilogue tells how the Indians recapture the stone and return it in triumph to the statue of the Moon God. 'I was not only pleased and astonished at the finale,' Collins admitted after dictating it from his sickbed, 'but did not recognize it as my own.' The preparation for Jennings's experiment, the account of Franklin in a dazed obsession under the drug, have a strange contracted lucidity and excitement. The Indian epilogue with its rituals and its imagery of moon and fire is an addict's vision and no less transparent and exact. The epilogue to the epilogue, an unconscious tribute to the medical theory that Collins quotes, is the spectacle of its drugged alert author sitting up in bed, stunned – like Franklin after the discovery of his actions under opium – by its presence in the novel.

The Moonstone is the summit of Collins's technique. Revolving perpetually around the single fact of a theft, its machinery has an apparently self-winding beauty. Each circuit, providing a new insight, doubt or argument, demands another circuit. The movements gradually become hypnotic, inducing a state of trance not unlike Franklin's. As in *The Woman in White*, conflicting evidence emerges from the different narrators' testimonies. The personal antagonisms are sharper than before – Betteredge warns the reader against Rachel; the lawyer comes to Rachel's defence, Franklin doubts Rachel all the same, then Rachel accuses *him* . . . Looking back, it seems inevitable that each character thought or behaved as he did at a particular moment. The truth of Collins's image of a trial becomes self-evident. Rivalries, ego trips, denials, secrets and factual accounts gradually coalesce in 'their march toward the same goal'. Characters reveal themselves as complex as the twists of the plot, yet neither violates the other. No subsequent detective novel matches this performance.

Through frequent changes of tone Collins extracts a variety of human experience from the basic episode. In its ironic passages *The Moonstone* achieves a style that Chandler once hoped to explore – he called it 'the comedy of manners about crime'. In its unfolding of a puzzle it conveys the suspense of imaginative deduction. Through Sergeant Cuff it suggests that the detective's profession is fundamentally lonely and disagreeable. In its atmosphere it reflects Collins's fear of the ambiguity and disturbances underlying so-called everyday life.

Since the impulse behind the comedy is caustic, it brings little relief. Like the elements of fear and mystery it derives from Collins's suspicion of the world in which he lived. Almost unique among his contemporaries in failing to respond to the dynamic thrust of Victorian life, he saw only subterranean movements, tremors, wounds, remnants, disguises, the warning that Rosanna feels in the Shivering Sand: 'It looks as if it had hundreds of suffocating people under it – all struggling to get to the surface.' The surface is repressive and prosaic. Collins attacks the hypocrisy of institutions, the ugliness of industry, the 'solid sameness' of the middle class, the pervading distrust of the 'individual member of the species who presumes to differ' – whether he smokes opium, studies the unconscious mind, rejects Christianity or merely withdraws from society. The haunted and solitary outsider-figures retreat or die. Rosanna the female outcast kills herself, Jennings the drug addict cries 'Peace! Peace! Peace!' shortly after the mystery is solved and goes into his last dream. As for Cuff, he escapes alive to a limbo of rose gardens, in the manner of Holmes's retirement to his bee farm.

Some further similarities between Holmes and Cuff will be discussed later. The major difference is that Cuff has no sense of mission. With many quirks of temperament that Conan

Doyle will also attribute to his detective – trained suspicion of human motives and behaviour, love of solitude, lack of sexual interest in women but a great courtesy towards them – Cuff is denied the consolations of idealism. He remains a brilliant, grudging professional, aware of his responsibilities but bored by them, longing to turn his back on what he calls 'this miserable world'. Holmes uses the same phrase, but believes the world would be even more miserable without his presence. Cuff turns his back on it as he's earned his last fee.

Like Hartright and Laura at the end of *The Woman in White* (though without Marian for a *ménage à trois*), hero and heroine marry and settle down in their country house. It is not the usual celebration of horses, dogs and walks through the woods. The couples seem to be rejecting the whole industrialized world – 'the deserts of Arabia are innocent of our civilized desolation'. Withdrawing to a fortress, they immure themselves against the city and its dangers, Fosco's villa where Laura Fairlie 'dies', the spy at the opera, the Indians hiding in the apartment building with its strange odour of spices, the seedy hotel room with the murdered man in disguise on the bed. The safety of retreat, Collins implies, is the greatest good fortune of the privileged classes – and their favoured retainers. Pensioned off by Rachel, Betteredge gratefully drops out in the servants' quarters with his copy of *Robinson Crusoe*. Even the malicious Clack, after a financial reverse, is exiled to a village in France 'possessed of the inestimable advantages of a Protestant clergyman and a cheap market'. No doubt that Collins connects the idea of survival with isolation.

The preface to the first edition of *The Moonstone* again insists on the documented research behind it. He gives a brief history of famous jewels with curses attached, and emphasizes that his 'physiological experiment' – the actions and reactions stimulated by opium – was endorsed by leading medical authorities. The preface to the second edition is more personal. He tells us that he awaited the novel's reception 'with an eagerness of anxiety, which I have never felt before or since for the fate of any other writings of mine'. (It was again the target of strong critical attacks and popular enthusiasm.) The preface also indicates, like Jennings in the novel itself, that Collins feared he was a dying man. As it turned out he had more than another twenty years to live, but they passed in a kind of creeping twilight.

His mother had died ('the bitterest affliction of my life'), and two years later Charles Dickens died. Towards the end they had felt more competition than sympathy, but the relationship was always an anchor, and without it Collins faced more isolation than even he cared to feel. He comes more and more to resemble Jennings. The abuse of laudanum leads him to spend part of his life in the company of apparitions. They take up residence in his house and multiply with time. During his last years one of them is particularly ferocious and menacing, a woman who waits at the top of the stairs each night when he goes up to bed. She has a greenish skin and is tusked like a wild pig. She likes to bite his shoulder.

His eyesight grows worse. Apart from laudanum, he doses himself with all kinds of remedies for minor afflictions, real or imagined. To what extent were these illnesses psychologically induced, to what extent the result of a gradually failing organism? The opium, the puny body, the decaying eyesight, suggest a combination of both. In any case the outward geniality continues, he keeps his 'unsought self-possession' and is amazingly prolific: a dozen more novels, half as many plays.

Too original a writer to repeat what he has already done (except, indulging his pleasure in the theatre, to dramatize his most successful novels), Collins seems in his later years to be groping for ways to extend himself. After *The Moonstone* he never attempts another 'pure' detective novel, probably aware that the book was a *tour de force* and had exhausted the best possibilities of a form destined to click into formula. But the pursuit and suspense of *The Woman in White* had allowed him complete freedom to explore his favourite theme, the isolated man faced with a secret that demands to be unlocked. Like the writers who follow him in what Greene is to call 'the new imaginative form', he sees that it has still a long way to go. Most of the later novels are at least in part suspense-orientated, but they are even more message-orientated. At this point in his life Collins becomes, of all things, a propagandist. He aims with fervent overkill at a variety of targets – the marriage laws, the criminal code, vivisection. It seems like an obstinate bid for the wrong kind of seriousness. But the strongest appeal to Victorian taste could only be made

28

through the monumental. Importance, like sermons, demanded a pulpit and official robes.

Collins had always refused these trappings, though he started to try them on when he wrote *No Name* in an attempt to disprove the critics of *The Woman in White*. Now, uncertain of his direction, he tries again to make them fit. Discomfort results. Collins the architect of tension remains in excellent form but Collins the lecturer constantly interrupts him. Laudanum clouds as well as stimulates, and the public figure is invaded by the private grotesques and phantoms that haunt his house. In *The Law and the Lady* (1875), suggested by a murder trial in Scotland, tendentious legal discussions interfere with a story that promises to develop excitingly – then a dime novel maniac enters, the legless poet lurching and plotting in his wheelchair, crazed with impotent lust . . . Collins hasn't lost his touch, only his confidence in it.

One novel in the later period, haunting in its wild and dead-end way, recovers the old sureness. It focuses on Collins's obsession with the crippled and afflicted, and shows – as *The Moonstone* glimpsed with Rosanna and 'Limping Lucy' – how a passionate relationship can spring up between them. In *Poor Miss Finch* (1872), a blind girl and an epileptic fall in love. Searching for cures, each submits to an experiment, one psychological and the other medical. The blind girl relives a trauma in her past and regains her sight. What she sees is that her love has turned blue from head to toe as the result of silver-nitrate infusions. The fantastic, ironic cruelty of the situation is justified by a personal metaphor at its base. Collins writes about opening his eyes for the first time and meeting a cryptic, distorted world. A psychic chord is struck that carries the sound of his own past, the experience of what he called 'those early lessons' – the childhood overcast by a gifted tyrannical father, the schoolboy desperately inventing stories to escape oppression, the sense of persecution and physical oddity, all the signs and warnings that his journey ahead lay through enemy country.

Out of this past, the private view slanted by pain and shock, the writer dreaming mystery, conspiracy, secrets: the symbols of quicksand, deformity, 'the dark cloud over London': the identification with victims, the discovery of people living in separate cells of aggression and fear, the fascinated dread of power expressed through creation of a master-criminal. Collins died in 1889, at the age of sixty-five, after a stroke. It had the usual physical effects. In his last hours he looked curiously like someone in a state of terror: mute, rigid, paralysed.

TWO
Final Problems

1

. . . I feel that there is something deeply, deeply wrong which nothing
but some great strong new force can set right.
                              Sir Arthur Conan Doyle,
                              The Wanderings of a Spiritualist

A pencil drawing by his uncle, Richard Doyle, shows Arthur
Conan Doyle at the age of five, a boy with huge dark eyes
and wistful, almost delicate features. By fifteen he's grown
husky, with the promise of stoutness. At twenty-seven another
photograph shows him seated at his desk during a pause in
the writing of *A Study in Scarlet*. He has already assumed the
official disguise of the age, and it grows only more impenetrable with time.

Frock coats tightly buttoned, collars primly starched,
moustaches sad or bristly, waxwork postures – the same
image is presented by many successful artists who grew up in
the late Victorian age. The style of clothing and grooming is
the last word in protective covering; nothing could be farther
from nakedness than this grave respectable armour. The man
himself remains equally hidden. You wonder if photography
in its cumbersome early phase made the posed portrait an
ordeal, or exaggerated the importance of the event. Then you
see the same features offering the same impassive look in the
1920s. Coats remain tightly buttoned and the poker face is a
mask of decorum, daring the camera to give anything away.

In a biography of Rider Haggard, his daughter quotes a
letter in which he records a conversation with Kipling. Past
middle age now, the two men have gone out fishing together.
Haggard suddenly remarks that he thinks this world is 'one of
the hells'. Kipling replies that he's certain of it and that he
lives surrounded by 'every attribute of hell: doubt, fear, pain,
bereavement, almost irresistible temptations springing from
the nature with which we are clothed'. Between two outsiders
the conversation would not seem surprising. Between the

31

authors of *King Solomon's Mines* and *Captains Courageous*, ripe and laurelled figures gone fishing, it becomes extraordinary. Like the age which produced them, these men found their ambition and confidence secretly eroded by anxiety. The crack in the times was apparent to relatively few when Wilkie Collins began writing, but fifty years later it looked dangerously wide. Maturing as the century ends, creative spokesmen for the confident age find its Christian beliefs shaken by Darwin and its social structure doomed to extinction by Marx. When the First World War breaks out, Freud has opened up another battleground, human beings at war with their own conscious drives as well as each other. On the far side of shock, bloodshed and middle age, even the establishment wonders if it's not living in a kind of hell. Buttoned and upright, the public surface refuses to give way, but private confession breaks through – Kipling's outbursts of hatred and bitterness, Haggard's preoccupation with death, the almost eerie melancholia in Elgar's music. Conscious or not, a requiem note is allowed to sound.

Of all these father-figures on a secret rack, Conan Doyle is at once the most composed and self-revealing. Belief in the future keeps him from being swallowed up by the past. In spite of aching personal conflicts he never betrays a strict yet generous code: kindness, courtesy, active support of what he considered moral progress, active opposition to the enormous list of things he considered cruel or unjust. As a writer he passes on this idealism to his most popular creation. Like his author, Sherlock Holmes steps into the threatened arena. 'Art in the blood,' he remarks, 'is liable to take strange forms', and Conan Doyle projects his personal sense of the necessary struggle between 'something deeply, deeply wrong' and 'some great new force' on the contest between criminal and detective.

The early years of Collins and of Conan Doyle contain similar experiences that provoke sharply different reactions. For Collins the power of terror leads to the creative thrill, but Conan Doyle believes in duty and part of that duty is the conquest of fear. 'One should put one's shoulder to the door and keep out insanity all one can . . .'

The father was again an artist, a water-colourist and architect, and again a remote and disconcerting figure. But where William Collins had been the successful autocratic head of the family, Charles Doyle was a nerve-ridden failure who eventually became an invalid. (His three brothers, however, all with 'Art in the blood', made reputations for themselves.) Mrs Doyle, descended like her husband from an Irish-Catholic family, was a remarkable mixture of puritan and romantic who glorified the spirit and distrusted the flesh. She believed in improving the world but also in the spirit of medieval chivalry. She told her young son tales of knight errants, sacred quests, King Arthur and Sir Lancelot, that could still make him 'goose-fleshy' when he remembered them years later. While Collins's prolonged attachment to his mother seems to have been purely emotional, Conan Doyle's was moral and imaginative as well. Blocked from contact with his apathetic father, he centred his whole early being on her fierce ideals and her contempt for the material world. He will often acknowledge her total imprint, which continues until her death.

Sent to private school, Conan Doyle passes a few seasons in hell. Unlike the small strange-looking Collins, he is strongly built, athletic and a capable boxer. The Jesuits who run the school, not the other inmates, provide the bullying. Their almost medieval system is based on austere discipline, corporal punishment and a wholly inadequate diet. Physically well equipped and morally prepared for endurance tests, he remains cheerful. Later he will remark that Jesuits 'try to rule too much by fear', but still agrees to complete his education at a Jesuit college in Austria. In a suitably gothic landscape of mountains and pine forests he discovers the writings of Poe, as overwhelming as his first taste of Sir Walter Scott.

At the age of fifteen he visits London for the first time. It is Christmas, 1874, the weather predictably frowning and freezing. This early glimpse of a shrouded metropolis will never be forgotten: an exhibition of fog, gaslight, black and secretive hansom cabs, slanting rain, rivers of mud in the streets – and Madame Tussaud's, perhaps the most riveting spectacle of all. Like Collins at the Paris Morgue, he feels a chord being struck. 'I was delighted with the Chamber of Horrors,' he writes to 'the Ma'am', as she comes to be known, 'and the images of the murderers.' The background to Sherlock Holmes is the schoolboy's initiating contact with the mystery and half-light of London.

After a ritual family conference on a choice of career, he accepts the Ma'am's suggestion to study medicine and goes to Edinburgh University. As with Collins and the law, the false start produces one of those accidents so vital that they seem to be predestined. Among his professors is Joseph Bell, a surgeon whose lectures stress the need for deductive logic in diagnosing a patient's symptoms. 'The trained eye!' is his repeated watchword. Conan Doyle witnesses this eye deduce even the character and professions of patients brought in for study. He is particularly impressed when Bell announces that one of them must be 'a left-handed cobbler'. Worn patches on a pair of corduroy trousers, extra wear on the right side indicating that he held his hammer in the left hand – these scraps of evidence are all the detective needs. Symbols of the power of reason, they also contribute to Conan Doyle's loss of faith.

He reviews the Catholic theology and rejects it. He doesn't swerve into atheism like Collins, but retains a vague generalized belief that God exists somewhere, beyond the reach of churches and the cruelty and intolerance of Jesuits. The decision appals most of his family, but the Ma'am is surprisingly calm. She agrees that ideals are more important than dogma and admits that she's never believed in eternal punishment herself. All the same, the graduate discovers the usual aftermath of a loss, whether desired or not; feels adrift; takes a job as surgeon on a ship bound for the west coast of Africa. He returns and sets up in general practice at Southsea on the English Channel, renting a modest house without a view. He decorates it with some gothic touches, the hallway windows tinted red to achieve a 'lurid and artistic' look, macabre little water-colours by his father, *The Haunted House* and *The Ghost Coach*, for the consulting-room walls. Unconsciously, it seems, he creates the décor for a very different life.

In the meantime he never doubts the Ma'am's ethic of hard and useful work, and believes he has a good chance of success. Since childhood he's written stories and descriptive essays; he loves literature and thinks it might prove an agreeable second string – but the idea of making it his central career would, at this moment, have astonished him. But since patients are slow to arrive, he can certainly experiment with pleasure in the absence of duty. He writes a few short stories and sends them to magazine editors. They are accepted, modestly paid for and modestly praised. At the same time he begins keeping notebooks, the jottings and confessions that are to become an expanding, indispensable habit of his (and Sherlock Holmes's) life. They show a mind leaping and speculating far beyond the surburban house with the M.D.'s brass nameplate on the door, collecting facts and theories on history, science, literature, all aspects of human existence. And at the end of a year his earnings as a doctor are below the minimum taxation line.

Two years later, a little farther from failure but still a long way from success, he feels secure and lonely enough to marry. Louise Hawkins, shy and self-effacing, seems as far opposed in temperament as possible to the Ma'am. The romance with a patient's sister has a distinct lonely hearts touch, more mutual sympathy than passion. It is sober and discreet, like Conan Doyle's reaction in 1886, his fourth year at Southsea, when he admits to himself that he's unlikely to go very far as a doctor. Wondering now if he could ever support himself by writing, he decides to try but continues his practice in the meantime. For this new effort, he tells himself, a new kind of release is necessary. He must go beyond the magazine story to something more compelling and ambitious. 'I know,' he confides in a letter to the Ma'am, 'I have it in me to make my name famous. . . .'

In the deliberate attempt to extend himself he discovers a faculty that he will later describe as erecting a 'mental curtain' to cut off the outside world. Without any artificial aid he can induce a heightened, isolated state of consciousness in which he feels himself becoming an imaginary character. This happens before he begins *A Study in Scarlet*. On the first page of notes for the novella that introduces Sherlock Holmes, he writes: '*I am a consulting detective.*'

I had been reading some detective stories, and it struck me what nonsense they were, to put it mildly, because, for getting the solution of the mystery, the authors always depended on some coincidence. This struck me as not a fair way of playing the game, because the detective ought really to depend for his successes on something in his own mind and not merely on adventitious circumstances which do not, by any means, always occur in real life.

35

The interview that appeared in the *Westminster Gazette* of 1900, fourteen years after Conan Doyle wrote *A Study in Scarlet*, gives the immediate reason why he imagined himself as a detective behind his mental curtain. His notebooks contain no titles of whatever nonsense he'd been reading, but there were quite a few English and American bestsellers of the period from which to choose. But the notes for *A Study in Scarlet* include some first drafts of comments that Sherlock Holmes will make on Poe's Dupin – 'more sensational than clever' – and on Lecoq, the 'miserable bungler' of a detective who figured in a series of internationally popular novels by the Frenchman Emile Gaboriau.

Conan Doyle was very conscious of the influences that shaped Holmes. His notebooks also refer to Collins and his autobiography describes the methods of Dr Joseph Bell. Holmes inherits his proud and aristocratic manner from Dupin, but a stronger touch of Poe appears in the gothic atmosphere, the menace of empty twilit rooms and the grotesque physical effects of death. Bell is the memory of a sharp face, angular figure and theatrical style, the 'trained eye' swooping on the detail that provides the clue to a character and a life. (But Conan Doyle's own eye, according to Bell, had been intuitively trained. 'You are yourself Sherlock Holmes!' he wrote to his former pupil.) The debt to Gaboriau is technical. This now almost forgotten writer was an expert on the routines and tactics of the Paris police. His detective moves like a turtle but can disguise himself brilliantly, an idea borrowed from Vidocq that Conan Doyle reappropriates for Holmes. Although Paris in the nineteenth century was as violent and lawless as London, Gaboriau's backgrounds have little flavour. His cases usually revolve around remote family scandals. To explain them, he interrupts his stories halfway through and makes long reconstructions of events in the past. Unfortunately Conan Doyle imitates the device in *A Study in Scarlet*, and it throws Holmes off-centre as well as allowing the suspense to grow fatally slack. The novella in fact is not the ideal frame for Holmes, and Conan Doyle never seems at ease with it. (*The Valley of Fear* is again broken-backed in the Gaboriau way, *The Sign of Four* too obviously lifted from *The Moonstone*, and even *The Hound of the Baskervilles* runs out of mystery after a powerful exposition.) The symmetry and concentration of the short story has to be discovered before Holmes can really take the stage.

The first half of *A Study in Scarlet*, all the same, contains a vivid first sketch of the great detective as well as a gripping account of a crime in suburban London. Conan Doyle swiftly establishes the physical image, the solitary disposition, the almost manic self-assurance of Holmes – 'No man lives or has ever lived who had brought the same amount of study and natural talent to the detection of crime which I have done.' In a few pages he indicates Holmes's peculiar stockroom of knowledge: the all-seeing eye, the passion for scientific experiment – when Watson first meets him, he's just invented a method of classifying bloodstains – and the alternating current of energy and apathy that makes the doctor wonder whether his friend might be 'addicted to the use of some narcotic'. In *The Sign of Four* (1890), this suspicion is confirmed. Watson comes to tolerate though not to approve Holmes's dependence on cocaine as an escape from boredom and frustration when 'cases are scanty and the papers uninteresting'. But the detective confides a more important reason. The drug acts as an energizer of body and brain, unbelievably stimulating and clarifying – a kind of x factor in the whole nervous system not unlike Conan Doyle's own mental curtain. For many years the shot in the arm will heighten Holmes's perceptions. While the author apparently never discussed how he arrived at this openly non-conformist touch, it may well have been by way of *The Moonstone*.

In Collins's novel two forces combine to solve the crime – the detective and the drug-addict: Cuff the logician and Jennings the man in a state of artificially heightened consciousness. In Holmes himself the separate forces combine to create a man of uniquely equipped talent. Without the other parallels between Cuff and Holmes that I discussed earlier, there would be less of a case for the connection. Together they suggest that Collins left not a few fingerprints on *A Study in Scarlet*. As in *The Moonstone*, a strange profession attracts a strange exponent, fanatical, isolated, with original powers and habits. Meditating on a problem, Cuff whistles a depressing 'Last Rose of Summer' and Holmes plays a dreamy violin. Each finally retires to the natural world, roses for Cuff and bee-farming for Holmes.

Like the faint opium glaze in Jennings's eyes, the needle marks that scar Holmes's arms and wrists are a symbol of his dark and secret side. They reveal one of the few chinks in the personal armour of a man who insists, 'I am a brain. Watson. The rest of me is a mere appendix.' The appendix in fact is 'all nerves', as Conan Doyle once described himself. A delicate substructure that the brain would prefer to keep hidden, it suggests the possibilities of disorder. In later years Watson will often refer to the breakdowns narrowly averted by periods of enforced rest. Without these inner tensions Holmes would lose his imaginative appeal. His character was conceived at a time when public opinion linked drug-taking with romantic enterprise, with the legend of Byron and Shelley in a castle in Switzerland. Watson confirms this when he associates his friend's addiction with his other 'bohemian' habits – picturesque untidiness, revolver practice in the sitting-room, playing the violin in the middle of the night. The rational man and impersonal observer sometimes betrays the popular characteristics of the poet.

Conan Doyle himself had a poetic imagination which the skill of the stories and the examples of Holmes's intellect at work tend to obscure. It comes through strongly in his settings, with their personal impressions derived from memories of that first astonished wintry visit to London. *A Study in Scarlet* is full of intense detail, like the description of the murder-house standing in a row of other dismal houses, all with 'vacant melancholy windows, which were blank and dreary, save that here and there a "To Let" card had developed like a cataract upon the bleared panes'. Terse atmospheric touches gradually create a panorama of the whole city, yellow gaslight merging into yellow fog, black cabs and grey skies, the long anonymous suburbs that conceal dramas of fatal violence. 'The detective story', Eric Ambler comments, 'may have been born in the mind of Edgar Allan Poe, but it was London that fed it, clothed it and brought it to maturity.' Conan Doyle's London, he might have added, with its particular fusion of security and menace, the cold partridge and white wine waiting on the table at 221B Upper Baker Street when Holmes and Watson return from viewing the corpse and the bloodstains in the villa behind the prim laurel hedge.

The aftermath of violence appears even more sinister than

the act itself. Watson is haunted for days by the 'malignant and terrible contortion' of the murdered man's face in *A Study in Scarlet*, the 'writhing, unnatural posture' of the body in the dusty room with its solitary red candle. 'There is a mystery about this which stimulates the imagination,' Holmes agrees. 'Where there is no imagination there is no horror.' Murder is the signature of an angry destructive impulse scrawled across its victims. Physical wounds take second place to the marks of fear. In the later adventures, confronting some sophisticated non-violent crimes, Holmes finds in them the same disturbing and (one of his favourite words) *outré* quality. The diabolic side of crime seems very important to Conan Doyle. It heightened his sense of living on the threshold of shock. Power politics and the new German militarism have just begun to touch off fears of a catastrophic major war. Anarchist conspiracies and bomb-throwings, spy scares, a dynamite attack on Scotland Yard and an aborted explosion in the House of Commons coincide with a passionate cold-bloodedness in private killings. During the so-called Golden Age of English murder a man rides across London in a hansom cab with his current girl-friend beside him and his previous girl-friend's severed head in a hatbox on his knees. A maid kills her employer, boils her body, renders down the human fat and sells it to neighbouring housewives as 'best dripping'. *A Study in Scarlet* appears only a few months after *Dr Jekyll and Mr Hyde*. Jack the Ripper appears only a few months after *A Study in Scarlet*.

Rejected by several publishers before it eventually appeared, *A Study in Scarlet* made little impression on the public or the critics. Without the interest of an American magazine editor, it is even possible that Conan Doyle would have abandoned Holmes. He branched away to write a long historical novel, *Micah Clarke*, which the critics preferred and which had a solid success. He followed it with another, *The White Company*, and produced several more over the next twenty years. Outlets for his romantic love of the past, he always found them more enjoyable to write than stories set in the present. For a long while he considered them his most important work, and here was a sign of the persisting battle within himself between the Victorian and the modern man. He only abandoned history when the future, first in the form of science-fiction and then of spiritualism, began to interest him more than past or present.

Deliberate and monumental, the historical novels are like offerings on the Victorian altar of importance. Their archaic manner is inherited from Scott, their ideals of bravery and chivalry from the Ma'am. The flashback in *A Study in Scarlet*, with its account of life in an early Mormon settlement, prefigures the general approach. Descriptive passages are solidly done, human elements remain stiff and remote. The characters of the medieval romances are self-conscious antiques, substituting 'deem' for think, 'devoir' for duty, 'quoth' for said. Varlets and caitiffs abound. The times are 'simple' and 'full of elemental passions'. It is easy and unnecessary to make fun of these obviously vulnerable works, better to understand the sincerity of their failure. For the novelist, the problem with history is that it cannot answer back. It turns too often into a kind of hold-all for nostalgia and becomes a way of avoiding the active creative tension of the present. After finishing *The White Company* an elated Conan Doyle said 'That's done it!' and threw his pen across the room. He felt sure that he was illuminating national traditions. In fact he illuminated only the side of himself that wanted to retreat into the past.

He returned to the present on commission from the American editor of *Lippincott's Magazine*, who invited both Conan Doyle and Oscar Wilde to dinner. After the safe plush and chandeliers of a London hotel, the signing of contracts: for another Holmes story of murder and vengeance, *The Sign of Four*, and for another fable of the human crack, *The Picture of Dorian Gray*. The Holmes novella created little stir in England, but it revived the author's interest in a character suspended for more than two years. Holmes found a sizeable vanguard of admirers in the United States, and his success there opened Conan Doyle's eyes to the new and profitable market in the large-circulation magazines springing up in both countries. Their editors' preference for the short story (from five to eight thousand words) had begun to rescue it from the limbo of the novel's poor relation. When Conan Doyle finally decided to abandon his medical career and concentrate on writing, his wife had just given birth to a daughter. *A Scandal in Bohemia*, the first Holmes short story, was born of financial need. Written a year after *The Sign of Four* appeared, it was conceived as one of a set of six for *The Strand* magazine.

At the same time an imaginative stimulus arrived from a writer nine years older than Conan Doyle, but in many ways younger. Many of Stevenson's stories were first published in the magazines. In open revolt against wordiness and slack, they offered the alternative of verbal marksmanship and the quick direct hit at the small centre. Although fascinated by the detective as a phenomenon of the times, a man who 'from one trifling circumstance divines a world', Stevenson deplored the long and laboured mechanics of the popular detective novel. He felt the pull of melodrama but liked it glamorous or unearthly, under the spell of buried treasure or the supernatural. *Dr Jekyll and Mr Hyde* was both instant folklore and seductive evidence of the short story's power of compression. It had the allure of a legend or fairytale, larger than life though small in scale. *The Suicide Club*, one of Conan Doyle's favourites at this time, revived the spirit of *The Thousand and One Nights*. The tales of Scheherazade were preoccupied with escape and pursuit (not surprisingly, since she invented them to distract her husband from murdering her), and they exist on the borderline of magic and reality. The stories of Prince Florizel, a young visitor to London who disguises himself in search of adventure, reproduce their pace and twists of plot, their last-minute rescues from the trap about to close. In the first short story that begins the Holmes cycle their imprint is clear.

King Wilhelm of *A Scandal in Bohemia* comes from the same country as Prince Florizel. On a winter's night his carriage stops in front of 221B Baker Street and he steps out wearing a long cloak, fur-trimmed boots and a black mask over his eyes. We are at once in a different world from the novellas. The surface is more fantastic, with a fairytale aura – but the power of reason will ferret out a logic and an actuality behind the most extraordinary events. The black magic of the old fairytale becomes an ingeniously planned crime, conquered by a greater marvel, the scientific spirit. Behind the mental curtain where he first thought of Holmes, the young Conan Doyle sifted through different layers of experience – inherited beliefs and acquired doubts, wide reading of books and of life, pressures, memories, fears. They connect in a final superimposition of form that allows the cycle to develop like a miniature epic, reaching from the personal to the collective unconscious. 'These are much deeper waters,' as Holmes likes to remark, 'than I had thought.'

Like the King of Bohemia subsequent visitors turn up at Holmes's apartment at all hours of the day and night, blown in by the wind, tramping through snow, umbrella'd against the rain. Veiled, breathless, cagey, indignant, all are in some kind of danger, threatened by murder or blackmail or involved in unnerving events they don't understand.

'Ha! I am glad to see that Mrs Hudson has had the good sense to light the fire. Pray draw up to it, and I shall order you a cup of hot coffee, for I observe that you are shivering.'
'It is not cold which makes me shiver,' said the woman in a low voice, changing her seat as requested.
'What, then?'
'It is fear, Mr Holmes. It is terror.'

As well as cross-examination of his story the client must expect intense personal scrunity:

'Beyond the obvious facts that he has at some time done manual labour, that he takes snuff, that he is a Freemason, that he has been in China, and that he has done a considerable amount of writing lately, I can deduce nothing else.'

The enormous success of the first stories led to another six and then another complete set of twelve for *The Strand* magazine. Collected as *The Adventures* (1892) and *The Memoirs* (1894), this first part of the cycle ends with Holmes's apparent death at the hands of his arch-enemy Moriarty.

In *A Scandal in Bohemia* the opening suggestion of masquerade develops as Holmes disguises himself as a groom and a clergyman, while his opponent, the brilliant adventuress Irene Adler, disguises herself as a man. At the end she rather surprisingly outwits him, and Holmes asks for her photograph as a memento of the experience. Watson comments that she remains '*the* woman' for his friend, but Holmes's admiration seems more intellectual than romantic. It has no real bearing on his celibacy, which always remained a matter of principle.

'As a lover he would have placed himself in a false position.' Holmes cut himself off from sexual feeling to protect his reputation for objectivity.

The idea of a king being blackmailed by his former mistress, whom he met when she was an opera singer, was suggested by the affair between the dancer Lola Montez and King Louis of Bavaria. Many of the stories that follow are derived from newspaper items, gossip, fragments of anecdote, and a few impose an original twist on a situation from Collins or Poe. *The Naval Treaty,* one of the most ingenious puzzles, comes from an actual case of a Foreign Office employee turned spy. The theft of *The Beryl Coronet* carries vibrations from *The Moonstone.* The crime is not always murder and in a few cases not even technically criminal – like the woman in *The Yellow Face* whose first husband was a negro and who keeps their child hidden in a cottage bedroom and a strange white mask. Settings divide evenly between London and the country. Disguises and impersonations recur. Some stories (like *A Scandal in Bohemia*) are more adventure than puzzle, and in others the basic mystery is human behaviour. The most powerful reiterated motive is greed. Desire for money and land provokes four memorable accounts of murder and cruelty. *The Reigate Puzzle* involves two country squires in a death feud over property rights. Girls with inheritances find themselves in particular danger. In *The Speckled Band* a stepfather contrives a diabolical murder with the aid of a trained snake. In *The Copper Beeches* a governess forced to cut her hair and wear a blue dress discovers that she's been hired to impersonate her employers' daughter, locked away in a barricaded wing of the house. In *The Engineer's Thumb* a group of counterfeiters traps the mechanic who threatens to reveal their secret in a nightmare dungeon reminiscent of *The Pit and the Pendulum.* Notably inspired by the challenge of *The Speckled Band* and *The Reigate Puzzle,* Holmes admits a preference for the bizarre. Its force will grow stronger and darker in the great stories of the later cycle.

Another recurring theme is of people living under false names to escape a criminal past. It leads to murders of revenge, of which *The Resident Patient* is a savage example, echoing the horror of *A Study in Scarlet*:

43

I have spoken of the impression of flabbiness which this man Blessington conveyed. As he dangled from the hook it was exaggerated and intensified until he was scarce human in his appearance. The neck was drawn out like a plucked chicken's, making the rest of him seem the more obese and unnatural by the contrast. He was clad only in his long night-dress, and his swollen ankles and ungainly feet protruded starkly from beneath it.

In this story Holmes is again at his most inventive. From a few insignificant details – cigar butts, a screwdriver, the angle of a footprint, a piece of rope – he reconstructs a murder made to look like a suicide, deduces the number of people involved, how they entered the house and in what order they went upstairs, even their movements in the room before Blessington was killed.

These tales dominate *The Adventures* and *The Memoirs* even though the lighter and non-violent ones in fact outnumber them. But the bizarre note and the profit motive persist in the absence of physical violence or punishable crime. In *The Man with the Twisted Lip* and *A Case of Identity*, a single clue – a missing coat and a typewritten letter – enables Holmes to expose outrageous dramas of disguise. An ex-actor pretends to be a businessman but really makes his money posing as a hideous and pitiable beggar every day in the London streets. To keep control of his stepdaughter's legacy and deter her from marriage, a wine salesman impersonates a gas fitter with tinted glasses, side-whiskers and moustache. He meets the lonely short-sighted girl at night, makes cautious love to her, then 'disappears' and breaks her heart. A precise sense of place and social background reinforces these fantastic situations, and pivotal touches make the central characters oddly plausible. Cosmetic scars stripped away, the beggar reverts to a sad young man with an apologetic and bewildered air. The suburban girl's myopic good-natured face, her clumsy and timid movements, mark her out as one of life's victims. Ironic examples of Holmes's belief that life is infinitely stranger 'than anything which the mind of man could invent', these two stories also expound his basic theory of detection. When the impossible has been eliminated, he explains to Watson, 'then whatever remains, however improbable, must be the truth'.

In the professional melting pot of pawnbroker and race-horse trainer, engineer and wine salesman, doctor and plumber, army officer and servant, governess and politician, only the derelict and the unemployed are absent. Halfway through the century Disraeli had called the rich and the poor 'the two nations'. Conan Doyle reflected the nation he knew and a state of affairs that had hardly changed by the 1890s. The upper classes still formed the garrison of power and the Labour Party had not yet been created. The 'great conservative politician' of *The Naval Treaty* represented an overwhelming type. Because Conan Doyle's imagination and experience stopped somewhere short of the poverty line, and he never suggested hunger or desperate need as a criminal motive, he has been criticized for giving a falsely secure impression of the period. But he was aiming at a different kind of impression. Watson sums it up when he remarks that Holmes's cases offer 'a perfect quarry for the student not only of crime but of the social and unofficial scandals of the late Victorian era'. Holmes takes the political system for granted because he operates in the world as he finds it. His attitude to crime is not exactly reassuring, but in the light of subsequent ideas and events it seems at times prophetic.

The two nations have now become two worlds, yet there is less crime in Morocco than in California. Economic motives defer to psychic problems, genes and hidden instinctual drives. *The Copper Beeches* and *The Reigate Puzzle* describe the greed of affluent people, and today their impulses would be classified as aggression by Conrad Lorenz, and as the territorial imperative by Robert Ardrey. In one of his rare general statements, Holmes refers to tensions created by 'the artificial state of society' and to the influence of heredity, under which 'the person becomes, as it were, the epitome of the history of his own family'. He sees the criminal as a symbol of psychic unrest and biological destiny at work in the tightly structured Victorian world. He leaves us to see a connection between the obsessive use of disguise and the houses with locked and guilty rooms.

The masked child, the imprisoned daughter, the false beggar and lover, the assumed names, the wigs and cosmetics are all cover-ups, literal and figurative. They point to the buried lives and secrets that haunted Wilkie Collins. The stepfather in *The Speckled Band* guards his house with a baboon and a cheetah, and the couple in *The Copper Beeches* train a huge dog to fly at enemy throats. In *The Reigate Puzzle* the land-hungry father and son react to the threat of exposure by violently attacking Holmes, one trying to break his arm and the other to strangle him. Extreme security measures do not suggest a secure period.

Watson's normality provides the reassuring note. One of Conan Doyle's most subtle effects is to make Holmes's biographer a man about whom the detective complains that he lacks imagination. The ideal solid citizen, Watson's virtues are common sense, dependability, and a cautious but open mind. Resisting the unpredictable only to face the shock of proof, he connects the man in the street with the deadly snake gliding through the ventilator. *The Musgrave Ritual* shows how much is lost when Holmes himself narrates a story. Without Watson's honest and sometimes dazed mental filter, only a technician solving a puzzle remains. Watson not only animates the character, he breathes his own fear and anxiety into the situation, then offers a touch of comfort. After the bloated corpse hanging from the ceiling, the Baker Street sanctuary with its brightly lit windows at night and the great man's thoughtful silhouette glimpsed behind the drawn blind.

While the 'quiet thinker and logician' becomes almost unrecognizable in action, examining footprints and sniffing clues with 'a purely animal lust for the chase', Watson always returns to the detective as artist and the eye as antenna of the mind. 'You see, but you do not observe,' Holmes tells him. 'That is the difference.' And again, when Watson says, 'You see everything,' he is briskly corrected: 'I see no more than you, but I have trained myself to notice what I see.' The trained eye leads first to a particular deduction – that a man takes snuff and has been to China – and then to a commentary on life. Since the improbable and the true are so often the same, the eye warns Holmes not to look for revelation in the commonplace but in the dangerous and unexpected and bizarre. Watson learns to apply this method when he examines Holmes's personal habits. The detective's untidiness – unanswered letters and residues of chemical experiments everywhere – reflects not a vague but a fantastically disciplined person. Working at constant high pressure, his brain has no time for middle-class proprieties and is completely indifferent to the cigar in the coal scuttle or the criminal relic that turns up in the butter dish.

Watson instinctively avoids treading on private ground. After the discussion about cocaine in *The Sign of Four* he drops the subject for many years. He records without protest the celibacy, the rejection of social life, the moodiness and driven quality that leads Holmes to the edge of breakdown. He's not even surprised that Holmes has no other friends besides himself, and accepts the fact that for the detective their friendship is simply another habit. He admits his own slowness but sees that it excites Holmes's 'flame-like intuitions' to burn even more fiercely. Most important of all, his devoted and admiring records will make Holmes into a legend, and the detective knows it. Although he disclaims interest in money and fame, Holmes agrees with Watson's view of himself as an artist and hopes for the approval of a trained eye beyond his own, for the nod of posterity.

Until the last but one story of *The Memoirs,* Watson describes a man who reasons strictly from cause to effect, discounts the supernatural and remains indifferent to the idea of God. In *The Naval Treaty,* a moment occurs that seems all the more significant because it has no bearing on the plot. The detective takes a rest from trying to unravel an espionage case and picks up a rose:

'There is nothing in which deduction is so necessary as in religion,' said he, leaning with his back against the shutters. 'It can be built up as an exact science by the reasoner. Our highest assurance of the goodness of Providence seems to me to rest in the flowers. All other things, our powers, our desires, our food, are all really necessary for our existence in the first instance. But this rose is an extra . . . It is only goodness which gives extras, and so I say again that we have much to hope from the flowers.'

Logically this is below the master's standard and sounds out of character. A mosquito, after all, is an 'extra', but it points to divine malice rather than goodwill. The idea comes from Conan Doyle himself, not Holmes, and provides the first sign of the author at odds with his protagonist. Conan Doyle's notebooks show that by the time he came to write *The Naval Treaty* his trained eye had begun to look beyond the visible. The struggling young doctor had attended a few spiritualist meetings. He came away mildly sceptical, but they sparked a fascination. By the mid-1880s he was reading Swedenborg and corresponding with Frederic Myers, the founder of the Society for Psychical Research. Approaching the occult like his detective, he set off on a long search for conclusive evidence. He wrote to Myers for advice on how to distinguish the genuine table rap from the accidental creak, and noted that if the truth of spiritualism could be proved it might 'break down the barrier of death'. The creator of the supreme rationalist was also privately investigating all aspects of the paranormal, mediums, clairvoyance, animal magnetism, extra-sensory perception. Although identified with an apostle of logic, he was slowly edging towards the unknown 'extra' missing from his life since he rejected the Christian church.

The situation has a touch of *Frankenstein*, and so has the way out that Conan Doyle chose. Naturally the Ma'am was the first to be told. 'I am in the middle of the last Holmes story, after which the gentleman vanishes, never to return!' He had already complained that Holmes interfered with his more important work as a historical novelist, but this in itself hardly justifies attempted murder. The hasty concoction of *The Final Problem* suggests a desire to be free at all costs from a character whose basic point of view is now in conflict with his own. A new and fanatic enemy of Holmes appears on the scene. Moriarty, the head of a secret murder network, pursues Holmes and Watson to Switzerland. The great criminal and the great detective are left alone at the Reichenbach falls. After both of them disappear, the police conclude that they toppled into the cataract together during a struggle. But there are no bodies. Holmes is only declared missing and presumed dead. In a farewell letter discovered by Watson on a rock, he confesses that his career has run its course and he finds the prospect of death perfectly acceptable. None of this works. The episode is clumsily contrived and the transformation of Holmes into a fatalist sounds unconvincing. All that survives is the image of a confrontation on the edge, the two antagonists above a black chasm and a torrent of melting snow. A touch of guilt is suggested in the way Conan Doyle left the country for a vacation before *The Final Problem* appeared in *The Strand*. He avoided some extraordinary public scenes, hundreds of outraged letters and black armbands worn in the street.

A real death and the threat of another provide a curious sequel. After many twilight years in a sanatorium, Charles Doyle dies in 1893. His son's exasperation with him had turned to pity before the end. He pays homage to 'Art in the blood' by hanging a group of his father's sinister little water-colours in the study of his country house. A few months later he discovers that his wife has tuberculosis. English doctors give her only a few months to live, but Conan Doyle seeks medical advice in Europe and she survives for another twelve years. During most of them she is a semi-invalid, and while they remain intimate companions, the physical marriage dies. In 1897 Conan Doyle meets a girl in her middle twenties called Jean Leckie. They fall instantly and passionately in love, a prelude to what Holmes would have called the most *outré* incident in his creator's life.

Since an affair would betray not only Conan Doyle's wife but his romantic ideals, Jean Leckie agrees to a test. They will re-enact the pure nobility of a troubadour's ballad, and as crusading knight and worshipped lady reach the heights of unconsummation together. Taken into their confidence, the Ma'am approves this revival of the spirit of courtly love that she'd instilled into her child from the beginning. She witnesses a solemn medieval legend played out in frock-coats and chignons as electricity begins to replace gaslight and Queen Victoria shrivels and dies. The knight goes on a journey and his lady fills the ship's cabin with flowers, tenderly kisses his pillows. He endures the ordeal of chivalric devotion and sexual abstinence for ten years. The few close friends who know about it remark that his posture gradually becomes as rigid as his determination.

As a refuge from private tension he begins to seize opportunities for public life. After a long lecture tour, the outbreak of the Boer War stirs his patriotism. For once ignoring the Ma'am's protests, the knight embarks for South Africa as an army physician and his lady flutters a handkerchief in farewell. Almost single-handedly he organizes a hospital and deals with an epidemic of typhoid fever. He writes a history of the campaign, attempting to refute stories of British atrocities and to justify the setting up of concentration camps. Supporting an openly imperialist war and its brave soldiers – 'such splendid chaps, bearded and fierce' – he becomes for a while the man of the past. And yet, noting the British army's out-of-date methods and suggesting new military tactics, he shows himself a keen analyst of the present. The Boer War episode locates the deep and troubling split in his whole life.

'My soul is naturally and inevitably rather wrenched in two all the time', he writes to the Ma'am, citing only the situation with Jean Leckie and unconscious of the wider reference. The wonderfully inquisitive mind that pioneered modern crimino-logy, digested scientific knowledge, relished the eccentric and explored the occult, could also surrender to dreams of a lost Victorian security and idealize a mercenary cause. While living through and recovering from the self-created ordeal with Jean Leckie, the contradictions in his life are frequently be-wildering. After his propaganda on behalf of the Boer War he is offered a knighthood. Fearing it would imply that he's been no more than a government spokesman, he turns it down. The Ma'am persuades him to change his mind, but when he brings Holmes back to life he makes the detective refuse a knighthood in the same year, 1902. He becomes a candidate for Parliament, opposing the Liberal anti-war platform, and loses after an obviously amateur campaign. Then, aroused by reports of torture and slavery by the Belgian regime in the Congo, he heads a committee of investigation and writes a powerful indictment of colonialism. Supporting a move to reform the antiquated divorce laws, he obstinately opposes women being granted the vote. Years before 1914 he foresees the dangers of U-boat warfare, yet he is near-sightedly shocked by the paintings of Cézanne and Matisse, finding that they go 'over the border of reason'.

After his wife's death in 1906 Conan Doyle himself nearly goes over the same border. A sense of guilt (had he neg-lected her, and did she suspect his love for Jean Leckie?) battles with a sense of release. It leaves him jittery and insom-niac, unable to concentrate. To avoid nervous collapse his doctor advises a period of complete rest. A year later he marries Jean Leckie. They are very happy, yet he feels an uncharacteristic lack of energy and produces little work for several more years.

In the long disturbed interval before his near breakdown, *The Hound of the Baskervilles* (1902) appears as a Holmes novella set in the pre-Moriarty years, and the actual *Return of Sherlock Holmes* (1905) naturally causes a sensation, though as a whole it's the least satisfactory collection in the series. But some of Conan Doyle's most personal and surprising work is contained in a few short stories mostly written around the turn of the century, all dealing in some way with the fantastic and the supernatural. (They were eventually collected as *Tales of Terror* and *Tales of Twilight and the Unseen*.) Their emphasis is on violence and the grotesque, those increasingly powerful hallmarks of the later years. *Playing with Fire* describes a spiritualist séance in which the writer makes his first imaginative statement on the possibility of two worlds existing at the same time, and on people moving like amphibians between them. The medium breathes and hisses, a strange luminous vapour hovers around the table in the ordinary surburban room, while cabs pass in the street outside, voices are heard in a sidewalk argument and dogs bark in the distance. A hideous monster is unaccountably conjured up, a huge black unicorn-like thing that stamps and snorts and rushes 'with horrible energy from one corner of the room to another'. In *The Terror of Blue John Gap* the monster is real, and much larger. A survivor from prehistoric times, it lives in a subterranean lake reached by a cave opening out of the peaceful countryside. Even more loathsome than the apparition of *Playing with Fire* or the Baskerville hound painted with phosphorus, it is ten times the size of a bear, has immense fangs and claws and pale malignant eyes like light bulbs. Local farmers finally block up the entrance to the cave, burying the creature in its own dark.

The prevalence of monsters is the most striking feature of these years. Glaring, snarling, smoking, they erupt with the force of unconscious images. When Conan Doyle describes the labour involved in sealing up the Blue Gap monster – dozens of people rolling boulders into the cave – the metaphor is unmistakable. It is also misleading, for the monsters have not been buried and in fact will never go away. They develop on a vicious human level in the later Holmes stories, and the theme of dark surviving prehistoric agencies will be explored in the science-fiction masterpiece, *The Lost World*. Meanwhile the public figure keeps up its impassive appearance. In a painting done as the century ends he sits very upright in a dark leather chair, pencil in hand, notepad on knee, a correct monument of the age: rich moustache with long waxed ends and a silver chain looped across his vest. You look at the stiff yet genial face and wonder how much he knows. Part of the fascination is that he will never tell. Occasionally he throws out a remark that may or may not be a hint. 'The best literature,' he tells his audience at a lecture, 'is always the unconscious literature....'

Was Conan Doyle unconsciously motivated when he killed off Holmes and failed to produce a body? In any case it eased the technical problem of a return to life, and the moment itself was clearly signalled in advance. While the detective remains missing and presumed dead, his creator is still haunted by the subject of crime. In 1901 he publishes a series of articles in *The Strand* that discuss some recent murder cases. *The Hound of the Baskervilles* appears a year later and proves that Holmes is still alive in the writer's mind. Although set in the past, this story naturally excites demands for Conan Doyle to reconsider the future. Big offers from America and British magazines for the return of Holmes are certainly an inducement. But they are not conclusive, for he will continue the cycle when he no longer needs the money. The strongest clue to a change of heart lies in the work itself.

Watson opens *The Empty House,* the story in which Holmes reappears, with a confession that seems to echo Conan Doyle's own situation: 'It can be imagined that my close intimacy with Sherlock Holmes had interested me deeply in crime, and that after his disappearance I never failed to read with care the various problems which came before the public. . . .' The best tales in the new collection show a darkening view of the criminal world. The imagery becomes fiercer. London is compared to a jungle in which monsters have to be tracked down like wild beasts. Unlike the shadowy Moriarty, the master-criminal Moran and the blackmailer Milverton emerge as antagonists with an appetite for evil far beyond any characters in the earlier part of the cycle. Holmes gives signs of a deep pessimism about human nature. In the context of the darkening view, Conan Doyle tries to close the religious gap between himself and his creation by making Holmes a kind of lay brother, using the detective to ventilate his belief that a special dominating force is now necessary to oppose the criminal. And since the British have always enjoyed staking the amateur against the professional, Holmes's status gives him a unique and rather mysterious position. His superior talent recognized by Scotland Yard and the government, both of whom frequently seek his help, he becomes like an elected mediator between authority and crime. On the side of the law, he is still powerful enough to break or ignore it when he feels inclined. For Wilkie Collins the main objective was never the solution but the experience of the mystery. Conan Doyle believes in the solution at all costs. A practical and symbolic act, it preludes the removal of an infection in the system.

The detective returns appropriately in disguise, and when the hunchbacked book-collector reveals his identity Watson faints for the first and last time in his life. Only Moriarty died in the struggle at the falls, but to avoid the professor's associates Holmes has been obliged to live in hiding. Now only one of the murder gang survives, Moran of the scarred face, iron nerve and cruel eyes. Speculating on how a man who was once an 'honourable soldier' could become a paid assassin, Holmes suggests that a secret deforming process may be at work in nature. 'There are some trees, Watson, which grow to a certain height and then suddenly develop some unsightly eccentricity. You will see it often in humans. . . .' With Watson's help the enemy is cornered and Holmes takes up his profession again.

Several unusually tame case-histories follow, then halfway through the collection gathers force. The plump and dandyish blackmailer in *Charles Augustus Milverton* has touches of Fosco in his frozen smile, glittering eyes and smooth conceit. To convey his peculiar repulsion, Holmes evokes memories this time of venomous serpents at the London zoo. In a surprisingly ruthless climax, Holmes and Watson witness the blackmailer's murder, hidden behind a curtain while an elegant and aristocratic lady empties her revolver into his shirt-front:

He shrank away, and then fell forward upon the table, coughing furiously and clawing among the papers. Then he staggered to his feet, received another shot, and rolled upon the floor. 'You've done me,' he cried, and lay still. The woman looked at him intently and ground her heel into his upturned face.

A draft of night air blows into the room and the beautiful avenger slips away with a rustle of skirts. Holmes makes no effort to detain her. When the police later ask his help in solving the case, he refuses. Milverton had ruined the woman's life – when she couldn't meet his price he sent some 'compromising' letters to her husband – and the detective feels that such a case reverses the usual identities of criminal and victim.

He feels it again in *The Abbey Grange*. A drunken aristocrat brutalizes his wife, even setting fire to her dog. Then someone murders him. Holmes discovers that Lady Brackenstall has a lover. He learns that Captain Croker kissed nothing more than the ground on which his lady trod, but killed Brackenstall after seeing him beat his wife across the face with a stick. As judge and jury Holmes and Watson pronounce pardon, and allow the young sailor to flee the country. Two cunning puzzle stories that show Holmes at his most alert also incline to the same view of criminal and victim. In *The Second Stain* a foreign agent blackmails a politician's wife on account of an indiscreet but 'innocent' event in her past. He forces her to help him steal a state document, but Holmes recovers it and again sets up his own court of justice. Respecting the lady's secret, he refuses to incriminate her. In *The Golden Pince-Nez* he is even prepared to be sympathetic to a murderous lady nihilist from Russia whose husband betrayed her to the police, but she resolves his dilemma by killing herself.

Condoning acts of private revenge, Conan Doyle begins to accept the inevitability of violence in the world around him. Defending 'pure' passion, he refers to the situation with Jean Leckie and perhaps even confesses his own fear of blackmail. In Milverton and Brackenstall he discovers a form of life low enough to justify the private executioner. But the really new element in these criminal fables is their underground of suffering. When he shows people trapped in situations from which the only way out is through violence or betrayal, he moves to the edge of a bitter territory that Simenon will later explore. More personally involved than before with the predicaments of clients and criminals, Holmes is often pictured by Watson as stern, haggard, preoccupied. His friends make the same point about Conan Doyle at this time. Resurrected and forgiven, the imaginary character seems closer than ever to the real one. Holmes in *The Second Stain* is deeply concerned when the prime minister describes Europe as an armed camp and admits his fears of a major war. Conan Doyle's private life apart, his interest in military tactics and propaganda on behalf of British rearmament betrays a quickening anxiety for a world he feels to be threatened. Soon after *The Return* is published, the author even turns detective himself. The case of a near-sighted and rather dim young Indian convicted of mutilating cattle suddenly arouses doubts in his mind. He conducts his own investigation, sifting through clues of weapons and bloodstains, brilliantly demolishes the police evidence, exposes the real criminal and frees an innocent man. Later he will rescue a gambler and pimp accused of murdering a rich old lady, will solve a jewellery theft and the mystery of a man who vanished apparently without trace from a London hotel. United by their drive to forage for truth and correct injustice, Conan Doyle and Sherlock Holmes are now moving together to confront some final experiences on what the detective calls 'a great and sombre stage'.

'What is the meaning of it, Watson?' said Holmes, solemnly, as he laid down the paper. 'What object is served by this circle of misery and violence and fear? It must tend to some end, or else our universe is ruled by chance, which is unthinkable. But what end? There is the great standing perennial problem to which human reason is as far from an answer as ever.'

This epilogue to *The Cardboard Box*, one of Conan Doyle's most disturbing inventions, sums up the mood of the great final tales in *His Last Bow* (1917) and *The Case-Book of Sherlock Holmes* (1927). The story that opens this last part of the cycle, *Wisteria Lodge*, finds Holmes discussing with Watson the associations of the word 'grotesque'. He detects in it some 'underlying suggestion of the tragic and the terrible', and remarks how often the grotesque deepens into the criminal. The cycle has already been laced with witty references to some bizarre cases that Watson feels for various reasons cannot be made public. Sealed away for ever is the journalist staring in

55

terminal insanity at a matchbox that contains a new species of worm, the banker sucked to death by a red leech, the affair of the giant rat of Sumatra and of the aluminum crutch. But now Watson releases a few other hauntingly strange episodes from the archives, and at moments they almost crack the composure of Holmes himself.

The last stories were written between 1912 and 1925, but with two exceptions the period is still late Victorian and early Edwardian England. Not only time and distance affect the view. Since *The Return* appeared, Conan Doyle's world has passed from the threshold to the centre of shock. Now he re-examines an earlier age in the light of the First World War and the 'feverish' twenties. The final part of the cycle also coincides with the years of his finest imaginative writing, the Professor Challenger series beginning with *The Lost World* (1912), a classic ghost story called *The Brown Hand*, and the extraordinary *Horror of the Heights* in *Tales of Terror*. During these years he also exhausts his long investigation of spiritualism and becomes a convert, certain that he's found the secret to 'the bridge of death, the assured continued journey in the world beyond'. Meanwhile the colours of the actual world grow darker and the atmosphere of violence and danger surrounding Holmes turns as thick as the fumes from his chemical experiments.

Mutilations and psychoses are uncovered in the old country houses and suburban villas. Many characters exist on the edge of deformity: a dwarflike creature with a bulbous head, a man with a curved back and convulsively twitching hands, a woman like a huge clumsy chicken. Holmes has developed a particularly sharp response to physical oddity. When Watson embarks on a rather imprecise visual catalogue of a murder suspect, he interrupts –

'Left shoe wrinkled, right one smooth.'
'I did not observe that.'
'No, you wouldn't. I spotted his artificial limb. But proceed.'

Holmes seems almost manic-depressive now. He slumps into near-despair: 'We reach. We grasp. And what is left in our hands at the end? A shadow . . .' Then he rouses himself to feverish activity, reaching the climax of a case after an attack on his life, pale as a ghost with a bandage around his head. One year finds him so exhausted that his doctor orders complete rest. During another case he feels so energized and relaxed that he can write a monograph on the medieval composer Lassus in the intervals of stalking prey. He watches Watson drowsing in an armchair, and from the expressions that cross his friend's face can deduce what he's been thinking about (getting a picture framed, and then the American Civil War). The portrait of the artist suggests a presence that broods over everything, on or off stage.

At the same time we seem to penetrate beyond the stare of the author's poker face, the patriot, the sportsman, the justice-collector, the family man, that composite 'normal' image purveyed by so many biographers and cultists. On the other side is a human being of extraordinary gifts, admired and successful, happy in his personal relationships, with a great capacity for pleasure, and yet in a deep sense alienated. No one who spends years searching for proof of a future life, then advertising his discovery of it, can be at ease with his present one. Even at his most secure Conan Doyle finds the ground giving way beneath his feet. He is haunted by that 'underlying suggestion of the tragic and the terrible'. In his newly discovered relation to the universe he looks across the bridge of death to a state of eternal progression, a movement farther and farther away from all human dangers and terrors, from the existence that Holmes now calls 'the schoolroom of Sorrow'.

Here are some events occurring in the schoolroom. In *The Cardboard Box*, Holmes solves a murder of jealousy which begins with a suburban spinster receiving through the mails a package that contains two human ears, one male and one female, freshly severed and packed in salt. In *Wisteria Lodge* he confronts a ferocious political vendetta involving the former dictator of a South American republic. Before the final assassination there is one barbaric murder and an attempt at another by a mulatto who practises voodoo in his kitchen, where Holmes discovers a pail of blood, a mutilated rooster and a disgusting fetish that suggests a 'mummified negro baby'. In *The Devil's Foot*, a sister and two brothers are found sitting around a table in a farmhouse, their faces convulsed with horror. The sister is dead and the brothers have been driven out of their minds. Chanting idiotically, they are removed to the nearest asylum. There will be yet another victim before

Holmes exposes a drama of revenge in which the criminal uses a poison derived from the root of an African plant. Thrown on the fire, its powder induces hallucinations that result in either madness or death. Jealousy with a circus background is the secret behind *The Veiled Lodger*, a woman who hides herself in a suburban apartment and always wears a thick veil to conceal the ruin of her mutilated face.

The cycle also describes some parallel acts of inner violence. In *The Creeping Man* a distinguished middle-aged professor falls in love with a young girl and goes to Europe to try a rejuvenation drug. Injections of monkey serum turn him into a kind of missing link, clambering up the walls of his house, attacked by his dog, flying into chattering rages. 'When one tries to rise above Nature,' Holmes drily remarks, 'one is liable to fall below it.' In *The Sussex Vampire* a man sees his wife attack her stepson, then suck blood from the neck of their own baby. When Holmes solves the mystery, appearances are almost magically reversed. 'Did it not occur to you,' he asks the husband, 'that a bleeding wound may be sucked for some other purpose than to draw the blood from it?' The young stepson, adoring his father and jealous of the new wife, has tried to kill their baby with an arrow dipped in poison. In *Thor Bridge* a woman commits suicide but makes it look as if she's been murdered by a girl with whom her husband is in love. Although there has been no affair, only a close friendship, the wife suffered from a 'soul-jealousy' as passionate as any 'body-jealousy'. Holmes remarks that he's never come across 'a stranger example of what perverted love can bring about'. Even the idea of a mental rival drove the wife to revenge and suicide.

Just below the level of these tales are two others in which the vicious and the grotesque make an equal impact. *The Illustrious Client* provides Holmes with another superantagonist, the murderer and sexual adventurer known as Baron Gruner. This sinister creature, with languorous eyes and waxed tips of hair under the nose that suggest an insect's antennae, exploits a rich young girl who finds him attractive. The beauty and the beast situation is resolved when a prostitute throws vitriol in Gruner's face, and it turns into something blurred and inhuman, like a painting 'over which the artist has passed a wet and foul sponge'. In *Shoscombe Old Place* a country squire has reasons for concealing the death of his wealthy invalid sister. He burns her body and hides it in the family crypt, then hires a manservant to impersonate her. Holmes becomes suspicious when he learns that the squire has given away his sister's dog. He retrieves the animal and sets it on the impersonator as 'she' appears on one of her rare outings, riding in a carriage:

> With a joyous cry it dashed forward to the carriage and sprang upon the step. Then in a moment its eager greeting changed to furious rage, and it snapped at the black skirt above it.
> 'Drive on! Drive on!' shrieked a harsh voice.

Even disguise has become macabre. Physical horrors in these stories are tersely but unsparingly described. They seem to spring from that awareness of spreading violence first noted in *The Return*, but are heightened by the new element of psychosis. *The Sussex Vampire* contains an unforgettable image of the father fondling his baby while Holmes glimpses the young stepson's face, maniacal with jealousy, reflected in a window that looks out on a peaceful garden. An even more chilling moment ends *The Veiled Lodger*. The woman has confessed how she and the circus strong man planned to kill her husband. The plan failed on account of her lover's cowardice, and she was left alone to be attacked by a lion. Angered by the memory of the strong man's weakness but still in love with him, the passionate relic compares herself to a wounded animal crawling into its hole to die. Moved to a rare and rather awkward display of sympathy, Holmes pats her hand and murmurs something about patient suffering:

> The woman's answer was a terrible one. She raised her veil and stepped forward into the light.
> 'I wonder if you would bear it,' she said.

The curious link between sexual desire and physical disfigurement is echoed by Gruner's fate in *The Illustrious Client* and by the lovers' in *The Cardboard Box*, heads battered to a pulp and ears cut off. (It recurs even more brutally in *The Case of Lady Sannox*, from the *Tales of Terror*, with a surgeon tricked into mutilating his mistress.) Lust also motivates the apelike regression of *The Creeping Man*. The final revelation is often of a submerged but violent sexual guilt, just as the 'soul-jealousy' in *Thor Bridge* alludes to Conan Doyle's fear, after his first wife died, that she might have suspected his love for Jean Leckie. Severed ears, squashed heads, dissolved and ruined faces, the academic capering wildly from branch to branch of a moonlit tree – the cycle closes with some terrible and grotesque symbols that ironically recall their author's remark about unconscious literature.

The same externalized fears continue in the final stories: violence, corruption, war. In *The Three Gables* Conan Doyle moves valiantly beyond his range to a sleazy underworld of prize fighters and gun molls. His subject is the rise of organized crime in London. But the portrait of the American millionaire in *Thor Bridge* is blunt and sardonic. The Gold King stands on the vanishing frontier between big business and gangsterdom and imposes like a prefigurement of one of Marlowe's rich ambiguous clients. Like many English writers, Conan Doyle has problems with American dialogue, but he brings off his effects all the same. Looking like a villainous Abe Lincoln, the millionaire talks about his interests – 'they are large, Mr Holmes, large beyond the belief of an ordinary man' – and warns of his power to influence not only individuals but 'communities, cities, even nations'. He tries to bribe Holmes and is deeply shocked to find one individual exempt from his influence.

The title story of *His Last Bow* is an inferior work, but ends with a strange elegiac scene on the eve of the First World War. Holmes has been called out of retirement to unmask a German espionage network. Mission accomplished, he stands with Watson on the terrace of a country house and gazes out at the moonlit sea:

'There's an east wind coming, Watson.'
'I think not, Holmes. It is very warm.'
'Good old Watson! You are the one fixed point in a changing age. There's an east wind coming all the same, such a wind as never blew on England yet. It will be cold and bitter, Watson, and a good many of us may wither before its blast . . .'

From this bleak future with its suggestion of 'God's curse' hanging over the world, Holmes has already decided to retire. He returns to his farm and absorbs himself again in philosophy and bee-culture, studying the insects' 'little working gangs as once I watched the criminal world of London'.

His creator begins another kind of withdrawal, a gradual imaginative departure from the planet earth. He has already looked beyond the ravages of war to the threat of cosmic disaster. After the desolate dream-landscapes and the reminder .of fierce primitive origins in *The Lost World* (1912), the Professor Challenger stories develop into doomsday parables. In *The Poison Belt* (1913), a current deriving its force from the stars causes the earth to drift into a cloud of deadly gas. All life goes into a coma during which many cities are destroyed and the world appears extinct. In *When the World Screamed* (1914), Challenger has decided that the world is a living organism, an animal that actually breathes and feels. The rise and fall of landscapes reflect the creature's 'slow respiration', and tracts of undergrowth suggest traces of its hairy skin. To prove his theory Challenger sinks a shaft through the earth's crust and enters its 'sensory cortex'. He provokes a dreadful cosmic-animal scream, followed by cyclones, spouts of evil-smelling tar, tremors and explosions from Central America to the Mediterranean. Since he describes the earth as feminine and her howl occurs at what he calls the moment of penetration, the ecological nightmare once again carries sexual undertones.

Imagination of disaster relates *The Horror of the Heights* to the Challenger stories. Lacking their ironic touch, it becomes undiluted paranoia. A young aviator takes his plane twenty thousand feet above the earth and encounters a terrifying aerial whirlpool. Escaping from it and going higher, he finds himself in an empty stratosphere. Objects begin to sail past, beautiful but sinister. An armada of creatures that look like jellyfish, each one larger than the dome of St Paul's, is followed by streams of huge, vaporous, serpentlike things. Then a colossal purplish beaked monster attacks the plane with blubbery tentacles. Others close in and devour the pilot. Conan Doyle suggests that in the interests of sanity it is better not to dwell on the nature and meaning of these organisms policing the upper air.

All these tales were written in the shadow of a catastrophe on earth. When the 1914 war breaks out Conan Doyle hears the sound of trumpets for the last time. As well as visiting the fronts and writing a history, he persuades the British navy to introduce a 'swimming collar', precursor of the inflatable lifebelt, and the army to issue steel helmets. He also loses a son, a brother and several friends. Unlike the Boer War, the experience is in no way reassuring but leads him to the centre of an 'agonized world'. Surrounded by death, he clinches his religious beliefs. Beyond the certainty of communication with the dead – the Ma'am dies in 1921 but later materializes at a seance – he foresees a spiritual evolution that will reject all the horrors of history. Apart from a few Holmes stories, his final years are dedicated to writing and lecturing on this world beyond the agonized world. In *The Vital Message* he discusses all the expendable 'unlovely aspects' of the human race. The catalogue of political, social and religious outrages echoes the private fears and cruelties that end the Holmes cycle.

In 1930, aged seventy-one, he has a second attack of angina pectoris. It leaves him mute during his last hours, but he signs to be lifted from his bed and placed in an armchair. His wife and his youngest son each hold his hand. He remains like this for a long time, gazing out of the window to the garden. He is almost certainly looking at or imagining another country. Inheriting as a child the idea that life exists to be improved, he reaches the ultimate conclusion and sees death itself as 'an improvement on life'. As well as his work, he leaves behind a fantastic number of personal effects and papers. Like the pile of relics at the end of *Citizen Kane* they represent a stockroom of the mind. There is a collection of rare coins, primitive art, military items, and a unique library of crime. Filed in boxes are family letters and documents, more than fifty notebooks containing anecdotes, ideas for stories, observations of history and current events, speculations and prophecies, psychic jottings. There are notes on his war experiences, on scientific inventions, on his own adventures as a detective, on Houdini, on secret codes and mind-reading techniques, on conversations with H. G. Wells, on the 'insanity' of Nietzsche, on the scheme for a Channel tunnel and the possible location of Atlantis.

There is even his 'Rosebud', a final clue to the puzzle. Found in his wallet, written on the back of an envelope: 'The Lord is on my side. I will not fear what man doeth unto me.' It signals the end of a journey out of fear. Romantic ideals had met the shock of an actual world. Against the dream of courtly love, the reality of sexual drives: over the crusade for honour and justice, the stain of criminal aggression. To combat thieves and murderers in the immediate arena, he conjures up a detective errant. When the conflict escalates in his mind and he imagines a wider conspiracy of darkness, he becomes a Holmes of the metaphysical. Sifting through clues discovered now in seances, dreams, precognitions, he solves the final problem by arriving at what he believes to be the supreme correct improbability. In the last moments, stricken with silence but fully conscious, he waits for it to be proved.

2

'I'm afraid I'm a practical man,' said the doctor with gruff humour, 'and I don't bother much about religion and philosophy.'
'You'll never be a practical man till you do,' said Father Brown.
G. K. Chesterton,
The Dagger with Wings

In December 1903, a year after publication of *The Hound of the Baskervilles,* another remarkable figure stalks another English moor. Already well known as a journalist and critic, the twenty-nine-year-old G. K. Chesterton has been visiting the north of England on a lecture tour. He hasn't yet acquired the charging dinosaur image of his middle and later years, but an expanding frame promises the hulk to come, and is decorated with a theatrical cape and slouch hat like a pirate's. Swordstick in hand, he towers above an immaculate little priest at his side. Curate at a nearby Roman Catholic church, Father O'Connor looks trimly understated, his only prop an oddly shabby umbrella.

Chesterton likes to sing as he walks. The priest sings along with him for a while, then starts to talk about sin. He describes the cruelty and cunning of the poor, and one anecdote especially fascinates Chesterton. A beggar woman stationed herself daily on the same street corner, holding a baby that always cried and always had a bandage over one eye. It was finally discovered that the bandage concealed a walnut shell, which concealed a spider that had gnawed a hole in the baby's eyelid. Impressed by the priest's cool way with a tale of ugly fraud, Chesterton decides that he's met a great expert on evil. But the end of a long walk he's also met a friend for life, the agent of his conversion to the Catholic faith and the model for his fictional detective, Father Brown.

The bandage, the walnut shell, the spider and the gnawed eyelid: one has to remove similar layers of disguise, the cape, the swordstick and the pirate's hat, to arrive at Chesterton himself. As with Wilkie Collins and Conan Doyle the paternal line carried 'Art in the blood'. Chesterton's father abandoned the idea of becoming a professional painter to enter the family real estate business, but he remained an inventive amateur artist and craftsman. He invited his children to share his private imaginative world. Its centre was a den at the back of the suburban London house, a secret laboratory that produced invention after invention, water colours, sculptures, photographs, magic lantern slides and an elaborate toy theatre. The young Gilbert focused his imagination on this theatre. In his *Autobiography* he says that his most powerful childhood memory was of a puppet kingdom with cut-out scenery, golden keys and paper crowns. It was to colour the style of his creative work as well as the figure he chose to present to the world.

From his mother he inherited a love of witty argumentative conversation, but he never seems to have been close to her. She dressed and kept house sloppily, and her indifference to the way things looked extended to her own teeth, hypnotically crooked and discoloured. She preferred her younger and less remarkable son, whom Gilbert also adored. From an early age Chesterton's strongest affections seem to have been directed towards men. At school he imposes as a benevolent oddity who prefers to be left alone. Exceptionally tall for his age, clumsy in movement and speaking in a high-pitched voice, he responds to joshing with the air of someone half asleep. Eventually the barrier of solitude is broken by the precocious Edmund Clerihew Bentley, later to invent the form of light verse named after him and to write a popular detective story, *Trent's Last Case*. They form a debating club and exchange ironically formal letters. Chesterton likes to sign himself, 'Your grovelling serf, villein and vassal'.

Curiously slow in learning to read, the future writer has made no progress until the age of nine. But his visual sense develops quickly and he covers his school textbooks with drawings. Two figures recur in them, a crucified Christ and an angel with a devil's face. When he decides he wants to paint, his father sends him to art school. By the time he reaches sixteen, secret drawings have become an obsession. To the notebooks he's begun to keep he confides a few verses and fragments of stories, but angel-devil figures crowd them out on the pages. There is increasing emphasis on the devil. A sado-masochistic element appears: naked men and women in bondage, a threatening apparatus of whips and swords. At eighteen he is exhausted, terrified, on the verge of nervous collapse, but the comfortably agnostic parents suspect nothing. Accustomed to his vagueness and solitude, they have no idea that Chesterton believes himself to be struggling with the devil.

The battlefield never extends beyond his mind. Until his wedding night Chesterton remains a virgin, in itself probably a struggle, for he notes with the gift of paradox that is to become typical: 'Even vice demands virgins.' After suppressing the devil within, he is left shaken but euphoric, like someone rescued from a mountain ledge or a shipwreck. From now on he will wear optimism like a cape, flourishing his belief that existence is the deepest and greatest fact of existence and everything in the world is ultimately 'all right'. An early poem celebrates the new mood. In the cry of a bird and the crackle of fire and the sound of the wind, he hears the same repeated word, 'God'. The conversion to Rome is still a long way off, but the voice of God is already orthodox Christian.

Photographs show him oddly handsome but not very optimistic at the end of adolescence. Rambling hair, haunted eyes and a strong full mouth give him the look of a sensual and delinquent scarecrow. The wild deranged air carries a touch of the young Rimbaud. Ten years later, like a transformation scene in his father's magic theatre, all visible traces of the mysterious adolescent have vanished. The assured and hearty young man is someone new.

Deciding that he wants to write, Chesterton abandons art school. Words take over from images in the notebooks, though the demonic sketches are never destroyed. He gets a job as a publisher's reader, then a friend arranges a commission to review books on art. An offer to write a column for a moderate left-wing weekly called *The Speaker* launches him as commentator on life and letters. And with a mixture of astonishment and fear he falls in love.

The first and last romantic experience of his life is Frances Blogg. Educated at an Anglo-Catholic convent, she is vaguely radical in politics, vaguely orthodox in religion, vaguely interested in art. In a word she is vague, and you see it in her pale blurred face, neither happy nor sad, in the muted uncertain colours of her clothes. Chesterton himself describes her as a 'queer card', but he courts her in letters and light verse that carefully mask the seriousness of his feelings. Her parents have reservations about the young man's lack of solid prospects and his untidy appearance, but Chesterton's growing success as a journalist soon takes care of one problem and Frances takes care of the other. Though muffled like everything else about her, the queer card's intuitions are strong. She sees that her lover must create his own fashion, persuades him to discard his usual dreary rumple and substitute a flowing cape and slouch hat. He enthusiastically adds a swordstick and a moustache, and the new public figure is born.

After the wedding they left for a honeymoon in the country. Chesterton stopped twice on the way to the station. The first time he bought and drank a glass of milk at a dairy to which his mother had often taken him as a child. The second time he bought a revolver and cartridges. In his *Autobiography* he explains the glass of milk as 'a fitting ceremonial to unite the two great relations in a man's life'. More facetiously, he accounts for the revolver by suggesting there might have been dangerous criminals at large in the countryside. Presumably, as often happened in Chesterton's life, the act of theatre disguised extreme nervous tension. Both sides were uneasy about the wedding night ritual, and some kind of unhappy scene occurred. Chesterton later wrote several articles about marriage in which he alluded to 'the aura around the virgin', 'the awful armour of ice' and the need for 'magnanimous compromise'. Although she wanted children, Frances was both barren and sexually frozen. After the failure of an operation that was supposed to make it possible for her to conceive, one imagines the physical temperature of the marriage dropped from subnormal to zero. But they discovered a profound tenderness for each other. It lasted for thirty-five years, until Chesterton died.

The glass of milk was the truly pregnant gesture. Chesterton became the child of his childless wife. Frances became the custodian of an enormous restless baby, and in the new role discovered practical motherly gifts. She acted as Chesterton's financial manager, doling out pocket money; she controlled every domestic detail of their life together, even ordering his cigars; she made travel arrangements and accompanied him on lecture tours, and when she felt that journalism was overtaxing his energies she moved him from London to the country.

Before relocation, Chesterton is Fleet Street's most picturesque figure. He debates and holds forth in pubs, starting to drink wine very heavily while celebrating the glory of life. He is famous for being able to write anywhere, in cabs and restaurants, even in the street. By the time he reaches his middle thirties he's produced an amazing amount of work. It includes a book of poems, containing notably 'The Donkey'; a brilliant study of Dickens; two novels and a collection of short stories; hundreds of newspaper and magazine articles. The novels, *The Ball and the Cross* and *The Man who was Thursday*, both dissolve in rather heavy-handed allegory, but they prefigure at moments the unique sinister imagination of the Father Brown stories. The occasional pieces range from professions of Christian belief through attacks on industrialism and centralized government to whimsicalities about cheese. Turned out with almost manic energy, a surprising number of them show Chesterton's mind at its most exuberant and original. *The Defence of Ugly Things* attacks the Greek ideal of physical beauty for its worship of an aesthetic stereotype and its 'terrible sin against the variety of life'. *Cockneys and their Jokes* begins as a study of popular humour, then discusses popular art as a whole. Noting its prophetic qualities, Chesterton himself becomes prophetic. When he writes, 'It is complete error to suppose that because a thing is vulgar therefore it is not refined; that is, subtle and hard to define', he strikes a note fifty years ahead of fashion. The pieces are studded with aphorisms that reflect his love of paradox. 'The people who are most bigoted are the people who have no convictions at all.' 'The way to love anything is to realize that it might be lost.' 'Silence is the unbearable repartee . . .'

Something forced and disturbing occurs only when Chesterton becomes oracular about the Christian faith. Early in his life he makes a basic rule: 'A man's minor actions and arrangements ought to be free, flexible, creative: the things that should be unchangeable are his principles, his ideals.' This seems to deny the possibility of development and limits the writer to following and repeating a party line. Chesterton insists so much and so often on his religious beliefs that you suspect he is trying to keep himself persuaded in the guise of persuading others. The longer Christian testaments, *Orthodoxy* and *The Everlasting Man*, are blustery and wearisome. He begins to sound like the hard-selling graduate of any life-improvement course. To make his point that Christianity is the only 'logical and workable' faith, he crudely misrepresents other religions. Underestimating the opposition is one mark of the fanatic, and the fanatic is essentially insecure.

For when Chesterton writes at the top of his voice it is because he fears the unbearable repartee of silence. The adolescent claimed to have exorcized his terrifying private demons, but he only locked them away. They remain in the closet and he knows they are there. To ease the burden he embraces Christianity and eventually the Catholic church, preserving his sanity as a human being at the expense of his free imagination as an artist. No wonder there are times when he is forced to bluff, like someone who knows what he thinks about the world without really knowing the world. The gibes at Darwin and at psychology, the boisterous homage to the 'normal' man and the exaggerated horror of 'decadent' art, are the gestures of a man caught in a steep emotional dilemma. Jorge Luis Borges has commented on the dangerous equilibrium of Chesterton's life and his 'precarious subjection of a demoniacal will'. He adds that the Father Brown stories are the emblems of his struggle. They are also confessional, which is not surprising in view of their original source. Goaded by the example of a priest who shed an urbane and consoling light on dark places because he wasn't afraid to enter them, Chesterton in these stories lowers his own voice, speaks as it were through a grille, abandons the pretence that belief is always easy and admits the demons behind the locked door.

In 1910, seven years after his first meeting with O'Connor, Chesterton wrote his first story featuring Father Brown. *The Blue Cross* had an instant success in *Storyteller* magazine.

Within a year Chesterton had written eleven more stories, and the collected *Innocence of Father Brown* (1911) led to the *Wisdom* (1914), the *Incredulity* (1926), the *Secret* (1927) and the *Scandal* (1935). After many conversations between writer and priest the basic idea crystallized: 'A comedy in which a priest should appear to know nothing and in fact know more about crime than the criminals.' In the germinating years Chesterton also read a great deal of detective fiction. He admired Collins and Conan Doyle, and developed conflicting theories about the genre in a number of articles. One of them suggests that the detective story is essentially an art of the city, since the city itself has become a vast cryptic maze and an image of mystery. Another links it to popular art and the fears of childhood, 'the healthy lust for darkness and terror which may come on any of us walking down a dark lane'. Chesterton also visualized the detective as 'an original and poetic figure', while dismissing criminals as 'placid old cosmic conservatives', as predictable and limited as apes and wolves. All this was happily dropped when Father O'Connor began to pass on his first-hand knowledge of crime. Hardly surprising, in fact, that during their first conversation on the Yorkshire moors the priest remarked on Chesterton's ignorance of the whole subject.

Much of O'Connor's knowledge of crime naturally derived from the secrets of the confessional, and when Chesterton created Father Brown he made him in every sense an insider. There is a vivid contrast between the early theories and the priest-detective's statement of intentions:

'I wait till I know I am inside a murderer, thinking his thoughts, wrestling with his passions: till I have bent myself into the posture of his hunched and peering hatred; till I see the world with his bloodshot and squinted eyes, looking between the blinkers of his half-witted concentration; looking up the short and sharp perspective of a straight road leading to a pool of blood ... And when I am quite sure that I feel exactly like the murderer myself, of course I know who he is.'

Although his intelligence about the world is extremely sharp, Father Brown solves his cases by intuition rather than deduction. He's had no training as a sleuth and ignores scientific evidence in a way that would appal Holmes. He relies instead on his 'uncommonly keen' animal senses that enable him to smell evil as a dog smells rats. Yet the amateur detective is

69

still a professional in the eyes of God. Since a priest's business is the saving of souls, Father Brown merely uses his gifts to extend his duties. He unmasks a criminal to save a criminal, treating him as a sinner to be set on the road to repentance. He also believes that what we call mystery loses its power to intimidate the moment it's demystified. Fear is a product of superstition, a quality that it amuses him to find non-believers associating with the church. With his love of paradox Chesterton portrays Father Brown (and the church) as an apostle of reason as much as of faith.

In *The Blue Cross* Father Brown encounters the master-criminal Flambeau disguised as a priest and intent on stealing a jewelled cross brought to a Catholic congress in London. He suspects Flambeau's disguise early in the game, but is only certain of it when the false priest attacks the power of reason. 'It's bad theology,' Father Brown observes, and Flambeau bows to a master. The priest-detective returns frequently to the idea that belief is a rational force and the lack of it leads to confusion. 'It's the first effect of not believing in God that you lose your common sense and can't see things as they are,' he points out in *The Oracle of the Dog*. The devil's trick is to horrify us with 'things half understood'. Secret societies, disguise, the locked door entered or escaped from, the headless body in the sealed coffin, the two voices speaking where only one person is present – the trappings of mystery generate more terror than the crime itself. Apart from hoping to rescue a criminal's soul, Father Brown's most important function is to dissolve the apparently insoluble in a clear and sacred light: the same light, Chesterton believes, that was his own deliverance. Behind the flamboyantly dangerous puzzles lie the student's fears, what the *Autobiography* calls the 'overpowering impulse to record or draw horrible ideas and images'.

'The criminal is the creative artist,' says the French chief of police in *The Blue Cross*, 'the detective only the critic.' Reversing one of Chesterton's earlier ideas, the aphorism shows him no longer prepared to dismiss the criminal as ordinary or shrug him off with a joke. Father Brown also looks at crime as a work of art. 'Every work of art, divine or diabolic, has one indispensable mark – I mean, that the centre of it is simple, however much the fulfilment may be complicated.'

Chesterton's most stunning demystification of mystery

occurs in *The Honour of Israel Gow.* The story takes place in a decaying country house, one of the author's favourite settings in spite of another early claim for detective fiction as the art of the city. Gloomy and isolated estates on the edge of Charles Addams country are a speciality of these tales. Their inhabitants are always sad and eccentric, disinclined to go out, drugged with superstition, unable to break the spell of some threatening family legend. Living out of time, unrelated to anything except their self-created prisons, they serve as a strange, powerful metaphor for a community of lost souls. In *Israel Gow*, the last Earl of Glengyle has just died at his castle in a remote part of Scotland. Having sealed him up in his coffin with indecent eagerness, the gaunt and deaf Israel Gow, his only servant, is suspected of murder. Father Brown and the police discover a number of baffling things in the castle. Diamonds without settings are strewn everywhere. Heaps of snuff have been dumped on mantelpieces and sideboards. Scattered on the floors are curious little remnants of steel that look like parts of dismembered mechanical toys. While the place is stiff with candles, not a single candlestick can be found. 'By no stretch of fancy,' says the inspector, 'can the human mind connect together snuff and diamonds and wax and loose clockwork.'

The mind of Father Brown instantly disagrees and suggests several possible startling connections. Then he dismisses them all as intellectual exercises. 'Ten false philosophies will fit the universe; ten false theories will fit Glengyle Castle. But we want the real explanation of the castle and the universe.' They open the coffin and find the earl's head missing from his body. The priest locates it in a potato patch that Gow is fond of digging. The wind screams, storm clouds gather, nightmare time approaches, but Father Brown goes confidently to sleep. Next morning he arrives at the real explanation. The last earl had promised his servant all the gold in the castle after his death. Since the Glengyles were notorious misers of gold, the innocent and simple-minded Gow found himself surrounded by a glitter of loot. Interpreting his master's promise to the letter, he stripped the gold from watches and diamond rings, emptied snuff from gold boxes and made off with all the gold candlesticks. Since one of his master's teeth contained a rich gold filling, he cut off his head to get at it. The eerie adventure

71

ends with a memorable image: Gow at his potato patch during a storm, conscientiously digging up the pillaged head to return it to its body.

The toy theatre of Chesterton's childhood is the clue to the atmosphere of *Israel Gow* and to all the Father Brown stories. Later in life he bought another theatre and staged many performances, officially to amuse the children of friends but basically to please himself. Where Conan Doyle's backgrounds are stylized and yet still real, Chesterton's are created from drop curtains and painted scenery. Puppet-types disappear through trapdoors to hell and are rescued on invisible wires to heaven. Wind machines and lightning sheets produce fantastic storms. Landscapes gleam in a violent theatrical light and the natural world twists into ominous shapes and shadows. *The Blue Cross* announces the technique:

The most incredible thing about miracles is that they do happen. A few clouds in heaven do come together into the staring shape of one human eye. A tree does stand up in the landscape of a doubtful journey in the exact and elaborate shape of a note of interrogation.

In another country house story, *The Doom of the Darnaways*, the priest looks out of a window and sees not the sky but only its reflection in a moat, as if he's looking at the world upside down in a mirror. The branches of two leafless trees in *The Absence of Mr Glass* are like 'demon hands held up in astonishment'. And in *The Oracle of the Dog*, though a man stands in distant shadow against the sunset, his white teeth gleam in the dusk to betray the fact that he's smiling. The same strange visual intensity extends to the murders. In *The Dagger with Wings* a victim lies in an endless landscape of snow, no footprints visible for miles. His black cloak makes him look like a huge dead bat. In *The Secret Garden*, surrounded by high walls and sealed tight as an air-chamber, Father Brown discovers first a corpse with a severed head, then that the head doesn't belong to the body.

'What we all dread is a maze with *no* centre,' says Father Brown, an effect which these images of death are designed to create. When he finds the centre, he banishes the dread. Human flesh creeps as the result of human confusion, usually abetted by some diabolic apparatus in the wings. But while the dragon has a kind of monstrous glamour, the St George is notably plain. Dumpy, neuter, unassuming, the little priest has a minimum of presence and will frequently be overlooked in a room. In his *Autobiography* Chesterton writes that 'his chief feature is to be featureless' and 'his conspicuous quality was not being conspicuous.' The external personality is not O'Connor's. Chesterton's mentor was angular and lizardlike. Far from unassuming, he possessed a forceful astringent manner. But in other respects the portrait seems to come directly from life. 'You combine so unusually in your single personality,' Chesterton once wrote to O'Connor, 'the characters of (1) priest (2) human being (3) man of science (4) man of the world (5) man of the other world . . .' The frumpishness of Father Brown conceals an idealization, but also makes a dramatic point. Chesterton likes to believe that modesty and self-effacement are essential parts of the faith that moves mountains. If the priest-detective appeared more of a hero, he would seem less of a miracle.

Chesterton illustrates this idea very effectively in *The Eye of Apollo*. Father Brown meets another kind of priest who calls himself Kalon and worships the sun:

'Their two great symbols are the sun and the open eye; for they say that if a man were really healthy he could stare at the sun.'
'If a man were really healthy,' said Father Brown, 'he would not bother to stare at it.'

Tall, magnificent, robed in white, this fashionably exotic guru betrays an American accent under stress. His chief follower, a wealthy Englishwoman, is going blind. He prescribes the sun cure and her condition gets worse. In a climactic scene, the dowdy priest forms part of the crowd while the magnetic Kalon orates from his office balcony. A terrible crash is heard from inside the building. Stepping into the elevator shaft under the impression the elevator was waiting, the blind woman has fallen to her death. Brown notices that Kalon has no reaction to the crash and the scream, but goes on with his speech. He accuses him of murder. Obviously the man was expecting the accident because he'd arranged it. 'The eye of Apollo can blast and blind,' Father Brown comments, his own clear eye seeing through to the dark side of the sun.

Behind the crime itself, a moral target exists for Father Brown to knock down. In *The Blue Cross* and *The Eye of*

73

Apollo he exposes false prophets. In the country house stories – apart from *Israel Gow*, the most ingeniously lurid are *The Perishing of the Pendragons* and *The Doom of the Darnaways* – he resists the terrors of superstition. Atheism provides another butt. In *The Three Tools of Death*, Chesterton's best fable about rich unhappy men trapped in the 'cruel religion' of unbelief, the priest investigates what looks like a highly imaginative murder. But he discovers that the millionaire philanthropist killed himself. Behind the cheerfully magnanimous speeches and deeds lay only the despair of an empty mind. In a further group of tales, most notably *The Dagger with Wings*, *The Oracle of the Dog* and *The Secret Garden*, Father Brown solves murders so cunning and impenetrable that they suggest supernatural powers at work. In the end, of course, all the stories make the same point. The particular light of Father Brown triumphs over a general darkness.

Effects overlap in the same way, for Chesterton's high points are nearly always visual rather than narrative. Echoing the adolescent's drawings, bodies catapult out of windows on fiendish ropes and slings. An unknown head with a wisp of bloodied hair lies in a moonlit garden. A postman leaves a block of apartments carrying a sack not filled with letters. A madman in a burning town impersonates a lighthouse and tries to guide a distant ship to founder on rocks. A photographer with a black cloak over his head apparently focuses his camera – only the unnatural posture of his leg reveals that he was murdered hours ago and propped up against his tripod.

Unlike the Holmes cycle, however, the Father Brown stories never develop into a cohesive work. Instead of a deepening exploration of life, they show a gradual imaginative decline. The first two collections, written before 1914, contain most of the best tales. *The Wisdom*, written shortly after Chesterton's conversion to Rome, contains the rest. The final volumes read like formula stuff, turned out for quick money. Throughout his life, Chesterton's uneasy prolific mind yields brilliant ideas that bore him after a while. A rhapsodic writer, the longer forms elude him. Themes somehow emerge from the wealth of improvisation. But after writing *The Blue Cross* he shows no interest in creating a frame for the Father Brown material.

The first story introduces the priest-detective, Flambeau the master-criminal, and the coldly sceptical Vallentin, head of the

Paris police and 'the most famous investigator in the world'. In *The Secret Garden*, which follows, Father Brown exposes the chief of police as a murderer and he kills himself. In the next story the priest encounters Flambeau again, and in the next persuades him to abandon his life of crime. Flambeau then sets up on his own as a private investigator. He and Father Brown work together as a detective team with undertones of Holmes and Watson. Each seems to be the other's only close friend, yet their relationship has little detail or intimacy. By the end of the first collection Chesterton has really shot his bolt. Having discovered his theme and played a few variations on it, all he can do is to provide more of the same. Of course he knows this. It explains his comment, 'I have never taken my novels or short stories very seriously,' a typically theatrical way of saying that he never cared about the form of the novel or short story in itself, only used it from time to time as a vehicle for his preoccupations.

But there was something else that perhaps Chesterton couldn't know. From the time that he first locked himself into an embrace with the church, the momentum of his work as a whole began to falter. He originally discussed conversion to Rome with Father O'Connor in 1911. After many hesitations on the brink he was received, swordstick in hand, in 1922. The church publicized the event as a surprise ceremony, but Chesterton and Rome were really like lovers who decide at last to get married. They'd already had several children, of which *The Innocence of Father Brown* was the first.

In Graham Greene's case, religious conversion was a creative as well as a private remedy. But where Greene has always been subtly unfaithful to his church, Chesterton's attitude reflects total submission. Hoping to escape from his demons, his secret masochistic nature substitutes one kind of bondage for another. 'I think I am morbid,' he confides to O'Connor, 'but I want to be told so by authority.' So the church appears as an instrument of correction, a spiritual whip. 'There is no other religious system that does *really* profess to get rid of people's sins. . . .' Having taken the miracle cure, the patient is condemned to advertise it for ever.

In the euphoria of obedience Chesterton comes to accept all the official claims of the system. One result is the sounding of a gradually false note in the character of Father Brown himself.

Turning too obviously into a spokesman for a cause, his air of certainty grows too rigid, his pleading too special. The history of his church is simply not as gentle and compassionate as all that. On the personal level he ends by offering an overdose of virtue, making one long for the pride and doubt and independence of Holmes. Read in a single continuity, the progress of the stories seems emotionally monotonous as well as lacking in design. As Father Brown continues to demonstrate an inflexible peace of mind, the suspicion grows that Chesterton is bluffing. His own life proves it right.

In *The Perishing of the Pendragons*, written at the end of 1913, Chesterton describes the priest-detective as having 'lately fallen ill with overwork'. His creator was in a much more serious condition. Overwork was part of the stress – in that year he'd written a play, several stories, a profusion of occasional pieces and one of his most stimulating books, *The Victorian Age in Literature*. But everything in his world was no longer 'all right'. Drinking too heavily to try and ease the basic unresolved tension, he becomes dangerously overweight. His wife had developed spinal arthritis and periods of melancholia. His brother's journalistic career collapsed after a libel action. The 1914 war was the final shock. The swiftness of the German advance into France appalled Chesterton. Having already lost his way in Catholic politics, he believed that France was a much stronger military power than Protestant Germany. The immense figure suddenly lost balance and consciousness, and capsized on his bed. It broke. For almost three months he lay in a semi-coma, unable to speak coherently, to read, to recognize people in the room.

By summer 1915 he had recovered and was writing columns for two weekly magazines. Something new and troubling appears. Before the collapse, his poem *Lepanto* crudely glorified religious war. Now he writes a patriotic biography of Lord Kitchener, the man responsible for the scorched earth policies and the concentration camps during the Boer War. And his reaction to the deaths of thousands of young men in France is to be filled with the sense of 'something beautiful, of men lying under a white light with their heads towards the morning'.

The rest of Chesterton's life is a dangerous tightrope act. In 1919 he goes to Palestine to write a series of articles later

76

collected as *The New Jerusalem*. The holy city excites less personal writing than a hypnotized visit to the 'empire of evil', the twin cities of the plain. 'Sodom lay like Satan, flat upon the floor of the world . . .' He continues to pour out essays, poems, lives of medieval saints, homages to Rome, and sounds a note of increasing crankiness. There are too many attacks on divorce, birth control, jazz, Jews, Shaw and Wells. Only a visit to America produces some unexpectedly shrewd and clear-sighted impressions. Physically he grows more and more dino-saurian, lumbering through the world as if it were a thick and difficult forest. His teeth rot because he hates going to the dentist. Advised by doctors to give up drinking, he becomes a 'secret teetotaller' for a while. For exercise he takes down a spear or javelin from his collection of medieval weapons and duels with flowers in his garden.

The *Autobiography*, worked on for several years and published after his death, confirms the truth of Borges's remark that the Father Brown stories are the emblems of Chesterton's struggle. It also reveals a struggle finally lost. Idealizing child-hood and its vanished innocence, he complains that 'it is man who afterwards darkens it with dreams'. Dreams, he insists, are 'dangerous' and 'morbid'. No doubt his own were unusually bad, but in his fear of them Chesterton tried to dismiss his unconscious altogether. This is like Don Juan trying to castrate himself.

In spite of the attempt, the unconscious surfaces. When he clings to the toy theatre, that emblem of childhood, and moves Father Brown across its stage, Chesterton projects an aching wish to be immune to the terrors of violence and untroubled by mystery and lust. Convincing himself that with the church's help the miracle has actually occurred, he sees his life as a detective story with 'its particular questions answered and its own primary problem solved'. Yet, as Father Brown says about the oriental dagger supposed to have been used as a murder weapon, something here is 'the wrong shape'. Chesterton still drives and drinks himself to a state of collapse. The demons continually rattle the locked door and the dark central thrill never loses its allure. Holding on to his priest's hand and as it were opening a private window, he returns to the view ouside, the severed heads, the corpse lying in untrodden snow, the murderer smiling in the dusk. Metaphors of what he calls the power that can be bought from hell, they haunt him as fiercely as the naked bodies lashed with thongs and pierced by swords haunted the adolescent unaware of heaven.

By 1936 Chesterton's tissues and organs (lungs, heart, kidneys, stomach, liver, brain) are all premature ruins. Exhausted and swollen, the sixty-two-year-old writer begins to fall asleep in the middle of work. Then the mind wanders out of control. It dissolves into the final coma and the end of a struggle against a long darkness with too many dreams. Perhaps a last blinding image erases the others, and the real solution of the detective story lies in his 'beautiful' vision of death on the battlefield, in a cruel wish for the white light and the head turned towards morning.

THREE

The Thin Protection

1

'Still I don't understand,' said Leithen. 'He's frightened of the wilds and yet he hankers to get deeper into them, right to a place where nobody's ever been.'

John Buchan,
Sick Heart River

In *Memory Hold the Door* John Buchan tells us that he was brought up in wild country, on the coast of Scotland. Although the family house facing the sea was backed by a railroad and small but growing industries, just a few miles beyond the coal pit and the linoleum factory lay dense woods and moorlands. Buchan's father, a Calvinist minister, ran a household of daily prayers and long strict Sundays during which he read aloud from the Bible and *The Pilgrim's Progress*. The child mixed up Calvinist dogma with his own mythology, with Bunyan and the Norse sagas he also read at an early age, and with the wild country itself. He privately located the human soul in a particular stretch of moorland, and sin (which he imagined as 'a horrid substance like black salt') in a secret part of the woods. In 1880, at the age of five, he fell out of a horse-drawn carriage and fractured his skull. He tells us that the accident improved his character. Becoming lean and tough, he understood the value of physical endurance. It was the first of many intimate connections in his life between ordeal and ideal.

Childhood summers were spent in even wilder country, at his grandmother's farmhouse near the English border. He remembers an isolation of huge and ancient trees, water-meadows, shepherds, mountains. Like his three brothers and his sister he became an enthusiastic walker and mountaineer. Climbing a higher mountain began as a challenge and developed into an ideal, with a new element added to the touch of danger and the austere physical test: the thrill of reaching the top ahead of everyone else.

Eventually he gave up climbing mountains, but not climbing. About adolescence the autobiography is veiled. It sketches a life of blustery winters, fishing, wandering, long hours with books, five-mile walks to school. The father emerges as a benign figure, thundering against the devil in church but happily reciting old Scottish ballads at home. Centred passionately on church-going and her children, the mother was the only member of the household with no time for books. Buchan implies that he was closer to this quirky indomitable countrywoman than to anyone else. Their relationship seems to contain undertones of *Sons and Lovers*.

Other incomplete accounts of this period appear in the memorial volume published after his death, *John Buchan by his Wife and Friends*. Between the lines they create an impression of someone growing up quietly self-assured in spite of a polarized nature. The romantic and the dreamer browses on solitary moorlands, loves wild weather, reads Stevenson, listens to the tales of shepherds and seamen, thinks of becoming a country minister like his father. The practical man thinks very differently. He is interested in some kind of fame, perhaps as a university professor or magazine editor. He admires Napoleon. He has a dream that people from all over the world come to ask for his advice. He reads Plato and is fired by the Greek ideal, that combination of discipline and freedom, the hardy perfect body and the controlled yet inquiring mind. He tells himself he must finish his education at Oxford, seeing it as a gateway to opportunity. This involves winning a scholarship, since his father's income is modest, and by the end of his time there the small, spare, eager student has not only won further scholarships and a poetry prize, but discovered a natural talent for making good connections.

From a remote world of wintry puritan kindliness he moves into a circle of young men marked for future importance as politicians, lawyers, publishers, generals, heirs to family estates. He cultivates their 'careless good breeding', a very English code of high spirits and veiled ambition. While success is the ultimate desirable thing, one must never admit to wanting it. Once achieved, it should be worn with convincing modesty and lightness. The shy charm, the casual manner, the slightly feminine voice, the inner determination – these gain Buchan a membership card. He sells articles on fishing and natural history to magazines, connects with two publishers, for whom he becomes a reader, and with an editor of the weekly *Spectator*, for which he reviews books. Yet literature, for all his love of it, doesn't appeal to him as a career. It's too suggestive of the dreamer, over whom the man of action has now taken precedence.

Like Conan Doyle he accepts the need for an immediately useful profession and decides to become a lawyer. But he also cements relations with the *Spectator*, is appointed a part-time editor and contributes occasional articles on politics. One of them reaches Lord Milner, colonial administrator in charge of reconstruction in South Africa at the end of the Boer War. A new important connection is made. Milner invites him to join his staff as an assistant secretary. Arriving in Johannesburg in 1901, Buchan enters another circle of confident young men. Some of these colonial aides will die in the First World War, others will become bankers, newspaper editors, ambassadors. They draft dispatches, draw up plans, ride horses and are nicknamed the Kindergarten.

In another wild country Buchan finds his most lasting ideal. Much of the land has been devastated. Continuing typhoid epidemics sweep the concentration camps. (After setting up the first hospital to deal with them, Conan Doyle has returned to England a year before Buchan's arrival.) The Boer farmers have to be resettled, equipped with livestock and machinery, mines and factories need rescuing from neglect. Buchan discovers his enormous competence for a new kind of work and acquires a political faith. He describes his new convictions as international, but they are really a pledge of public service to the Empire. Like Milner he accepts the principles of Victorian imperialism and sees Britain still leading the way. A liberal note may be sounded, adm'   ᵓses like 'self-determination' though usually ⌐   ⌐ them   ith 'eventual', but the world still divides ⁱ   ⸴uled. Following Milner, Buchan wil¹   of the rulers. He meets Cecil Rhoᵈ   ʰe great states   who has also made himself a diaʳ   ⸴, and Buchan comes away with   ‒‒‒   ⸴e but crippled power'. *Power* beᵉ   ˢ an ⌐   ⸴rrent word. The pilgrim has reᵃ   ⸴rridors, and will move along theʳ   ᴊⁱ ᴄ.

As the priv   ᵈˡᶠ   ⸴s into the public figure, Buchan's autobiography takes on an official tone, mellow yet steely. It constantly assesses people in terms of fame, influence, money and birth. The natural reticence of the early passages freezes into a cautious mask. Photographs reflect the new image. The childhood accident had left a deep scar on the left side of Buchan's forehead. Later portraits usually show the right profile. In an occasional full-face pose the scar is touched out. The frontispiece of *John Buchan by his Wife and Friends* reproduces a sculpture of his head. The artist has included the scar but the head reposes on a pedestal, the subject's natural location in his final years. The elder statesman is now distinguished enough to acknowledge the mark of a childhood ordeal. Perhaps he has even grown fond of it. By the time the bust was made, of course, he was Lord Tweedsmuir, G.C.M.G., Governor General of Canada, and had scaled the highest mountain of his life.

It would be too simple if the dreamer disappeared after South Africa, if the private man became lost in the succession of careers – lawyer, publisher, Member of Parliament, deputy chairman of Reuters, senior politician. It would be too simple if all the books Buchan wrote never rose above the correct and carefully researched level of his biographies of Cromwell, Julius and Augustus Caesar, Sir Walter Scott and George V. It would still be too simple if the private man revealed himself only through a few of his novels. In fact he surfaces at different moments and in different ways throughout Buchan's life.

One day in South Africa, on vacation from work and exploring the country by himself, he is walking alone on the bushveld. Mules and servants have been left some way behind. He wanders into a small forest, then stops suddenly, overcome by the feeling that he's been here before. Something disturbing happened then, and is going to happen again. He senses a hidden enemy presence behind a clump of trees and feels his heart in his throat. Then panic subsides as the mules emerge from behind the trees.

A few years later he is mountaineering in the Tyrol with a young Austrian. They have finished their climb and are walking back towards the valley, through a pine forest. There is no one about. Glancing at his friend, Buchan sees that the young

Austrian's eyes are glazed with fear, his face white and sweating. A moment later he runs off wildly. Without a word spoken the fear passes to Buchan. He runs too, both of them racing through the empty shadowed forest, bumping into trees and each other. They emerge into open country, leap and skid over rocks, desperate to reach the village below. Exhaustion finally kills the panic. They finish their walk in silence, unable to discuss what has happened; no word was ever exchanged about this mysterious visitation, the sudden terror of space and solitude.

Not long after this Buchan is the guest of friends in the Highlands, sleeping on a yacht at anchor in a lake. He dines at their house, dressed in a kilt, and is ferried back late at night. Glancing down at his buckled shoes, he moves through a time barrier and finds himself in an earlier century, at a moment of great danger. Hidden enemies surround him. The yacht looms mysteriously ahead, a strange threatening figure on deck. As he starts to climb the ship's ladder, Buchan forces himself to look up. He is deeply disappointed as well as relieved to see the skipper with a welcoming scotch and soda in his hand.

When the menace is concrete Buchan feels no fear. In 1936, aged sixty-one, he is flying in a private plane over the northern wilds of Canada. The weather turns bad, glaciers and mountains darken, then the plane develops engine trouble. It lurches above a narrow valley, amost skimming jagged snowy peaks. Buchan's companion, who hates flying and suffers from vertigo, is unable to speak. At first Buchan merely studies the map and confers with the pilot. They pass bumpily over a mountain top shaped like a bowl, with a forest and a frozen lake and stunted vegetation. Buchan points it out to his companion and says it would make a wonderful site for a house. A plane could bring in provisions and the place be kept wholly secret. The companion forgets his fear long enough to reflect that Buchan has always had a curious vivid response to sanctuaries, as if he were a fugitive.

Although he dismisses introspection as 'morbid', Buchan reads a great deal about psychoanalysis. In his middle thirties he develops a painful duodenal complaint that treatments and an operation fail to cure. Told that illnesses of this kind are

83

often psychosomatic, he agrees to consult an analyst. The distinguished Freudian pronounces him free of neuroses and says the disorder must be physical. When it persists, doctors can find no physical cause. By this time Buchan is surrounded by professional and personal success. He has returned from South Africa to become first a lawyer, then director of a publishing house, then Conservative Member of Parliament. He has married Susan Grosvenor, great-niece of the Duke of Wellington, resident in a privileged social world. He is widely popular in the corridors of power. The energy that provokes so much admiration, the charm and openness that appeal to so many different kinds of people, will flourish for the rest of his life. So will the internal symptoms and the pain. They become acute at moments of tension and shock – the early death of one of his brothers, the outbreak of war in 1914, the loss of another brother during the war. At other times they settle into a dull residual ache. As he grows older the long nose and shrewd alert eyes suggest a minor Roman emperor.

As with Wilkie Collins, the illness and its origins remain a mystery, but imply some obstinate rebellion within the organism. Buchan is known to have endured his condition with a minumum of complaint. Almost certainly he accepted it as another element of ordeal. Still, he must have been disappointed that in spite of the early rigorous training his body never reached a healthy classical perfection. (The adult preferred to keep it immaculately covered, reluctant even to wear an open collar on a fishing trip or a picnic.) Throughout his twenties he would disappear from the public world for long bouts of exercise combined with nature-immersion. During vacations from Oxford he went back to Scotland and surrendered again to the wild country, tested himself with walks of sixty and eighty miles a day, lived in a primitive shepherd's cottage or slept on the frosty ground. In the same way he found time to forget Milner and the Empire in South Africa, exploring velds and deserts and mountains and caves with underground rivers, celebrating their fierce aloofness from human life. In his sixties he was drawn to the forbidding north of Canada. He reached a frozen edge of the world by boat and plane, in a canoe and on horseback, and was moved after a long interval to climb a last mountain. He scaled the top before several younger members of the party.

A happy marriage, devoted children, a multitude of friends, public recognition, the favour of presidents and kings – important and desired as all these are, some vital essence remains to be tracked down in remote and isolated places. The fantasies of danger in forests and on the lake at night, the weird arctic sanctuary spied from a crippled plane, echo the child who believed that sin and the human soul inhabit a wood and a patch of heather. The adult's best novels create a landscape of suspense, fear behind a line of trees, in a distant figure climbing a hill or an empty street with shuttered windows. 'I felt the terror of the hunted on me,' says Richard Hannay in *The Thirty-Nine Steps*, alone on the Scottish moors. 'How thin is the protection of civilization,' reflects the lawyer Leithen in *The Power House*, on the run in a London, park. But the violence and the networks of enemy power concealed in natural or familiar surroundings are an invitation as well as a threat. Beyond the comfortable world lies a test. To refuse it brings the curse of mediocrity.

Buchan often admitted his horror of 'suburbanism'. The prospect of the anonymous office and the middle-class villa appalled him. His heroes agree, preferring the cult of the last chance. With the same deceptive façade of normality as Buchan himself, they are seduced by the idea of stepping outside the protection of civilization.

The early *Prester John* (1900), written after some attempts at historical romance, was conceived as a boys' adventure story in the manner of Stevenson's *Treasure Island*. Like that novel it found an audience far beyond its intentions and was even read in prison by the African nationalist leader Jomo Kenyatta. Buchan had moved into publishing when he wrote it, but the political experiences with Milner were still on his mind. It is the first example of his mesmerizing gift as a storyteller, and he was surprised at first to find that he possessed it.

In *Memory Hold the Door* he supposes it developed from a habit of 'always telling myself stories when I had nothing else to do – or, rather, being told stories, for they seemed to work themselves out independently'. The idea of 'hurried journeys' had always fascinated him, and the conflict born of living simultaneously in time and space. 'A hundred yards may be a breathless business if only a few seconds are granted to complete it.' He suggests that the excitement of a horse race and of a man trying to reach sanctuary before his pursuers overtake him appeals to the same ancient instinct. He might have added that he invented the same kind of excitement in his own life when he set himself the task of walking eighty miles in twenty-four hours.

The narrator of *Prester John* is David Crawfurd, a minister's son in a remote Scottish village around the turn of the century. A travelling black preacher called John Laputa has given a sermon at a neighbouring church. That same night the boy sees him on the beach, a huge knife in his hand, performing some kind of black magic ritual. The image haunts him. A few years later Crawfurd's father dies and the young man has to earn a living. He rejects the idea of office work and accepts a job at a trading post in South Africa. In a village consisting of a few buildings and huts, he finds himself on the edge of civilization. Laputa reappears, and Crawfurd discovers that the preacher believes himself to be a reincarnation of Prester John, the legendary king of Abyssinia. A vast Kaffir uprising is threatened, its slogan Africa for the Africans. Laputa has acquired Prester John's ruby necklace, a symbol to himself and his followers. Crawfurd's decision to become a spy for the British has little at first to do with patriotism. Fascinated by the black man, he is 'strung up to the gambler's pitch of adventure' at the intimation of primeval stirrings in the wild country. The forest conceals stealthy movements and watchful enemy eyes, mysterious drums tap out messages. 'The brain in the life of action,' Crawfurd remarks, 'turns more to the matter in hand than to conjuring up the chances of the future.' Like the other whites in the story – the breezy young British agent who disguises himself as a stoned old Kaffir, the nervous schoolmaster, the drunken storekeeper – Crawfurd is a fairly ordinary person. But he is tempted in a very ambiguous way by the extraordinary.

Laputa was brought up in America, but has wiped out his civilized past to invoke magic and superstition in the name of a mystic destiny. He is intelligent and beautiful. Buchan insists on his splendid physique, six feet six inches tall, with a face more Arab than negroid. He has a deep chest and massive shoulders although his slender hands are like a 'high-bred woman's'. Looking at him, Crawfurd forgets everything else and is lost in admiration. While he knows him for a dangerous enemy he is unable to resist the physical allure and mysterious dignity that excites a longing for submission to 'a leader who should master me'. Perhaps aware of this, Laputa strips naked in front of his antagonist. The current of sympathy certainly passes both ways, for when Laputa first captures Crawfurd he has every reason to kill him, but instead he snaps a thong on the young man's wrist and attaches it to the saddle bag of his horse. After hours of bondage Crawfurd can only feel passive and helpless 'in the grip of these great arms'. Several escapes later, he finally confronts Laputa in the secret cave with a thundering waterfall. The dying black man wears nothing except Prester John's ruby necklace. Still hypnotized, Crawfurd offers him water, but Laputa only suggest that they die together. Not infatuated enough to accept, Crawfurd watches the noble agonized figure hurl himself into the falls and be swept to the chasm below.

Released by his glamorous enemy's death, Crawfurd turns back to 'the matter in hand' and remembers he's a patriot after all. The threat of rebellion is over and Africa has been made safe for the British again:

I knew then the meaning of the white man's duty. He has to take all risks, recking nothing of his life or his fortunes, and well content to find his reward in the fulfilment of his task. That is the difference between white and black, the gift of responsibility, the power of being in a little way a king; and so long as we know this and practise it, we will rule not in Africa alone but wherever there are dark men who live only for the day . . .

As if this were not enough, Crawfurd becomes a millionaire. For helping to save the dark continent from the blacks he is awarded a share of Laputa's buried treasure. One of the British agents stumbles on a diamond mine and ends up a millionaire as well. The white man's duty pays off in more than moral satisfaction.

In spite of this greedy and unpleasant materialism *Prester John* remains in several ways a prophetic novel. Looking far beyond the immediate issues of the Boer War, it foresees the rise of black nationalism in Africa. (Five years after its appearance, the Reverend Chilembwe tries to organize a similar revolt in Nyasaland.) It describes Islam breaking through the imposed Christian surface, and the chapter called 'The Cave of the Rooirand' provides a powerful glimpse of 'desperate things, mysteries of horror long shut to the world'. Witnessing Laputa's coronation as the new Prester John, the disguised Crawfurd is enveloped in a haze of ritual, incantation, animal sacrifice, jumbled texts from the Koran and the Old and New Testaments, anger, joy, fire. Here Buchanan touches a nerve of racial aspirations and memories still raw and exposed today.

The novel finally betrays these aspirations, but the portrait of Laputa survives. The power of the unconscious is on his side. It gives him a curious daydream quality, like the later figures in *Greenmantle* and *The Three Hostages.* Crossing to the unprotected side of the frontier, the Buchan hero discovers a man of personal splendour, linked with danger and magic.

After writing *Prester John* Buchan re-enters political life and for several years Laputa lies buried. At the outbreak of war in 1914 he and his wife are living in a rented house on the east coast of England. A severe duodenal attack confines him to bed. He begins telling himself stories again, and remarks to his wife that he'd like to take 'real pains' with a thriller. A central character occurs, a composite drawn from various members of Milner's Kindergarten. He comes from South Africa and Buchan calls him Richard Hannay. A short way up the coast some relatives of his wife are living in a house with a flight of wooden steps leading down to the sea. It strikes him as a good location for the headquarters of a terrorist group. He doesn't know how many steps there are, and nobody knows why he decided on the number 39. It sounds mysteriously right. And he was thirty-nine when he started writing the novel.

'I never consciously invented with a pen in my hand; I waited until the story had told itself, and then wrote it down, and, since it was already a finished thing, I wrote it fast.' *The Thirty-Nine Steps* appears in the spring of 1915. Even more swift and compressed than *Prester John*, it also sheds the earlier work's mannerisms, the archaic turns of phrase, the self-conscious use of Scottish and Afrikaans expressions for local colour. From the opening sentences the writing establishes Hannay's character and a new tone of voice:

88

I returned from the City about three o'clock on that May afternoon pretty well disgusted with life. I had been three months in the Old Country, and was fed up with it. If anyone had told me a year ago that I would have been feeling like that, I should have laughed at him, but there was the fact. The weather made me liverish, the talk of the ordinary Englishman made me sick, I couldn't get enough exercise, and the amusements of London seemed as flat as soda-water that has been left standing in the sun.

A bearded American arrives at Hannay's apartment and asks for shelter. He explains that he's discovered the exist ence of an international terrorist group and now fears for his life. The group plans to assassinate the premier of Greece, due to arrive in England in three weeks' time, and provoke a world war. Half incredulous and half intrigued, Hannay allows the stranger to stay. The next night he comes home and finds him murdered. Staring at the white face and the body skewered to the floor by a knife, he has 'a fit of the horrors'. The police will suspect him of murder and the terrorists will be after him because he knows too much. He slips out of the building, boards a train without knowing its destination and jumps it in the middle of Scotland, finding himself alone on the moors. The rest of the story is a sustained chase-sequence. On the run from two sets of pursuers, Hannay has three weeks during which he must avoid capture, locate the enemy agents and prevent a war. The situation neatly illustrates Buchan's theory of suspense.

Hannay has few clues to follow up. The dead man's notebook is all in code. One memory that stands out is his description of the terrorist leader as an old man with a young voice who can hood his eyes like a hawk. In the meantime canny peasants and innkeepers, the single car moving along the empty road and the private plane swooping down from the empty sky create instant and justified paranoia. Hannay's world becomes an unending tight corner from which he is forced to improvise escapes. When the police close in, he seeks refuge at a farmhouse owned by an affable bald archaeologist. Something about the old gentleman makes Hannay feel 'not comfortable'. He understands why when the eyelids tremble and the keen grey eyes go hooded. A virtuoso escape scene follows. Imprisoned in the farmhouse cellar, Hannay discovers a store of dynamite. He decides to lay a charge, calculating the exact strength necessary to blast away a wall without 'blowing myself to the tree-tops'. The next sanctuary is more friendly. An affectionately satirized Kindergarten type, hearty and snobbish, believes Hannay's story and puts him in touch with his godfather at the Foreign Office. (Good connections can be useful in the most unexpected circumstances.) Experts try to crack the notebook code. The government calls an emergency meeting to discuss the impending danger. As the First Lord of the Admiralty leaves, Hannay glances at him and receives a hooded flicker of recognition. The terrorist leader disappears with the government's plans already developed in his photographic memory.

The enemy's technique of impersonation is seen at its most perfect and insolent when Hannay finally locates the group's headquarters. At the house with the thirty-nine steps he finds only three classically suburban Englishmen. Feeling 'the greatest fool on earth', he accepts their invitation to a round of bridge. The kind of talk you might hear at a country club continues over cards and drinks until the clock strikes ten. Hannay happens to look into the eyes of the cheerful old man called 'Uncle'. They seem imperceptibly to change, to harden, to grow brighter. As they guess what Hannay is thinking, the lids drop like a hood.

A theory of disguise that he heard from a Boer friend in Rhodesia flashes into Hannay's mind. Success in this art is not a matter of false beards and dyed hair. The great masters turn a handle and pass 'into another life', creating deception by atmosphere alone:

If a man could get into perfectly different surroundings from those in which he had been first observed, and – this is the important part – really play up to these surroundings and behave as if he had never been out of them, he would puzzle the cleverest detective on earth.

In the first Hannay novel the antagonist is physically unremarkable and almost anonymous, since he's known only under the bland aliases of Uncle and Mr Appleton. But his knack of disguising himself with no visible props links him again to a kind of magic. The paranormal touch completes Buchan's imaginative updating of the whole apparatus of the spy story, and prefigures later techniques of hypnotic suggestion and brainwashing.

90

The Thirty-Nine Steps is based on an idea that occurs in many popular novels of the 1890s, the existence of secret groups determined to destroy the world:

> Away behind all the Governments and the armies was a big subterranean movement going on, engineered by very dangerous people ... I gathered that most of the people in it were the sort of educated anarchists that make revolutions, but that beside them there were financiers who were playing for money.

But this is already some distance from the paranoid fantasies by William Le Queux and others that warn of diabolical new weapons, airship invasion, cigars that explode, adventuresses with smoky voices. In any case the popular myth contained a quota of truth. Mainly as a result of anarchist outrages and the Dreyfus affair, all the major European powers had developed a complex espionage system by 1900. In 1907 Conrad's *The Secret Agent* appeared. An anti-thriller containing many elements of the thriller, its tone is sardonic and analytical. The squalor of Conrad's political terrorists overrides any possible fascination with danger and violence. His shabby, almost grotesque conspirators are such moral outcasts that it comes a a shock to realize they live in the everyday world. Buchan never mentions that he read the novel, yet it seems to have left a mark. (Before starting *The Thirty-Nine Steps*, he read several thriller writers whose work he found careless and lacking in believable characters. They were probably Le Queux and Edgar Wallace, the great successes of the time.) His approach echoes Conrad's in several ways: the factual and sometimes ironic tone, the lack of conventionally sinister props, and above all the sense of undercover operations in familiar surroundings, among ordinary people who never suspect their existence.

As a stranger in Britain, Hannay's isolation is established from the start. Resourceful in action but limited in imagination, he is always making frantic mental adjustments to extraordinary events. He has to come to terms with emergencies before he can deal with them. His first reaction to a threat is to call its bluff, but once he understands it's serious he can be a formidable antagonist. Buchan draws on his memories of Milner's Kindergarten to render social attitudes. Hannay feels at home with the upper and lower classes, but naturally cannot abide the 'great comfortable, satisfied middle-class world'. He is a casual patriot with a touch of anti-Semitism. His personal code accepts killing in war but not 'cold-blooded indoor business'. His sex life is something he would never talk about and has no place in the story anyway. Once the pressure is on, he rather likes the idea of himself as a hero.

When everything is understated, anything seems possible. Hannay tells his story in a laconic and non-literary prose which transforms the most outrageous coincidence into something inevitable and even invests the fantastic with common sense. At his most desperate moments he is 'in the soup' or 'not feeling very happy'. After rounding up the terrorists too late to prevent a war, he dutifully joins the army. 'But I had done my best service, I think, before I put on khaki.' The off-hand manner fails to conceal an important conviction. War is only a necessary bad business. The higher and purer excitement of personal ordeal lies in open country.

The next two Hannay novels seem to have been written with Buchan's left hand. *Greenmantle* (1916) is very uneven and *Mr Standfast* (1919) almost self-parody. Only *The Three Hostages* (1924) completely recaptures and sustains the original verve. In spite of this, Hannay's adventures form a developing cycle like the Holmes stories. Over a ten-year period he moves from outsider to establishment figure and gathers around himself an unofficial secret society of like-minded friends. The protector of civilization is caught in some very strange undercurrents. After the First World War a new power-figure emerges, an enemy with paranormal gifts and a super-organization dedicated to creating world chaos. The climax of Hannay's experiences, and his strongest emotional involvement, is with this 'type and genius of deep crime'.

Greenmantle begins promisingly. Buchan found a point of departure in the early activities of his friend T. E. Lawrence as an intelligence agent in Egypt. Major Richard Hannay, having distinguished himself at the battle of Loos ('no picnic'), receives a secret service assignment that will take him across German-occupied Europe to Istanbul. He is briefed by Sir Walter Bullivant, the Foreign Office contact who materialized in *The Thirty-Nine Steps*, now one of several important officials with whom Hannay (like Buchan) is on intimate terms.

Scattered and enigmatic clues suggest that the Germans are plotting to bring Islam – the whole Middle East and possibly India – into the war on their side. Ready to launch a Jihad, a holy crusade, the Moslems await only the moment of revelation. The Germans apparently believe they have the means of supplying it. Rain patters against the windows and taxis hoot in the London street outside as Bullivant pieces together the scraps of information from his network of agents – Afghan horse-dealers, pilgrims to Mecca, Greek traders, sheikhs in North Africa:

. . . 'Supposing they had got some tremendous sacred sanction – some holy thing, some book or gospel or some new prophet from the desert, something which would cast over the whole ugly mechanism of German war the glamour of the old torrential raids which crumpled the Byzantine Empire and shook the walls of Vienna? Islam is a fighting creed . . .'

Hannay's job is to discover the mystic card up the German sleeve. He turns for help to a friend who has travelled widely in the East under a series of disguises. The Hon. Sandy Arbuthnot is a breezy but shrewd adventurer with 'brown eyes like a pretty girl's'. (Buchan based the character on a friend from Oxford, Aubrey Herbert, who later served under Lawrence in Arabia.) Along the way Hannay joins forces with another friend mentioned in *The Thirty-Nine Steps*, the Boer with a theory about disguises. Fresh from an espionage mission in South Africa, Peter Pienaar is another man of action with a feminine touch, 'a face as gentle as a girl's'. Bullivant provides a third aide, the American John S. Blenkiron. Rotund, jovial and cunning, he is one of Buchan's rare comic creations.

In Germany Hannay passes himself off as a pro-German Dutchman and gains the confidence of a member of the General Staff. As tall as Laputa, brutal and magnetically ugly, Stumm takes a liking to Hannay and in an ironic scene even introduces him to the Kaiser. But when Hannay arrives at the castle that Stumm uses as headquarters, he finds the colonel with the Iron Cross pinned to his huge chest living among framed embroidery and other objects that suggest a lady's boudoir:

It was the room of a man who had a passion for frippery, who had a perverted taste for soft delicate things. It was the complement

to his bluff brutality. I began to see the queer other side to my host.
that evil side which gossip had spoken of as not unknown in the
German army.

Queer as a slang word for homosexual was not at all current
until the twenties, and Buchan's use of it here seems only an
ironic accident. The handling of these scenes is prudishly uncertain and they don't escape absurdity. Stumm surprises
Hannay naked in his bath and is roused to playful sadism.
The hero becomes like a heroine trying to gain information
without losing her honour. Finally Stumm grows suspicious
and the sadism ceases to be playful. Eric Ambler has commented slyly that the climax of this ambiguous cat-and-mouse
game turns into 'an unconscious rape scene'.

Buchan recovers his touch after Hannay has escaped and
made his way across Europe to Istanbul. Winter strips the
enemy city of its fading exoticism. An icy wind stirs the
garbage in a labyrinth of muddy streets. At a seedy café filled
with Turks and Germans, Hannay watches the Companions of
the Rosy Hours, dancers who whirl themselves into a trance.
Turkish officers arrive on Hannay's trail. He is mysteriously
rescued. A carriage takes him through the falling snow to a
house in the suburbs. The leading Companion appears and
shakes his hand. It is Sandy Arbuthnot.

In another decaying house with a neglected garden Islam's
new prophet – known as Greenmantle because of the cloak he
wears – lies dying of cancer. Sandy has managed to talk to
him. Full of admiration, he describes a man who understands
the Arab desire to be lifted out of a subtle lethargy:

'They want to prune life of its foolish fringes and get back to the
noble bareness of the desert. Remember, it is always the empty
desert and the empty sky that cast their spell over them – these,
and the hot, strong, antiseptic sunlight which burns up all rot and
decay . . . It isn't inhuman. It's the humanity of one part of the
human race.'

But the prophet of a new austerity is being manipulated by
the fanatic Hilda von Einem. While Greenmantle wants to
save the souls of his people, von Einem is part of a Germany
that aims to rule 'the inanimate corpse of the world'. Sandy
sees her as a kind of Superwoman, refusing to be defeated by
the prophet's approaching death and already training one of

94

his ministers as a replacement. Always tuned in to power, Hannay finds something outside the 'routine of nature' in von Einem's eyes. Like Laputa, she arouses fear and a reluctant eroticism.

Although Greenmantle never appears in the story, his aura hovers over its second half. Buchan conveys very effectively the sense of an offstage force and the intrigues centred upon it. Unseen and dying, the leader figure still retains his magnetism. Then, as in *Prester John*, there is a gross conclusion. Greenmantle dies, von Einem is killed, Sandy assumes the prophet's turban and mantle, then he and Hannay lead an army of duped followers into battle on Britain's side. At the moment of victory over Turks and Germans Hannay reflects that life belongs to the strong. Even the odious Stumm 'was a man'. The compliment suggests an unconscious link between them, since the British have manipulated Islam just as contemptuously as the Germans. The world, Buchan reminds us, is divided into rulers and ruled.

Mr Standfast opens on this force-oriented note and never relaxes it. In late 1917 a bullish Brigadier-General Richard Hannay, D.S.O., again goes on leave for a secret mission. Blenkiron will make a welcome reappearance but Arbuthnot is in Mesopotamia and Pienaar has been captured by the Germans. When Hannay thinks of his South African friend he feels like 'a girl who longs for her lover'. Maybe this accounts for the rather bitchy tone of pacifist-baiting. Briefed by Bullivant, the spy-hunter sets out on the trail of a man who's been leaking vital information from England to Germany. As the pursuit moves from Scotland to Europe, Buchan draws laborious parallels with *The Pilgrim's Progress*. There is another master of psychological disguise. Hannay dislikes the cool English dilettante but is suddenly aroused when he metamorphoses into a proud German aristocrat. Unconscious rape is averted this time, however, since Hannay has fallen in love with a girl.

Faced with the Superwoman in *Greenmantle*, he admitted that he knew nothing about women, although 'every man has in his bones a consciousness of sex'. He longed to excite her cold and beautiful interest and moped when she ignored him. Mary, the girl he will later marry, is very different. First of all she moves with 'the free grace of an athletic boy'. She works for Bullivant, comes from a titled family and appears as virginal as her lover. Until the mission is accomplished they have no time for more than a few restrained embraces. Their conversations seem as amazingly high-toned as some of the dialogues between Buchan and his wife recorded in *Memory Hold the Door*. It becomes less a case of the writer failing to handle the emotional intimacy that leads to sexual fulfilment, than of the condition apparently not existing for him.

Both these novels were written at irregular intervals, when Buchan was preoccupied with work he considered more important. As soon as his health improved he became a correspondent on the French front for *The Times*. He wrote to Chesterton to tell him that he heard his poem *Lepanto* recited in the trenches. He embarked on a history of the war. In 1916 the government appointed him Director of Intelligence. The job brought him into direct contact with the world of espionage as well as of high diplomacy. To influence opinion and policy in other countries, and to make effective propaganda, he sifted through all kinds of information, secret and official. He attended meetings of the War Cabinet and met 'every foreigner who came to London'. During an assignment in France he collapsed after a duodenal attack, was given morphia at an emergency hospital behind the battle lines and put to bed for several weeks. Pages of *Greenmantle* piled up on the blankets while gunfire sounded in the distance.

The war atmosphere accounts to some extent for the jingoistic elements, but private attitudes are also becoming blunted in the pursuit of success. The kind of success Buchan wants is measured less in terms of money than of the approval of people he considers important. He remained at exactly the right distance from Hannay in *The Thirty-Nine Steps*, then allowed his hero to develop into a spokesman for the ruling class. Like Buchan himself, Hannay acquires a pious respect for national leaders, inherited wealth, people who come from the right families and go to the right schools. The outsider from South Africa reflects the outsider from the wild country as he becomes the intimate and employee of established power.

The same attitudes underlie *The Three Hostages* but hardly interfere with the action, which is sustained on Buchan's highest imaginative level. By 1922 Sir Richard Hannay, having won a title some years in advance of his creator, is living in the country. (So, incidentally, is Buchan. *Memory Hold the Door*: 'I wanted quiet after turmoil.' *The Three Hostages*: 'I felt that I was anchored at last in the pleasantest kind of harbour.') But the world outside is even more dangerous than in time of war. People live in an atmosphere of dissolution and eroded beliefs, and the 'moral imbeciles' thrive:

A large part of the world had gone mad, and that involved the growth of inexplicable and unpredictable crime. All the old sanctities had become weakened, and men had grown too well accustomed to death and pain. This meant that the criminal had far greater resources at his command, and, if he were an able man, could mobilize a vast amount of utter recklessness and depraved ingenuity.

The new organization interconnects 'all the contemporary anarchism' and aims at the overthrow of civilization. While its leader is unknown, the group has adherents in many countries. Great bankers and small businessmen, magazine editors and aristocrats, sportsmen and actresses are among the fanatics manipulating the stock market, murdering opponents, engineering strikes and backing minor revolutions. They are now poised to create important chaos in America and Italy, after which the members will disband and monitor the panic from separate hiding-places.

Alerted to the danger, the British government has started investigations, but the group strikes back by taking three hostages: the daughter of a Jewish-American banker, the sons of a famous general and of a titled politician. Hannay comes out of retirement to rescue them and to expose the leader before he can press the doomsday button. Once again he calls in Sandy Arbuthnot, 'still absurdly young and girlish' and now the heir to a family title and estate. Later he summons other allies, wealthy brother officers from the First World War, and a former secret agent, his wife Mary.

Hannay suspects the leader's identity fairly soon. His problem is to prove his suspicion without arousing his antagonist's. Dominick Medina, 'the handsomest thing in mankind since the Greeks', is a young Conservative politician. Popular in fashionable society as well as government circles, he chats amiably across the dinner table with the parents of his victims. Hannay first meets him at an exclusive London club, and becomes fascinated 'as a man is fascinated by a pretty woman'. Flattered when Medina responds to his interest, he walks his new friend home and is invited inside for a drink. A few minutes later he feels a disturbing aura in the room. Medina is trying to hypnotize him.

An intractable hypnotic subject, Hannay's antennae signal danger. He pretends to succumb. Medina starts to give away his secrets, the plan for 'the control of human souls' and the occult technique acquired from an Indian master. It amuses him to make a slave out of Hannay. Simulating bondage and acting out post-hypnotic suggestions, Hannay clinches their relationship and begins to gain information about the terrorist group. Although he has to endure sado-masochistic rituals, kneeling and grovelling in front of his new master and allowing Medina to spit in his face, he finds the man 'abominable but still wonderful'. Sandy explains the compelling attraction:

'... There is one kind of fanatic whose strength comes from balance, from a lunatic balance. You cannot say that there is any one thing abnormal about him, for he is all abnormal. He is as balanced as you or me, but, so to speak, in a fourth-dimensional world. That kind of man has no logical gaps in his creed. Within his insane postulates he is brilliantly sane.'

Medina wants to break down the whole structure of Hannay's personal code, his belief in family and country, his concepts of duty and honour. (He has begun work in the same way on his hostages, obliterating their memories and identities.) He sees Hannay as a microcosm of the world that he plans to throw into confusion. His motive is abstract, a demonstration of power carried to its ultimate point, of the trained hypnotic will that can reduce everything to flux, impotence, panic. He creates an atmosphere 'like a cold bright air in which nothing can live'.

Pretending to be his victim, Hannay begins to appreciate Medina as a figure of total perfect evil and to understand why 'mankind has had to invent the notion of devils'. Like Stevenson in *Dr Jekyll and Mr Hyde*, Buchan echoes a Calvinist upbringing. In both cases motiveless cruelty is released by a kind of magic, the drug that transforms Jekyll into Hyde and the 'secret knowledge' from the East that enables Medina to control the unconscious. But Medina is much more sophisticated. He knows who he is and what he's doing, and has no need to split himself in two. Jekyll disowns his criminal side, separating it into Hyde and becoming a nocturnal animal propelled by uncensored instincts into some fairly simple acts of brutality. Medina's criminal side is his true self, and he develops it through a mind-expanding technique. Admired and handsome, he combines the destructive urge and the respectable surface, operates in broad daylight in the London of Mayfair and Claridge's.

Beneath the successful mask may lie some 'ghastly throwback', but Medina's life is the opposite of primitive, all discipline, intelligence and austerity. (He has no interest in women and Hannay believes him to be asexual). Buchan again insists on the power of mental disguise. Hyde fails because he's a naked throwback. The enemy agent in *The Thirty-Nine Steps* has a trick of merging into his surroundings and being accepted as part of them. Medina goes further and starts to take over the surroundings that accept him. In the West End of London, with its solid houses and air of security, Hannay sees a fortress-symbol, a sanctuary against the danger and mystery that lies across the frontier. When the sanctuary admits Medina, the frontier and the thin protection dissolve. On a suspense level *The Three Hostages* is Buchan's most hairbreadth achievement. Medina plays Trojan horse to society and Hannay plays Trojan horse to Medina.

In some hauntingly improbable episodes that describe the rescue of the hostages, the novel reaches a free form melodrama. 'It occurred to me that anything might happen,' Hannay remarks on a desolate Norwegian mountainside at night. A wild young man springs at his throat. It is Lord Mercot, unkempt and semi-amnesiac, kept prisoner in a hut by one of Medina's agents, a reputable Harley Street doctor. The ten-year-old Warcliff is discovered in a suburban house belonging to another agent, a Swedish lady who gives hypnotic massages. He has been brainwashed into a girl and works as her assistant. At a private supper club the banker's daughter, dazed and dressed like a whore, dances with Medina's butler. The fake oriental atmosphere, the 'nigger band', the men as heavily made up as the women, suggest Berlin rather than London in the twenties. The dancers are all either victims or agents, automata or puppet-masters, the post-war world as Buchan sees it.

For its climax *The Three Hostages* moves to a wild part of Scotland again, an isolated stretch of moorland, forest and mountains with steep precipices. In total silence Medina and Hannay stalk each other for several hours. As the light fails they meet on opposite sides of a cliff face. Medina shoots off Hannay's left thumb and smashes two of his fingers, yet when he loses his foothold and starts to slip, Hannay's instinctive reaction is to try and save him. Like Laputa with Crawfurd, the enemy still attracts.

Then the body falls and disappears. A dull sound follows. Hannay faints, partly from his own pain, partly at the thought of Medina's. The story ends with the two men still disturbingly linked, Medina dying and Hannay unconscious as darkness falls on 'the most solitary place on earth'.

Although Buchan produced another twenty books after this novel he considered himself only a part-time writer. For a few years he devoted his main energies to business, as an executive at Reuters, then became a Member of Parliament again in 1927. In 1935 he was appointed Governor General of Canada and received a peerage. He resigned in 1939 because of weakening health and died a year later. Until he went to Canada he set aside weekends and two summer months at a rented house in Scotland to create a series of historical romances and biographies. Like Conan Doyle he valued his studies of the past more highly than the rest of his work and he used history in the same way as a vehicle for propaganda. In Buchan's case the propaganda is mainly for himself.

He abandons the original, mysterious fantasy about criminal power and its hidden presence in the world around him. It is replaced, as he becomes fully entrenched in public life, by a fantasy about what he calls 'benevolent dictators'. He makes a conscious connection between the two only a year or so before his death. In the meantime he moves from the fictional figures of Laputa, Greenmantle-von Einem and Medina to biographies of Cromwell and of two great Roman colonial administrators, Julius and Augustus Caesar. In his romances he creates imaginary political leaders, men who become kings and rulers and inspire devoted followers. In his own life he gathers

100

around himself a group of admiring young men and 'adopted godsons', keeps in touch with prime ministers, royalty and financiers, and eventually represents the king of England in Canada.

Although his closest friendships are with politicians, one figure outside the establishment who continues to attract him is T. E. Lawrence. Buchan could hardly fail to be fascinated by his legend and Lawrence admired the Hannay novels, comparing their style to 'athletes racing'. Both men had in common a talent for writing to which they refused finally to commit themselves, a taste for physical austerity and an energy that pushed them to the edge of their strength. They also shared, according to Buchan, 'the same philosophy of Empire'. But their lives moved in opposite directions. Buchan suppressed the private man, Lawrence tried to bury the public image. Buchan never ceased to regret his friend's decision to escape his own legend and become an anonymous outsider. Watching hopefully for a change of heart, he thought he detected it the last time they met, a few weeks before Lawrence's death:

When he left I told my wife that at last I was happy about him and believed that he might become again the great man of action – might organize, perhaps, our imperfect national defences. She shook her head. 'He is looking at the world as God must look at it,' she said, 'and a man cannot do that and live.'

Apart from its portrait of conversational style in the Buchan household, the episode is vividly self-revealing. The only solution for Lawrence with which Buchan can identify is a return to the exercise of power. He connects the solution with national defence, still dominated by the image of sanctuary from *The Three Hostages*. Two years later he centres his biography of Augustus Caesar on the idea that the right kind of dictator can 'provide against the perils'. The rest of his life is haunted by the enemy figures of his imagination. One of his last speeches as Governor General of Canada echoes Leithen in *The Power House*. He recalls the First World War and says that 'it revealed how thin the crust was between a complex civilization and primeval anarchy'.

In the last novel, *Sick Heart River* (1941; U.S. title *Mountain Meadow*), Leithen becomes a metaphor for the writer himself.

101

He first appeared in *The Power House* (1916). Set in pre-1914 London, it describes the young Scottish lawyer's encounter with a secret anarchist group and contains the famous pursuit-scene through the London park and the furtive narrow streets behind a fashionable square. Apart from this gripping passage it reads like a first sketch for *The Three Hostages*. After a walk-on part as a casual acquaintance of Medina in that novel, Leithen settles into the hero of a bland adventure about grouse-shooting and fishing. Further novels trace his rise to success, a knighthood, the position of Solicitor General. A scholarly bachelor, the apt quotation always ready, Leithen is the prisoner of a dry and reserved nature. But many people respond to his courtesy and kindliness, and as a public servant he moves easily among the ruling élite, knows Hannay and shares several of his friends.

Buchan wrote *Sick Heart River* at a time of increasing anxiety about his health and of constant physical pain. In the novel Leithen is also dying and in pain. Blenkiron, slimmed down from the days of his missions with Hannay and now 'a sort of industrial dictator' in South America, makes a brief reappearance. He tells Leithen about a wealthy young business-man in New York who recently fled to the wilds of northern Canada. It would take a 'combination of detective, psychologist and sportsman' to find out why he threw up his job and what he'd gone to look for. Leithen welcomes the adventure because he believes it will take his mind off his approaching death. He sets out with a guide into the subartic wastes and the reality of dying suddenly overwhelms him.

He begins to look back on his life. He reflects that he escaped from a Calvinist background without losing faith in Christianity, yet his religion never touched daily experience. It stayed aloof from his life. Aloofness in general is the keynote to his past. He seems unable to recall anything about love, very little about human relationships. He wonders about opportunities that may have been missed – his friends often said that with a little more effort he might have become prime minister. He cannot decide if his modesty is a genuine or a false front. He remembers the solitary wildness of the Scottish highlands and the prizes he won at school. He admits that he has sometimes been dominated by the idea of success. Then he moves deeper into deserts and mountains of snow, and feels only a twinge of fear. The mystery of the vanished man becomes less important than his own self-analysis and preparation for death.

In a silent frozen world all the exits gradually close. Leithen somehow crosses the frontier of panic. Doubt and pain begin to recede, sub-zero temperatures and a pitiless landscape revive him. The young guide strips him naked and gives him a massage. He feels even better. The missing man is sighted, crawling down a rocky hillside like a wounded animal. Disillusioned with money and power, he has run away in search of primitive isolation and found terror instead. A nearby Indian tribe is at the end of the same tether, dying from starvation and what its chief calls 'fear of the North'. But Leithen diagnoses this as fear of life. In a final bout of authority, he rehabilitates the Indians, brings the fugitive back to sanity (or banking), then withdraws into a satisfied coma. He has conquered the North:

> The most vital forces in the world are in the North, in the men of the North, but only when they have annexed it. It kills those who run away from it.

The writer's portrait of his *alter ego* shows a relentless and driven old man, as coldly compelling as the atmosphere in which he moves. The last reflexes of a leader-figure echo the youth who dreamed that people came from all over the world to ask his advice. Imposing puritan Christianity on the helpless Indian tribe, sending the businessman back to New York to make more money, Leithen embodies the link between Buchan's two fantasies. 'What is the secret,' a character wonders at the end, 'that gives one human being an almost mystical power over others?' Leithen finds in the North something more than a fear of hidden enemy forces. He feels that he's approached the centre of unexplained horror and cruelty. Then he 'annexes' it, and the curse turns into a blessing. Yet it remained a curse for Laputa in the African forest and for Medina in the Indian mountains. The wild country seems to transmit power like a magnetic field. How you use it depends on whether you pass or fail the test of fear.

Did Buchan spend his life trying to resolve the issue for himself? The young novelist describes the minister's son barely escaping from the grip of Laputa. The middle-aged one shows Hannay threatened and fascinated by the Superwoman and Medina. The later politician wears a mask of distinguished public solitude. He is benevolently preoccupied with great affairs, shoring up defences and warning of danger. There is something 'not comfortable', as Hannay would say, about this aspect of Buchan. In fact he was never more than a figurehead politician. The personal assumption of importance and power was really a fantastic role-playing adventure. Like the agent in *The Thirty-Nine Steps* he lived up to a chosen part and imposed it on his surroundings.

In *Sick Heart River* he raises Leithen's mask. The admired and honoured public servant is still a fugitive, moving deeper into the wilds, impelled to reach the 'place where nobody's ever been'. Preparing himself for death in the North, he is also Hannay facing Medina across the precipice. Even farther back he is the child Crawfurd on the beach at night, glimpsing the huge black man with the knife. In the past, says the doctor in *The Three Hostages*, the barriers between the conscious and the subconscious stood firm. Now they have started to break down, and two worlds are getting mixed.

Alone on the moors, Hannay was always looking behind and around, expecting to see what he feared. Buchan expected to die from his duodenal sickness. But he slipped and fell and fractured his skull for the second time. In spite of a brain operation he never recovered consciousness. The two accidents occurred sixty years apart, cryptic and arbitrary as the presence behind the moors. The first, he believed, moulded his life. The second killed him.

2

In most human beings the ideas of spying and being spied upon touch fantasy systems at deep and sensitive levels of the mind.

Eric Ambler,
To Catch a Spy

A fifteen-year-old schoolboy, on holiday with his parents in the south of England, has just read *Crime and Punishment*. In a nearby village a murder has been committed. The young Eric Ambler has a sudden desire for solitary communion with the scene of the crime. He bicycles to an ugly little cottage overlooking sand dunes and the sea. Already invaded by police and sightseers, its mystery has been destroyed. The spy in the house of crime leaves in disgust.

Elsewhere, in 1924, more spectacular crimes are in preparation. In prison after his first abortive attempt to seize power in Germany, Adolf Hitler writes *Mein Kampf*. Lenin dies in Russia, and Stalin immediately begins a struggle of succession with Trotsky. In a few months it becomes clear who the winner is going to be. These events make only a minor impact in England. Even H. G. Wells, whose *Outline of History* has just been reprinted for the twentieth time, prophesies in its last chapter that German militarism is finished. And even the murderer reflects a weariness with violence. Conan Doyle has seen a flamboyant dawn, but by the time of Ambler's adolescence the Golden Age has reached a discreet twilight. Arsenic in the sandwiches or the breakfast cereal furtively eliminates the unfaithful wife or the mean affluent mother-in-law. After astrology and spiritualism, the middle classes colonize another profession. Only a few of them commit murder, but thousands of them read about it. Detective novels flood the market while the murder rate stays remarkably low. Ignoring this and many other realities of the outside world, the novels are only one symbol of a prevailing mood.

The schoolboy pedalling to the cottage in the dunes reacted against the mood. He had read Dostoyevsky and was looking for serious terror. Perhaps the disappointment explains why he never found England stimulating. A few years later he realized that the seaside murderer was only one more average psychotic, part of the dullness of another Sunday afternoon.

Imaginative people born into a theatrical background carry it around inside themselves. Two of its vital elements, insecurity and impersonation, make a strong early effect. Ambler's parents were partners in a variety act and spent much of their lives touring the music halls. After being educated at a minor elementary school, Ambler won an engineering scholarship to London University. But the prospect of an engineering career struck him as literally mechanical. He abandoned the idea to tour the music halls as a comedian, writing his own acts and songs. Restless but adaptable, he followed this with a job as an advertising copywriter and found it no problem to create effective campaigns for baby foods, metallurgical products, theatrical agencies. During these years of the 1930s he also took time off for some modestly budgeted travelling. He gravitated towards the Balkans and the Middle East, following the Orient Express route to Belgrade, Athens, Istanbul. He reconnoitred Beirut and Cairo, and in Tangier he met a blowsy motherly Central European refugee who ran a beach café and turned out to be a spy.

It was only one of many theatrical encounters that revealed apparent backwaters as focal points of espionage. Cities of the underdeveloped world spilled over with evidence of the major powers preparing for another major war. Each minor country manoeuvred for position and provided a dingy rehearsal room for the super-production to come. Like Wilkie Collins tracking the disguises of crime in Victorian London, Ambler discovered the slouchy nonentity in the café at the end of the secret alley, worming out locations of an airstrip or minefield. He learned that the man with the air of a mediocre bureaucrat was a paid assassin, employee of a casually illegal business. Since passports and identity cards can be manufactured to conceal identity, the dead remain as anonymous as the living. Allegiance, like information, is only something that costs money. Behind this looking-glass world, like the darkness surrounding a lighted stage, lies the certainty of war and perhaps the end of a civilization.

The same instinct that awakened the schoolboy directed Ambler to settings already celebrated in popular fantasies of foreign intrigue. Like the wish suddenly granted in a fairytale, an imaginary fulfilment became actual. There were many unexpected solitary communions with the scene of a real crime. *The Mask of Dimitrios* will echo Ambler's first reaction:

The world of escape, the fantasies you created for your own comfort were well enough if you could live within them. But split the membrane that divided you from the real world and the fantasies perished. You were free and alive; but in a world of frustration.

In the frustrating thirties England seems more than ever a remote province, and the mean side street in Athens or Istanbul the true centre. But Ambler has to continue making a living. There are few things more incongruous than pushing baby foods in a society that you see edging blindly towards destruction. Still, he goes on turning out expert copy and by 1936 has become director of a London advertising agency. A year later he publishes his first novel, *The Dark Frontier*, and changes his life again. Leaving England and his job, he settles in Paris.

The young Englishman often seen at some shabby Paris bar in the early hours of the morning looks neat and quiet, almost dapper. People comment on his resemblance to the Duke of Windsor. Sometimes he sits and drinks alone. On these occasions he is probably turning over a new discovery, this time about himself. It started with 'guilt feelings', murderous private fantasies intense enough to make him wonder whether he might be personally capable of murder. He notes how often people say 'I wish he were dead' and mean it. The impulse to kill has grown alarmingly common. It seems to come from the surrounding air.

Psychoanalysis helps to relieve his anxieties about himself, if not about other people. The fantasies persist but some internal censor prevents him from activating them. From the resulting deadlock he comes to believe that 'there is a criminal and a policeman inside every human being'. It is not a comfortable view, particularly if one takes the human being as a metaphor for the current world and sees the criminal winning. In Europe in 1938, aggressors are everywhere in the driver's seat.

Violent people continue to fascinate him because he wants to know what they're going to do next. He assesses them with a streak of envy. Free of internal censorship, they can kill 'without passion and without remorse. They are the emotionally *un*disturbed' – an ironic thought which offers no consolation to the neutral and peaceful. It leaves *them* emotionally disturbed and leaves Ambler with an alert sense of fear at what he remembers as the 'crummy bricktop bar' in the middle of the night.

If he's not a murderer, is he a potential victim? Perhaps, like the criminal and the policeman, they are two faces of the same coin. His novels as well as his analyst become the vehicle for these fears. While *The Dark Frontier* and *Epitaph for a Spy* (1938, written after he moves to Paris) use too many conventional suspense devices, they contain most of the ideas that Ambler will develop later. Individuals are lost and isolated in a power struggle on a new scale. The physicist in *The Dark Frontier* not only forecasts the use of atomic weapons, but identifies the international cartel and the armaments firm as leading players in the war game. The big business corporation and the tycoon seem even more deadly than the totalitarian leaders with their blood purges and secret police. Financiers manipulate money and disturb whole economies. Industries produce immense stockpiles of guns and bombs. The profit motive creates the social chaos and the means of violence that lead to war. Although the Marxian argument reflects the intellectual left-wing climate of his time, Ambler uses it to convey a very unMarxian feeling of personal helplessness.

A world of paranoia opens up in *Epitaph for a Spy* when the hero's passport is stolen in a foreign country and he discovers the anxiety and humiliation of being officially nobody. Is there a plot against him? Will the police believe his story? How do you prove identity without evidence? Why should anyone listen to you if they don't even know who you are? The traffic in false passports leads to further questions. If identities can be bought, sold and stolen, is anyone really what he seems? How can you tell whose side anyone is on? And does it finally matter, since 'sides' are only reflections of a hostile and indifferent authority? Espionage, the small business behind the big business, deals in illusion and reality as well as the specifics of the submarine base or the military plans.

This is why the novelist who actually works as a spy finds himself inside a novel. For Somerset Maugham, a British agent in 1916-17, the experience was at first so like the average thriller that 'it took most of its reality away from the war'. Ten years later, in the linked stories of *Ashenden,* he gained a perspective on another kind of reality. The episodes based on his year in Geneva are particularly compelling, with their moral atmosphere that echoes the neutrality of Switzerland. He describes how the undercover world judges people only in terms of their ability to betray, dissemble and kill. No one is admirable or despicable, merely useful or useless. A 'human' reaction can only be an admission of failure. When Ashenden admires the courage of an enemy agent, his affably ruthless superior R. is rather shocked. He advises Ashenden to forget his 'morbid' ideas and concentrate on tracking the man down and shooting him.

Ambler takes the existential approach of *Ashenden* a stage further. He spies on spies, seeing around and beyond them. A trained engineer, at home with plans and documents, he knows how to pass on accurate information. But since fears and fantasies exist immediately below the level of the cool mind, he can grasp imaginative secrets as well. Unlike Maugham-Ashenden who returns untouched to his life as a writer, Ambler's protagonists never shake off the smell of their experience:

Fear and be slain. Or were you slain anyway, whether you were afraid or not? Yes, you were. 'Good' did not triumph. 'Evil' did not triumph. The two resolved, destroyed each other and created new 'evils', new 'goods' which slew each other in their turn. The essential contradiction . . .

The clear emotional blueprint from *Epitaph for a Spy* applies to Ambler's world as a whole. The essentially Victorian idea of security has disappeared. There is no question of outwitting criminals to protect a superior moral order. The problem is how to save one's own life from the 'essential contradiction' and the flux of violence.

In *Cause for Alarm* (1938), an engineer goes to Milan as the representative of a British company that manufactures shell cases. He also represents the British middle class, amiable and insular, firmly out of touch with his time. Like all of Ambler's best work this novel is about a rite of passage. It begins with the Fascist police demanding Marlow's passport for a routine check and then 'mislaying' it. His letters to and from England are steamed open. Someone follows him when he walks home from a restaurant at night. He receives a visit from an enigmatic Yugoslav general who carries a swordstick, wears make-up and a monocle, adores the ballet, and leaves after hinting at a proposition that he never actually makes. Then he meets Zaleshoff, a hearty and genial Soviet agent brought up in America, who peppers his Marxian talk with Chicago slang. He explains that Marlow's predecessor had been in the general's pay and supplied him with information about new shell cases, which Vagas relayed to Germany. Furthermore, he didn't die in an automobile accident but was murdered when he tried to back out of the deal.

Both sides now bid for the newcomer's services. Although Marlow thinks of himself as simply a businessman engaged in selling machinery and wants no part of 'politics', the uncommitted man finds himself caught between fiercely committed forces. General Vagas points out that a good business-man should always be open to a new proposition. 'Patriotism is for the *caffé*. One should leave it behind with one's tip for the waiter.' Zaleshoff points out that a businessman like Marlow is already a criminal. If he sells machine parts that will be used in case of war, he has joined the armaments conspiracy. The neutral technician finds himself no match for the Russian's frontal attack and the general's deviousness. When he realizes that the police have pretended to lose his passport as a way of keeping him under surveillance, anxiety becomes his only conviction.

Marlow doesn't share Zaleshoff's views, but likes and trusts him personally. They make a pact. He will pretend to accept the general's offer, passing on subtle misinformation and reporting back to Zaleshoff on the enemy's moves. Ambler's gift for ironic tension is deployed for the first time as he shows Marlow approaching the profession of double agent with the same careful, blinded efficiency that he brings to his job as an engineer. Living precariously in a secret world of deceit and impersonation, of assignations on a deserted highway at night and code letters sent to *poste restante* addresses, he refuses to abandon his prim businessman image. The general destroys it cruelly when he presses Marlow for information about the Italian arms factories he has to visit:

> When at last I spoke it was to utter one of the feeblest remarks of which I have ever been guilty.
> 'But that,' I said, 'would make me a spy.'
> His reply was delivered in terms of infinite contempt.
> 'My dear Marlow,' he said deliberately, 'you already *are* a spy.'

A few days later the police agree. They issue a warrant for Marlow's arrest and General Vagas flees the country. The second half of the novel is Buchanesque, an escape-episode that takes Marlow and Zaleshoff across the mountains into Yugoslavia. Marlow's delayed self-recognition underlies the physical suspense. He can no longer congratulate himself on 'a sound piece of work' after skilfully deceiving Vagas, but has to come to terms with his new reality as a fugitive – hiding in train lavatories, stealing clothes, running down side streets to avoid police patrols, toiling through snowdrifts that reach to his waist. Without Zaleshoff's capacity for endurance and improvisation, he would never survive. He has nothing to fall back on except his English middle-class belief in muddling through, ludicrously inadequate in a crisis. 'Change your system and you change your man,' says the tireless communist. 'When honesty really *is* good business, you'll be honest.' The point of view infuriates Marlow, but its strength saves them both.

He returns to an England unchanged from the time that he left it. In spite of a depression his employer is concerned only with improving his golf game. When Marlow first encountered the world of espionage, it seemed unreal. Now the so-called normality of England seems unreal. The strongest echo in *Cause for Alarm* comes from Vagas's sinister monologue on the ballet. Dancing and preparation for death, he told Marlow, have been linked since pre-history. Ballet remains the most accurate prophet of destruction:

'In the years before nineteen-fourteen it drew larger audiences than ever before. In the early nineteen-twenties, when Diaghilev was doing his best work, it became a more esoteric pleasure. Now it is popular again. If I never read a newspaper, Mr Marlow, one evening at the ballet would tell me that once again society is preparing for death.'

Ambler has said that politics interest him as much as espionage. Underlying the melodrama of Marlow caught between Soviet and German agents and Italian police is the suggestion that England should make a political marriage of convenience with Russia. In spite of his simplified ideology, Zaleshoff makes more sense than anyone else at the time and offers a chance of avoiding war with Germany and Italy. Soon after the novel appears, the British government begins negotiations with Russia for a non-aggression pact. They are broken off after pressure from big business interests who believe that communists are far more dangerous than fascists. Stalin signs with Hitler instead. Late in the same year, Neville Chamberlain abandons Czechoslovakia and comes to terms with Hitler at Munich. There is a move to make him a candidate for the Nobel peace prize and Lloyds gives odds of 32—1 against war breaking out within the next twelve months. Trenches in Hyde Park are covered over, temporary air-raid shelters abandoned, gas-masks stored away. England, like Marlow, continues to muddle through. *Cause for Alarm* has its prophetic side. It gives the last word to General Vagas, spokesman for Germany and the ballet.

The Mask of Dimitrios (1939; U.S. title *A Coffin for Dimitrios*) is the last novel Ambler writes in Paris. It creates a powerful suspense with a minimum of violent action, yet the atmosphere of a society preparing for death is richer than in *Cause for Alarm*. The protagonist, Charles Latimer, has been a university professor and written several books on political history, then discovered the more lucrative career of writing detective novels. They are of the kind that have been popular since Ambler's youth, emphasizing that murder will out and justice will always triumph. On vacation in Istanbul he meets an admirer of his work who happens to be chief of the Turkish secret police. Colonel Haki wonders if Latimer is interested in '*real* murderers'. The body of a man named Dimitrios Makropoulos has just been discovered in the Bosphorus. Since the early 1920s he had been involved in all kinds of crime: murder, political assassination, espionage, the white slave and hard drug traffic. Latimer feels a stirring of curiosity. He accompanies Haki to the morgue and has a moment of solitary communion with a corpse wrapped in a mackintosh sheet, its hair tousled and its face grey as putty. Haki warns him that the murdered murderer is not 'artistic', just one more criminal at the end of a squalid road.

In this ironic scene lies the beginning of an obsession. The writer of detective stories fabricates unreality, the dead man under the sheet contradicts it. Latimer suddenly decides to find out all he can about Dimitrios. He embarks on a passage to a different world, and the story of Dimitrios becomes a handbook of criminal activity in Europe between the two great wars.

The structure of *The Mask of Dimitrios* is Ambler's most brilliant achievement. From police records and newspaper archives Latimer learns of Dimitrios's early life, his escape from Smyrna after its destruction in the 1922 Turkish–Greek war, his first murder, his part in a political assassination. From La Preveza, an ex-prostitute who now owns a seedy nightspot in a back alley in Sofia, he hears about Dimitrios as pimp and blackmailer. An underworld figure tells of his partnership with Dimitrios in white slavery and heroin smuggling. A retired spy, living in Switzerland and writing a life of St Francis, describes Dimitrios the double agent. The multi-narrative technique develops from *The Woman in White*, but Ambler shifts time and viewpoints more freely. The mystery that Latimer sets out to unravel is not a single crime but a man whose life is the sum of all his crimes. (A year later Orson Welles will take the same approach with the journalist who investigates Citizen Kane after his death.) The past catches up with the present, and the novelist becomes a character in the mystery he's trying to solve.

As Latimer pursues Dimitrios, one of the dead man's former associates pursues Latimer. A man who calls himself Mr Peters believes that Dimitrios had money hidden away and that the writer is on its trail. He contrives to share Latimer's sleeping compartment on the train from Athens to Sofia. Peters is a criminal type directly descended from Count Fosco. Wonderfully odious, slippery and fat, he looks as if he eats too much and sleeps too little. His manner suggests an unfrocked priest. He displays brilliant false teeth in a permanent smile, as if 'some obscene plant had turned its face to the sun'. He always carries a paperback volume called *Pearls of Everyday Wisdom* and quotes its oily sentiments with a missionary's conviction. God and Destiny lie heavily on his mind:

'Leave the Great One to answer the questions beyond our poor understanding . . . If the Great One wills that we shall do unpleasant things, depend upon it that He has a purpose even though that purpose is not always clear to us. If it is the Great One's will that some should become rich while others should remain poor, then we must accept His will.' He belched slightly . . .

Since the Great One has seen fit to make Peters a criminal, all his vices are predestined. Greed, treachery, the prostitution racket, smuggling and diluting heroin – he accepts them with patient resignation. Like Fosco he rationalizes the most repulsive acts and disguises his nature to appear plausible to himself as well as to others. At his most dangerous he needs the mask of lovability.

A final witness ends the parade of testimonies. With a classic twist of plot Ambler introduces Dimitrios himself. The body in the morgue was only one of Dimitrios's victims, a false identity card sewn into the lining of his coat to mislead the police. 'A dirty type, common, cowardly, scum,' had been Haki's verdict, but Latimer is confronted by a distinguished-looking gentleman who might be a guest at a diplomatic reception. Unexpected on every level, this confrontation enables Ambler to reflect on a favourite subject, appearance and reality:

A man's features, the bone structure and the tissue which covers it, are the product of a biological process; but his face he creates for himself. It is a statement of his habitual emotional attitude; the attitude which his desires need for their fulfilment and which his fears demand for their protection from prying eyes . . . If he is afraid, then he must be feared; if he desires, then he must be desired. It is a screen to hide his mind's nakedness.

In *The Thirty-Nine Steps* Buchan suggested that a man can disguise himself by a paranormal trick of taking on the colour of his surroundings. Dimitrios performs the same act, but without any element of magic. Before his analysis, Ambler had become interested in Jung, and the 'mask' of Dimitrios is really an illustration of Jung's theory of the persona, the role that a person assumes in order to express his idea of himself. Dimitrios's life has been a struggle for money and power. At first desperation made him crude, so people like La Preveza found him crude. With success he became devious, an image reflected by the retired spy. Finally, after informing on most of his associates and changing his name, he appears on the board of directors of a banking corporation registered in Monaco and known as the Eurasian Credit Trust. In his early days he had been its employee, for Ambler reveals that the Trust financed both the heroin trade and the political assassination. It is less important, he comments, 'to know who fired the bullet than to discover who paid for it'. Under the mask of Dimitrios crime and big business merge as two aspects of the same face. 'The dirty type' and the respectable financier have become the same person.

114

Covering his different identities by a frequent change of surname and passport, Dimitrios is presumed dead on account of a false identity card. Peters has also blurred his origins. Born Petersen in Denmark, he travels on a passport issued by a South American republic that sells them to international criminals on condition they never set foot in their adopted country. Illusionism is the hallmark of espionage and drug traffic. Grodek the retired spy points out to Latimer that Europe in 1939 contains twenty-seven independent states, each secretly engaged in collecting information about the military strength of the others. He estimates the European spy population at around 50,000. The amount it is paid in different currencies runs into 'millions'. At first incredulous, Latimer makes his usual adjustment: 'Did governments of adult men and women behave like children playing Red Indians? Evidently, yes.' Peters confesses to Latimer how he smuggled heroin for Dimitrios in a coffin that he personally accompanied on the boat from Bulgaria to France, dressed in a suit of mourning clothes. 'I was most moved by the simple respect for my grief shown by the stevedores who handled the coffin at the dock.' As the membrane dividing Latimer from the real world splits a little farther, his own fantasies appear prosaic against the fact of this criminal underground. He begins to suspect that his imagination is simply unequal to the quest for the 'truth' about Dimitrios.

In a rare moment of plain speaking Peters accuses him of being secretly shocked by Dimitrios. Latimer agrees, then points out: 'It is just because I am shocked that I am trying to understand, to explain him.' After the parallels between Dimitrios's life as a criminal and the methods of big business, there remains the mystery of his personal drive. 'All men can be dangerous,' says La Preveza, 'as tame animals in a zoo can be dangerous when they remember too much.' She finds a clue to Dimitrios's nature in his eyes, brown and anxious, 'that made you think of a doctor's eyes when he is doing something to you that hurts'. Peters reveals more about himself than about Dimitrios. He drops his own mask of sentimentality and wobbles with hate at the thought of the man who outwitted and informed on him. The almost-last word comes from a left-wing journalist whom Latimer meets in Athens. Like Zaleshoff, he is portrayed with a mixture of admiration and irony. 'Special sorts of conditions,' says Marukakis, 'must exist for the creation of the special sort of criminal that he typified.' Europe since the First World War, with its gathering chaos and 'gospel of tooth and claw', provides these conditions. To say anything more is to apologize for Dimitrios. No further 'truth', however bitter, can be extracted from the life of a man who dedicates himself to crime and violence.

Somehow the aggression of Dimitrios and the aggression of society interact. Eugene Marais's *The Soul of the White Ant* describes a colony of termites living inside a solid pillar of earth. The queen termite controls and perpetuates her colony. In a way that Marais sees happening but can't explain, each termite is able to communicate with the other and the whole society shares what he calls a soul. In Ambler's novel Dimitrios and society communicate in the same mysterious way, telepathically linked in a single organism that shares the soul of the pimp and the murderer, the dealer in drugs and lives, the spy and the financier.

The Second World War broke out a few months after *The Mask of Dimitrios* was published. Ambler returned to England with the American girl he had recently married. His novels predicted war, but it still provided a shock because it didn't happen in the expected way. Instead of a holocaust, months of prolonged inaction followed the quick defeat of Poland. During the so-called 'phony war' armies remained behind their lines and more searchlights than planes pierced the sky. *Journey into Fear* (1940) reflects Europe's last season punctuated by air-raid sirens sounding false alarms.

Low-key prose conveys a high state of panic. Within a tightly controlled structure Ambler shows a man almost out of control with fear. The protagonist is a slightly older Marlow from *Cause for Alarm*, an engineer employed by a British armaments firm. After many trips abroad Graham has become less insular than Marlow and even enjoys discovering the strangeness of a strange city, but he is narrowly centred on his work, has made a successful passionless marriage and relaxed by reading detective stories. A 'Do Not Disturb' notice hangs on the door to his mind. It is due to be removed.

In early 1940, after England and Turkey have signed a treaty of alliance, Graham's employers send him to Istanbul to help re-equip the Turkish navy with new guns and torpedos. On the last night of his mission he returns to his hotel and several shots are fired from his darkened room, one of them gashing the back of his hand. A silhouetted figure disappears through an open window. Graham imagines he's surprised a hotel thief, but Colonel Haki of the secret police believes the intruder was a German agent. 'It is perfectly simple. Someone is trying to kill you.' Graham's death would leave the Turkish navy idle for several months while another expert came out to reconstruct the plans. Insisting that he must leave the country in secret, Haki puts him on board a cargo boat carrying a few passengers to Genoa.

Cramped, shabby and uncomfortable, the *Sestri Levante* is a microcosm of Ambler's world, a vessel for the ambiguous and the rootless. Three of its passengers travel on false passports, two are secret agents, and a hired killer comes on board at Athens. Apparently a Greek businessman, he wears a peculiarly strong and sickly perfume that Graham remembers sniffing in his hotel bedroom just before the shots were fired. The journey into fear begins at this moment. Graham tries and humiliatingly fails to convince the captain that his life's in danger. He tells himself, 'There's a way out of this', repeating the litany of the hopelessly trapped. His only consolation is that he's packed a revolver in his suitcase. When he takes it out and looks at it, the technician no longer feels neutral. Before the threat to his life he'd regarded any weapon simply as a piece of machinery, 'a series of mathematical expressions', no more symbolic than a vacuum cleaner:

> His interest in the men who had to fire the products of his skill as in the men who had to suffer their fire (and, thanks to his employers' tireless internationalism, the same sets of men often had to do both) had always been detached . . . His attitude towards them was as uncomprehending as that of the stoker of a crematorium towards the solemnity of the grave.

The gun in Graham's hand now ceases to be an impersonal object. There is 'a relationship between it and the human body'. It offers the choice between killing and being killed. He feels better for most of the day. In the evening he returns to his cabin and finds the revolver has been stolen.

The next stage is a masochistic fascination with the character

117

of the man who intends to kill him. Graham knows little except that he's a paid assassin, he comes from Roumania and his real name is Banat. Haki has said that his asking price is five thousand French francs plus expenses. 'He is very fond of gambling, and is always short of money.' His appearance is crumpled and mediocre. He wears a shabby raincoat, has pouches under his eyes and leaves this permanent incongruous trail of perfume. At dinner, trying to pretend he's not afraid, Graham forces himself to speak to him. Banat mentions that he was recently in Rome, where he saw 'a magnificent parade of the Italian army with guns and armoured cars and aeroplanes'. It made him think of God. Graham reflects that the law doesn't consider a hired killer insane. Yet if Banat feels the majesty of God in dive-bombers, he must be insane. Unfortunately he is not a fool. His professional reputation is excellent.

Inevitably Graham looks for someone on board to trust. Among the people who may or may not be what they seem, he finds one appealing. Josette's life is taken up with travelling to and from engagements as a second-rate dancer in second-rate nightclubs. Her Spanish husband and partner is always trying to fix her up with men who look as if they have money. But there is something innocent in her sensuality and her air of being bound for a destination that she will never reach. Her lack of surprise at Graham's situation also fascinates him. Used to living in a dangerous world, she tells him that her husband likes to quote a German proverb that says man is an ape in velvet:

'Jose says that if a person *really* needs to do something he will not trouble about what others may think of him. If he is really hungry, he will steal. If he is in real danger, he will kill. If he is really afraid, he will be cruel. He says that it was people who were safe and well fed who invented good and evil so that they would not have to worry about the people who were hungry and unsafe.'

Josette finds this 'simple'. She finds an equally simple answer when Graham asks if she likes her husband. 'He is my partner. With us it is business.' The same rule applies to affection as to killing. She likes Graham, but if he didn't have money she couldn't afford to be interested in him.

The novel's suspense derives its power from the way that Ambler extends Graham's fear of his immediate situation to a fear of society as a whole. On one level is the menace of **Banat**, and of the archaeologist who turns out to be a German agent and matter-of-factly announces, 'You will be dead within a few minutes of your landing at Genoa': on another, a world in which it is 'stupid' to talk of good and evil. Terror in itself is humiliating, and its physical sensations (nausea, the cramped chest, the crawling of the spine) disagreeable. But it also exposes certain illusions. Trying to escape with his life, Graham begins to question it. Is it really as enjoyable and important as he thought? Might not a bullet now be better than months of decay and illness in old age? After he's escaped, he feels a twinge of regret at not meeting Josette in Paris as he'd promised:

She was part of the world beyond the door: the world into which he had stepped when Banat had fired those three shots at him in the Adler-Palace: the world in which you recognized the ape beneath the velvet. Now he was on his way back to his own world; to his house and his car and the friendly, agreeable woman he called his wife. It would be exactly the same as when he had left it. Nothing would be changed in that world; nothing, except himself.

The Mask of Dimitrios ends with Latimer on a train that disappears into a tunnel, and *Journey into Fear* with Graham on another train, looking through a window at searchlights probing the sky. Both have come back from 'the world beyond the door'. But in 1940 Ambler himself re-enters it. He enlists as a private in the British army and will not write another novel for eleven years.

From suspecting the existence of a potential murderer within himself, Ambler has arrived at the idea of a potential murderer within everyone. Buchan's image of 'the thin protection' has been re-examined in the light of psychoanalysis. In the first of *The Lizzie Borden Memorial Lectures* written for *Holiday* magazine, Ambler recalls the schoolboy's trip to the murder cottage. He'd hoped then to come to 'closer grips with the problems of good and evil with which my anxiety-laden mind was preoccupied'. But the human biologist replacing the moralist of fifteen believes that Anglo-Saxon culture is built on 'studious denials of the existence within us of the primitive. The revelation that there is, after all, an ape beneath the velvet is perennially fascinating.' The revelation has come

119

through fear. Ambler admits that he's always 'frightened of what's around the next corner', and in this sense his neutral technicians (including Latimer, who manufactures detective stories) are metaphors for himself. They reach a point at which acute fear eliminates the idea of good and evil. For Marlow in *Cause for Alarm* the words only rationalize an unending struggle, 'the essential contradiction'. Dimitrios convinces Latimer that they are 'baroque abstractions'. Josette's husband persuades Graham that they are concepts invented by the fortunate in order not to worry about the unfortunate. When Graham tells himself that if he surrenders to panic he'll be lost, he begins to find his situation stimulating. When Ambler enlists in the army, fear and curiosity again interact.

War licenses the potential murderer and the ape can step out of his velvet to the sound of applause. There will be many new opportunities for solitary communion with the scene of a crime. Transferred to a combat filming unit, Ambler looks at battlefields through a keyhole, noting a few strange and ironic postures of death. The images usually connect with victims. In Italy he confronts a soldier pointing a rifle directing at his face. But the man is frozen in a death spasm. Nearby he sees another soldier carried away on a stretcher, one arm extended rigidly towards the sky. 'They couldn't get the arm down. He had a ring on his finger with a hieroglyph of the sort you buy in Algiers.' The humour that has always been dark grey turns to black. He hears about the bombing of London and is disturbed for the safety of houses in which famous murders have been committed. Must war sweep away all traces of the individual killer? A report comes through that Dr Crippen's former home has been reduced to a hole in the ground. Ambler checks it out after the war and finds that while respectable neighbouring houses have been destroyed, the old place still stands, 'a little shabby, perhaps, a little run down, but still proudly intact'. Since Crippen was an American murderer living in London, Ambler salutes in this surviving criminal landmark 'an enduring emotional link between our two democracies'.

A meeting with Carol Reed in the army film unit leads to a collaboration. Ambler writes the adroitly propagandist script for *The Way Ahead* (1944), a study of young men wrenched from civilian life and trying to adjust to military training. His interest in screenwriting continues after the war, but he never works with another director of Reed's calibre. The results convey little of his personal temperament. Screenwriting provides, all the same, a useful substitute during a creatively fallow time. Graham Greene once said that Ambler analyses danger as carefully and seriously as other novelists analyse guilt or love. But guilt and love are a fixture of human relations. Danger, as Ambler approaches it through the power play of politics, grows more or less intense according to season. When the war broke out, it was a fact already conceived in Ambler's imagination. There could be nothing vital left to say. When it ends, he has to wait for a glimpse of fear in a new shape.

By the end of the 1940s politicians had rebuilt their community of distrust. The cold war looked ominous. Ambler wrote *Judgement on Deltchev* (1951). A few years later colonized countries in southeast Asia began their struggle for independence. *The Night Comers* (1956; U.S. title *State of Siege*) and *Passage of Arms* (1958) report on terrorist movements, military and communist takeovers. Ambler is the kind of writer who depends on bad news, but sometimes bad news reaches only the conscious level of the mind and fails to touch the imagination. With their portraits of quiet, buried, astonished men in a jam, the pre-war novels conveyed a sense of psychic as well as physical danger. In the novels of the fifties the protagonists seem like pieces of literary cement to hold the action together. Facts receive more emphasis than people and settings are only topical backdrops.

Restless and displaced again in England, Ambler went to Los Angeles in 1959 to write a script for Hitchcock. The film was shelved but he remained in California. By this time he had divorced his wife, and made a second marriage, to Joan Harrison, a screenwriter who began as Hitchcock's personal assistant. He also covered for *Life* the murder trial of Dr Finch and Carole Tregoff. Raymond Chandler might have invented this gaudy suburban melodrama with its background of dusty palm trees and the kidney-shaped swimming pool. In the character of the casual criminal whom the doctor and his girlfriend offered $1,400 to kill Mrs Finch, Ambler sees and vividly sketches an emotionally undisturbed 'amoral realist'.

121

Briefly back in England in 1961, he writes about another case known as 'the A6 murder'. A gunman wearing black gloves forced a man and a woman to drive their car off the main highway into a field at night. After boasting that he'd 'done the lot' in the twenty-five years of his life, he killed the man, then raped the woman and shot her several times. She survived, paralysed from the waist down. Here Ambler reconstructs a scene of apparently motiveless violence in the same way as Capote's later *In Cold Blood*. After sketching the gunman's background as loner, thief and attempted suicide, he finds that the trial centres around a problem of identity.

Two witnesses who claimed to have seen James Hanratty driving the car erratically next day identified two different men at a police line-up. At another parade, the woman identified an innocent man before pointing to Hanratty as the man who raped and shot her. Hanratty's psychotic background and criminal record matched the gunman's in the field, and he could produce only a shaky alibi, but he pleaded innocent. After a long consultation with the judge on the meaning of 'reasonable doubt', the jury declared him guilty. Although Ambler agreed with the verdict, he had other reservations:

But when we are taking the irreversible step of executing a man, should there be *any* permissible kind of doubt?
Well, doubtless there has to be. Otherwise, nobody would *ever* be executed.

Five years after Hanratty's execution, another man confessed to the crime. The evidence was re-examined, the area of doubt found to be more reasonable than it seemed at first, and a committee formed to secure Hanratty the final irony of a posthumous pardon. Ambler's comment on capital punishment gains in persuasiveness *because* he believed in Hanratty's guilt.

In these cases, and in his portraits of other murderers in *The Ability to Kill* (1963), Ambler finds troubling echoes of Dimitrios. (Hanratty wasn't the A6 murderer, but apparently would like to have been. In prison while awaiting trial, he boasted that the man and the woman were among several of his victims.) Human beings who ignore moral issues, who know what they're doing but don't consider it wrong, are beyond the imagination of the law. Ambler notes that unless certifiable mental disease can be proved, the law falls back on 'the concept of unmitigated wickedness'. Listening to the judge denouncing the murderer before passing sentence of death, and hearing the court chaplain add his dutiful 'Amen', he feels only that uneasy minds have purged themselves of some of their own guilt secretions.

The experience of watching criminals on trial lies behind Ambler's creation of the acidly comic non-hero of his next two novels, *The Light of Day* (1965) and *Dirty Story* (1967). He has defined the calloused criminal type as a 'moral defective' and suggested a similar moral defection in the surrounding world. The survival of the fittest now turns into the survival of the criminal. Arthur Abdel Simpson is the illegitimate son of a British army sergeant and an Egyptian girl, both dead. At fifty he's an impresario of minor swindles, occasional pimp and pornography merchant. Once again the passport situation provides a metaphor of identity. No country wants Simpson. Living in Athens on an Egyptian passport that is running out and will not be renewed, he applies for British nationality and is turned down by the vice-consul as a 'disgusting creature' whose life is 'nothing but a long, dirty story'. Soon his Interpol dossier will be his only valid identity document.

Education at a second-rate English school has left Simpson with a nostalgia for middle-class values and a hatred of authority. As an adult he transfers the hatred to bureaucrats and power figures in general. Shocked by the crimes he's offered to commit, he accepts them out of greed and desperation. Pathetically eager to be liked, he is usually despised. Clinging to the illusion of respectability, he remains hopelessly mediocre. The affable surface conceals a hive of resentments:

The outside of the body can be washed of sweat and grease; but inside there are processes which produce other substances. Some of these smell. How do you wash away the smells of the inside of the body?

In *The Light of Day* he accepts a commission to drive a limousine from Athens to Istanbul, then to act as chauffeur for a group of people at a villa on the Bosphorus. The Turkish police stop him at the frontier and discover an impressive

123

cache of arms in the car. Simpson's terror is so naked that they incline to believe in his innocence. Suspecting that he's become involved in a political conspiracy without knowing it, they release him on condition that he acts as an undercover agent. Once again Simpson is forced to become more guilty than he would like. He arrives at the villa sick with fear, a radio transmitter concealed in his luggage. The scenes that follow have a double suspense: Simpson's attempt to spy on his employers and his dread of being caught by them. He overhears curious fragments of conversation, sees them consulting a map, drives them around the city, but cannot fit the pieces together. The police bombard him with insulting threats on the radio, mistaking incompetence for intent to deceive them. Finally he discovers that the group is planning a jewel robbery at the Topkapi museum. Indifferent to the crime itself, Simpson is horrified that he's expected to take part in it.

At this point the tension drops. The atmosphere of secrecy has promised a more original secret. But it recovers once the robbery is under way because of the cruelty with which Ambler focuses on Simpson's panic and confusion. At the climax he has to make his way along the narrow edge of the museum roof. Almost fainting with vertigo, his mind flashes back to a school experience. He remembers how he hated diving lessons. 'When my head went under water I was always afraid of drowning.' It becomes a moment of total humiliation and despair, and it sums up Simpson's life. There can be no more absurd yet horrible example of the moral defective who has always resented his situation but sees no way out of it. The others shout at him not to look down or sideways, only straight ahead. It is the one direction he would like to avoid, but all his options have run out. He lurches to safety, then betrays his rescuers.

For his part as informer Simpson receives $500 from the Turkish government and is deported on a plane to Athens. The payment hardly covers his own expenses in fear. Both sets of employers, police and thieves, regard him with contempt. Indelibly disgusting is the memory of his interrogation and search at the frontier when the adventure began:

People who run jails are all the same. When I was naked, he searched the inside of the clothes and the shoes. Next, he looked in my mouth and ears with a flashlight. Then he took a rubber glove and a jar of petroleum jelly from the wall cabinet and searched my rectum.

Caught between a wretched past and an unpromising future, Simpson wonders whether he should appeal to the U.N. for a passport. 'I refuse to go on being an anomaly. Is that quite clear? I *refuse*!'

An anomaly he remains in *Dirty Story*, a little shabbier and paunchier, haunted by phobias and indigestion. When he thinks about his life he recalls the vertigo on the museum roof. Still in Athens, the old passport expired, he knows where to buy a 'passport of convenience' but not how to find the money. He becomes casting director (pimp) for a Frenchman making an art (blue) movie. The authorities crack down and he has to flee the country in an old, creaking freighter bound for the Red Sea. He is technically in transit, but in transit to where? For a moment he even considers suicide. 'You don't need an entry permit for the sea.'

As in *The Light of Day* a minor misadventure opens the door to a major one, and in Djibouti the penniless stateless non-person signs up as a mercenary for a Swiss-based company known as SMMAC. He is flown in a derelict unpressurized plane to the new independent state of Mahundi in central Africa. Here SMMAC aims to exploit, by force if necessary, some rich deposits of rare earth (metallic elements used in nuclear weapons). These deposits lie in a frontier region claimed by a neighbouring state. Since Ugazi is backed by a rival American-German company known as UMAD, Simpson has the chance to betray the plans of one side to the other. His problem is not to betray the winning side. 'I don't know which is worse when you're dreading the future: to know too little or know too much.'

Back in the familiar territory of furtive meetings at night and contacts by secret radio transmitter, Simpson is once again the anxious spy trying to piece information together. The atmosphere this time is almost infernal. The remote tropical country seethes with aggressive insects and fetid smells. A dense and scrubby landscape competes in ugliness with the industrial wreckage scattered across it: temporary buildings, machinery and gashed hillsides. Even the forests are

125

rancid with decay. 'The smell of corruption, of things rotting beneath fungus growths, was very strong.' In Mahundi and inside Simpson's body the same processes of nature are at work, creating tumours and stench.

When a minor war breaks out between the two countries, it is really a war between the two rival corporations. Ambler describes it from the traitor's and coward's point of view, like the robbery in *The Light of Day*. Simpson tries at the same time to calculate the battle's outcome and to avoid the field of action. His keyhole view of the dead man with his head blown off and the body mutilated by a mortar shell recalls the images Ambler brought back from a more serious war. In the end Simpson's intrigues and terrors are all wasted, for the rival corporations combine forces and sign a merger. Once again he has played each side against the other and found himself rejected by both:

If I pinch a wallet in a washroom, that's stealing and everyone yells blue murder; but if SMMAC or UMAD pinches two hundred million dollars of rare earth, that's 'acquiring an interest' and nobody says a word. Why?
How do they get away with it?
How could I get away with something like that?

The only consolation is that Simpson has managed to steal some passports from a safe in a wrecked government building. He escapes to Tangier and sets himself up in the business of selling 'passports of convenience'. Keeping one for himself, he not only retrieves his identity but is made over into someone new and false. A sense of guilt transforms itself into a sense of mission, ludicrous but dynamic. Simpson comes to believe that in selling false passports he is aiding 'the stateless person in his quest for formal identity and his struggle against the powers-that-be'. His prices, he adds, are very reasonable.

Simpson's personal dirty story parallels the dirty story of business and politics, and his point about 'getting away with it' seems completely valid for a moral defective in a morally defective world. Smell is the human sense most often referred to in *Dirty Story*, and all its smells, from sweat to swamp, are dirty. Simpson even recognized twilight by its stink. Wondering how to wash away the smells of the inside of the body, he imitates the example of corporations and powers

126

and pretends to be performing a public service. Like them, he accepts spying as a natural function. When buying and selling is a means of survival, the secret radio transmitter becomes an image of the bugged life.

In this compelling sour novel, hatred is the underlying criminal motive. The schoolboy tormented by bullies and teachers grows into the swindler, pimp, informer and spy who hates society. He also hates criminals more successful than himself, and as a mercenary naturally hopes to betray his employers. His real mission is revenge. In the casual way that he reserves for his most barbed comments, Ambler has said that many people identify with Simpson. 'Because he's odious, it's easy. Most people are more odious than they think. Not wicked, just odious.'

By 1968, Ambler and his wife have moved to Vevey, over-looking Lake Geneva. Fifty years earlier, Maugham-Ashenden crossed this lake on the steamer to France. Simenon's home is a few miles away. On the surface the atmosphere is peaceful. Behind its isolation lies something closed and secret. Switzer-land is a small neutral country with an unusually large population of spies.

The neat, alert young man in the shabby Paris bar of the thirties has become a rather scholarly figure by the shore of the lake. Wary and spectacled, his eyes suggest that the longer you study appearances the more deeply you mistrust them. In the more than thirty years between *The Mask of Dimitrios* and his first novel written in Switzerland, *The Intercom Conspiracy* (1971), there is more than a warning link. Ambler's two finest novels use the same protagonist, Charles Latimer, and the same multi-narrative technique.

A foreword introduces a series of documents, letters, taped interviews and statements, and sections of an unfinished book by Latimer. We learn that the writer of detective stories held a minor post in British intelligence during the war, then con-tinued to produce successful novels and bought a villa in Majorca. As in the case of Dimitrios, he became fascinated by an actual mystery. In the middle of writing a book about it, he vanished. All efforts to trace him have failed. Apart from a few name changes 'to protect the guilty', Ambler says that he's left the unedited material to speak for itself.

127

It speaks of an undercover world now controlled by icy remote specialists. They employ the most advanced detection and telecommunication devices, and like famous statesmen and criminals are strictly shadowed when they travel. Secrecy fetishists with access to all kinds of technical knowledge, back-room rulers who despise legal limits, these government employees are beginning to control their employers:

They acquire more authority than their responsibilities warrant. They are accountable virtually to no one; and the longer they remain in their posts the stronger they become. Inevitably they also tend to become arrogant ... There have been directors who became king-makers, who have subverted the governments they were pledged to serve and helped plan the coups which brought them down. There have been those who have seized power for themselves, and those who have preferred to act as the *éminences grises* of puppet rulers. And there have been those whose arrogance has expressed itself in more eccentric, less familiar ways.

The story that Latimer began to unravel concerns two middle-aged colonels, Jost and Brand, directors of intelligence for minor unnamed NATO countries. With the world organized into opposing superpower blocs, the colonels feel left out of the game. Prestige and influence eroded, they become increasingly bitter. 'To their way of thinking, the way to oppose great force was to find out how to destroy its cohesion.' Jost and Brand know that modern espionage goes far beyond gathering information. It has subtle psychological techniques of creating *mis*information. Various groups financed by governments and angry political exiles manufacture false reports and documents to undermine the superpowers' confidence. The colonels decide to acquire a lie factory of their own.

Intercom is a private subscription newsletter printed in Geneva and financed by a former U.S. general with paranoid right-wing views. Its editor doesn't share them, but as an intelligent alcoholic has resigned himself to a well paid demeaning job. When the general dies, Carter is astonished to hear from *Intercom*'s lawyer that someone actually wants to buy the newsletter. Apparently a German businessman, the new owner remains a voice at the other end of the telephone and a signature to a letter. He instructs Carter to continue as before, but sends him brief news items to print in each issue.

128

Presented as 'intelligence leaks', they give details of aircraft and nuclear missile units currently being tested by the major powers. Sometimes (when Jost or Brand wants to get a rival into trouble) the source of information is named. Downfalls, suicides and murders result in the undercover world. Carter soon suspects that he's being used, but can't make out the nature of the conspiracy. He's warned and threatened in turn by the C.I.A., the K.G.B. and B.f.V. of West Germany, all convinced that he knows more than he will tell. Finally he is kidnapped, and escapes after being beaten up. In hospital the Swiss police question him as a potential spy and the doctors study him as a psychotic.

Alternating between Carter's and Latimer's points of view, Ambler stretches out two lines of tension. He shows Carter bewildered and then terrorized by a situation in which names and pretences are false but violence is real. He contrasts this with Latimer's unwise decision to investigate the case. The writer's curiosity has acquired a touch of malice with age. He enters the game in a game-playing spirit, diverted by the thought of a cunning fantasy that has imposed itself on so many minds. But what amuses Latimer is extremely unamusing to the colonels. A disappearance is arranged. At the same time, the major intelligence agencies combine to arrange the disappearance of *Intercom*. Acting for an unnamed 'consortium', a Swiss bank makes an enormous offer for the newsletter. When the lawyer accepts, the consortium closes it down. The only remaining conspiracy, as Carter notes, is one of silence:

Intercom *was silenced.*
Charles Latimer was silenced.
Those who silenced them are themselves now mute.
Mine is the only voice left.

Drunken and scared, it is not much of a voice, but Ambler implies that Carter is lucky to survive at all. Comparing him to an innocent bystander caught in a bank hold-up, Latimer found himself in the same position. Anyone involved with the new centres of power runs the same risk. The espionage machine has created a world of lethal and computerized danger. Agents operate under bogus names and accents, authority remains unknowable behind the elaborate protocol of secrecy. Information and misinformation have become almost impossible to separate, motives are as disguised as identities. The devious structure of *The Intercom Conspiracy* parallels the structure of the new power. The editor never meets his employers. The lawyer never meets his clients. The clients don't even know who they are silencing. 'Intelligence' means the use of mind to confuse and intimidate.

In an epilogue, Carter goes to Majorca and finds Jost happily retired after making his contribution to world alarm. He doesn't know what happened to Latimer, since Brand arranged the disappearance and is now in hospital, dying of a kidney disease. But he points out that specialization has produced the rigidly professional killer:

'The one who can use a knife will always prefer it to a pistol. The poisoner never strangles, and the strangler does not carry a bludgeon. In time of war, when there is a wider choice of weapons and the killing is legal, it is the same . . . Brand was no exception to the rule. He always thought tactically in terms of ambush and burial.'

Jost remembers his friend watching concrete as it poured into a construction site and remarking how effectively it could hide a victim for ever. Afterwards he always thought of construction sites as graves waiting to be filled. It seems certain that Latimer, like the rest of his story, lies buried somewhere in the foundations of a new office block.

With this drily unnerving and beautifully executed novel, Ambler states his case for politics as conspiracy. The view of apes in political velvet is developed in *The Levanter* (1972), where some rather laboured dialectics overwhelm the story of a Palestinian terrorist, and in the sinister fable of *Doctor Frigo* (1974). Preparing to stage a coup in a Central American republic, a band of predators converges on the exiled son of an assassinated political leader, determined to make the apolitical young doctor into a figurehead. The doctor himself tells the story through a diary that he kept during the few weeks of intrigue preceding the takeover. At the end he discovers the shabby truth about his father's murder and witnesses a second assassination under almost identical circumstances. Slight but ruthless, *Doctor Frigo* echoes Marx's idea that history repeats itself first as tragedy and then as farce. Its group of conspirators stakes its future on a derelict country that has struck oil after years of nothing more than bananas.

Returning briefly to his homeland, the doctor finds it in a state of suspended decrepitude, the legacy of corrupt and violent regimes. Jungle weeds push up through asphalt surfaces and buildings are still gutted from the last outbreak of street fighting. Like Graham in *Journey into Fear*, the doctor is a neutral struggling not to be involved; and by now Ambler approves the struggle. Since there is no cause beyond greed and competition for power, the unheroic man preserves his self-respect as well as his life by refusing to enter 'the world beyond the door'.

Ambler has always written his stories like intelligence reports, the prose spare and lucid, the surface exact, even the atmosphere informational. When the waves of Lake Geneva remind Colonel Jost of 'slopping bath water', the moment sums up Ambler's dislike of the romantic or literary image. Equally, there is nothing overheated in his accounts of violence and brutality. By the time of *The Intercom Conspiracy* he seems to regard them as impersonal necessities and shows no concern for the victims. Fear has reached the frozen state.

Latimer could see only 'cloak-and-dagger foolishness' in the colonels' conspiracy. He missed the handwriting on the wall, as he missed it before with Dimitrios. His greatest mistake was not to have been more afraid. Fear improves the critical sense as well as the imagination. It takes nothing for granted. On a visit to the Chamber of Horrors at Madame Tussaud's, thinking he detected something familiar in the criminal wax figures, Ambler wondered what it could be. He studied the real faces looking at the wax faces and decided he knew.

FOUR

The Double Agent

A child was crying in a tenement . . . too young to have learnt what the dark may conceal in the way of lust and murder, crying for no intelligible reason but because it still possessed the ancestral fear, the devil was dancing in its sleep.

Graham Greene,
Journey Without Maps

At the age of five he begins to suspect what the dark conceals. The dreams always begin with a door that edges open of its own accord. He knows that an unseen mysterious force waits behind it. Then, according to his autobiography, *A Sort of Life*, he dreams of a shipwreck at night. That same night, in April 1912, the *Titanic* hits an iceberg in the north Atlantic. That same year, his nurse takes him out for a walk and a man runs across a canal bridge with a knife in his hand. The figure disappears into a house, reappears at a window. Watched by a small crowd, he cuts his throat.

Not long after this the serious nightmares begin, single and connected, persisting companions of his life. At seven a witch dances in his sleep. The same door always opens suddenly and he throws himself on the floor in terror while she attacks him with long fingernails. This happens just before he's due to start school, to enter a new country through 'a green baize door' – the door that leads from his father's study to the school itself.

As the headmaster's son he belongs to the wrong side. The others immediately see him as an enemy agent and potential betrayer. He finds himself 'a foreigner and a suspect, quite literally a hunted creature'. Life itself is like the moment when he passes the witch's door in his dreams. For the condemned outsider relationships become an expectation of torture and his only friend deserts him. Obsessed for a while with thoughts of revenge, he turns them on himself. He tries to cut open his knee with a penknife, but the blade is too old and worn.

In a dream he finally escapes the witch and she never

returns, but other powers are waiting behind the door. Dark-skinned girls offer flowers that turn out to be poisonous, an old Arab and a Chinese detective advance on him, and a group of armed men with shaved heads. The new enemies seem to echo his deepening discovery of fear and hate in the corridors and stone stairways of school. Dreams and memories accumulate so powerfully that the adult becomes obsessed by the idea of childhood as a flytrap of imprisoning experience. Neither parents nor friends can break through a forced soli-tude. In Graham Greene's finest short story, *The Basement Room* (1936), the symbol of the green baize door recurs, separating the child Philip from the basement quarters of Baines the butler. Opening it, he goes downstairs to confront the mystery of an adult passion and the violent quarrel that creates a death. The child never recovers from the early experience, growing up into a cold haunted dilettante. Greene never recovers either, but grows up into a novelist. The writer becomes a fugitive from the emptiness and boredom of Philip who spent all his courage and remained forever crying in the dark.

In adolescence the lure of self-destruction persists. He survives eating deadly nightshade and taking twenty aspirins before going swimming. At eighteen he finds a loaded revolver in a cupboard. Out in the countryside he places the muzzle in his ear and plays Russian roulette. After several clicks, the thrill wears off. The role of double agent having been forced on him at school, he deliberately chooses it while a student at Oxford. In 1924 the French still occupy a small zone of Germany which they plan to turn into an independent state. Greene persuades the German Embassy that he can be a useful anti-French propagandist, since he writes occasionally for the Oxford newspapers. A trip is financed. He arrives in the zone and decides to inform the French authorities of his mission. But the political situation evaporates and the lust for betrayal remains unsatisfied.

As the warning dreams continue, they begin to colour reality. From his hotel window at night he watches a man and a woman in coitus under a street lamp. They seem to him like people in pain trying desperately to comfort each other. But a year after the trip to Europe he is apparently lost to ordinary respectability, working as an unpaid apprentice to a newspaper in Nottingham, living alone with a dog in the city that will later become the Midlands setting of *A Gun for Sale*. Since he's met a Roman Catholic girl called Vivien Dayrell-Browning and proposed marriage, he feels curious about the nature of her religion. Although the supernatural holds no appeal and he has no intention of being converted, he takes instruction from a fat priest who was formerly an actor. Unable to resist the double game, he never reveals his motives. Then his bluff is called. As he rides in a bus around the ugly foggy city, talking of the Immaculate Conception, he gradually discovers in the priest the challenge of 'inexplicable goodness'. The spy in the church ends as a believer. Intellectually, Greene is ready for belief in heaven since he already believes in hell. But unlike Chesterton who joined the church to escape from hell, Greene will continue to live in it. After the official ceremony he feels grimly apprehensive and has none of the convert's elation. Convinced that God created the world, he knows that among God's creations are the torturers at school and the suicide at the window.

Greene will later remark that Catholicism might have presented him with serious problems as a writer if he hadn't been 'saved' by his disloyalty. Part of the church's attraction, perhaps unconscious at first, is the opportunity to betray it. Even the marriage that led to conversion fails to last. After a period of happiness Greene and his wife agree to a friendly separation, and he has lived by himself for almost thirty years. Another irony: soon after he becomes a Catholic the dreams grow even darker and he recognizes the figures in them as evil – an old woman with ringworm scales covering her head and a gold-toothed man wearing rubber gloves.

Fear had convinced the child that hell existed, but the excitement of sex was bound up with fear. A beating by his father aroused an early sexual response. There were secret guilty passions for governesses and nurses. The priest who instructed him warned against intercourse before marriage and forbade the use of contraceptives. Until he married, Greene seems to have lived an intense sexual fantasy, much of it centred on a frightened longing for prostitutes. In Nottingham he used to watch the town whore crumbling on her foggy beat. In London he spied on the young and insolent tarts in bars and doorways, and during his travels in Europe he even noted a subtle out-of-date quality in the whores of Estonia with their corsets and garters and black silk stockings. (His fiction will contain an extraordinary gallery of prostitutes: at first the lurid or pathetic incidental figures in the London novels, then the ambiguously appealing Phuong of *The Quiet American* and Clara of *The Honorary Consul*.) The novels of Rider Haggard and Buchan fed his imagination of danger as Browning fed his imagination of sex, the poet's world of furtive assignations and violence providing a further link between the two. A historical melodrama by Marjorie Bowen, *The Viper of Milan*, stirred him with its 'sense of doom that lies over success', completing the circle of tension and mistrust. In 1938 Greene ends a short story, *Across the Bridge*, about a swindler tracked down by detectives in a Mexican border town, with a comment on 'our baseless optimism that is so much more appalling than our despair'. This sentence, and *The Basement Room*, tip off the novelist as a detective of hell, searching for the dark at the end of the light.

In 1926 Greene moved to London, having landed a job as sub-editor on *The Times*. During his four years on the newspaper he wrote two novels that were never published and a third that he never finished. The last sounds the most interesting: a detective story in which the murder is committed by a little girl in love with her governess. After the false starts, *The Man Within* (1929) was well received, and its sales encouraged Greene to leave *The Times* and set out as a long-distance literary runner.

The Man Within has a conventionally romantic setting of Scotland in the early nineteenth century, and its dialogue is often stilted. But the central character, a young smuggler who informs on his best friend, shows Greene edging towards the territory that he will make his own. The man outside is on the run from his enemies, but the man within from his secret fears and bitter lusts, intensified by the act of betrayal and the consequences of pursuit. The mood is similar in *The Name of Action* (1930) and *Rumour at Nightfall* (1931), political melodramas burdened by an obvious infatuation with the style of Conrad. When they fail with critics and public,

135

Greene recognizes the problem and stops reading Conrad for almost thirty years.

In the meantime he needs money and has lost confidence in himself. His diary notes 'a feeling of lurking madness, of something swelling in the brain and wanting to burst'. With a recording of Honegger's *Pacific 231* played over and over while he works, he writes *Stamboul Train* (1932; U.S. title *Orient Express*). The pressure point is like Conan Doyle's when he first determined to extend himself as a writer, withdrew behind his mental curtain and found he was Sherlock Holmes. Settling private accounts in order to release private feelings, Greene makes a return journey. Beyond *The Viper of Milan* and Rider Haggard and Buchan and *Dixon Brett, Detective* lies the first and lasting experience of life as flight and fear and anger, the primal response to 'the terrible living world'. (Books read in childhood, he will comment later, have the deepest influence of all.) When he rediscovers himself he finds his own language, its rhythm free and almost colloquial, its images sprung with inner violence. Since the cinema has always fascinated him, he begins to adapt movie devices, sharply intercutting events and impressions. *A Sort of Life* recalls the mood of fusing 'movement, action, character', and of technical discovery:

Excitement is a situation, a single event. It mustn't be wrapped up in thoughts, similes, metaphors. A simile is a form of reflection, but excitement is of the moment when there is no time to reflect.

The events that overtake the passengers of *Stamboul Train* are drawn from Greene's personal mythology, success soured by guilt, love that dissolves to the image of the couple writhing painfully under a street lamp, fear waiting behind a closed door. A minor character remarks that trouble usually starts in the Balkans, and the train plunges at high speed into disturbed country. It becomes a metaphor for society, 'breaking the dark sky like a rocket', as the cold hardens outside, snow falls thickly, nights grow blacker and passengers looking through the glass can see only their own transparent reflected faces. By day landscapes take on a fugitive ghostly quality, the wilderness of suburbs in a drift of smoke, the outlines of a solitary barge on a river blurred by ice forming on windows. When the train stops at a station, the view outside has the sudden clarity of danger. The middle-aged Austrian climbing on board at Vienna is plump enough to conceal the revolver bulging in his pocket and poker-faced enough to hide his stupid conceit at the murder he's just committed. News filters through of an attempted political uprising in Belgrade. In motion again, the train seals off its passengers from the violence outside, but its frosted windows offer only a thin protection.

The longest and most powerful episode takes place in the unprotected world. At the Yugoslav frontier the police arrest three passengers. The English schoolmaster is really Czinner, the revolutionary and hunted exile who planned the unsuccessful coup in Belgrade. Mistaking her for an accomplice, the police also arrest Coral Musker, a chorus girl on her way to a nightclub engagement in Istanbul. The Austrian is held with them after a customs inspection turns up his revolver. With nothing in common except anxiety and isolation, the prisoners sit in a locked waiting-room, the view from its windows blinded by snow. Coral, the most innocently derailed, has surrendered her virginity the previous night to an ambitious young Jewish businessman, with whom she now imagines she's in love. After Czinner is shot while attempting to escape, she will be rescued by a butch lesbian journalist whose girlfriend has just deserted her.

The element of farce underlying melodrama suggests the tone for many of Greene's later novels, and Czinner is the first in a series of tired, failing men who cling to the lifebelt of idealism. A lapsed Catholic, he longs momentarily for the release of confession. Just before dying he realizes that his mistake is to have lived as an idealist in an opportunist world, 'damned by his faithfulness'. Ironically he is saved by a vision of futilty that extends far beyond himself:

The world was chaotic; when the poor were starved and the rich were not happier for it; when the thief might be punished or rewarded with titles; when wheat was burned in Canada and coffee in Brazil, and the poor in his own country had no money for bread and froze to death in unheated rooms; the world was out of joint and he had done his best to set it right, but that was over.

Faithfulness is not a problem for the others. As Coral's fantasy of life with a rich man fades, she settles for the alcoholic possessive Mabel. The businessman decides to marry Mabel's former girl-friend because she's the niece of an important colleague. The girl herself dismisses Mabel's fierce devotion by confessing how tired she's grown of living with a woman. The role of chorus to a succession of betrayals is taken by the popular novelist Savory, whom Greene observes with a telling mixture of dislike and respect. Although his talk of reviving the spirit of cheerfulness and adventure embodies the glib optimism that Greene loathes, he is also a shrewd experienced professional. Looking out of the train window, he plans how to convey in prose the cinematic speed and movement of landscapes passing by, and he introduces an idea of the novelist to which Greene will often return:

"E's a spy,' Mr Savory added with confusing drama, dropping aitches right and left. "E 'as to see everything and pass unnoticed. If people recognized 'im they wouldn't talk, they'd pose before 'im: 'e wouldn't find things out.'

With its strong linear suspense and sharp focus on the contemporary, *Stamboul Train* prefigures the direction of Greene's most exciting work. But he seems unsure of this at the time. He subtitles the novel 'An Entertainment' and will later place some important achievements in the same category, among them *A Gun for Sale*, *The Confidential Agent* and *The Ministry of Fear*. About *Brighton Rock*, a novel on its first appearance and an entertainment when it's reprinted, he shows ambivalence. In 1970, opposite the title page of *Travels With My Aunt*, he finally lists all his fiction in a single category. The gesture seems to end a prolonged apology to critical fashion. In Wilkie Collins's time the most influential critics refused to take suspense novels seriously. They encouraged Conan Doyle, as I mentioned earlier, to concentrate on historical novels rather than Sherlock Holmes. When Greene started writing they had begun to attack story-telling itself as outmoded, and in the wake of *Ulysses* experiment was a new author's most likely passport to attention. *Stamboul Train* derived from an apparently safe formula, *Grand Hotel* on the Orient Express, and Greene claimed later that he only wrote it for money. For many years he seems to have feared that one of his strongest talents might be interpreted as a weakness. The signs include an attempt to inflate the melodrama

138

of *England Made Me* with Joycean interior monologue, and as late as 1959, in the *Congo Journal* that contains his notes for *A Burnt-Out Case*, he still worries about 'the abiding temptation to tell a good story'. The final result is ironic. By creating the categories Greene gave his critics an opportunity to make a case for them, and by dissolving them he neatly betrayed it.

It was never much of a case. For many years you read that in the entertainments the religious element is only incidental. Yet it remains just that in *The Quiet American* or *The Comedians*. The real point is that Greene's work as a whole shows a varying skill in combining ideas and stories. When a religious argument intrudes centrally, his art contracts and grows static. He has always objected to being labelled a Catholic writer rather than a writer who happens to be a Catholic. But *The Heart of the Matter* and *The End of the Affair*, moving oddly close to the old-fashioned problem novel, justify the label he dislikes. They dictate emotional response instead of inviting it.

You also read that the entertainments are much more preoccupied with violence and melodrama, and depend too openly on coincidence of plot. The idea falls down after a comparison of *The Honorary Consul* with *Stamboul Train*, or of *The Comedians* with *The Confidential Agent*. More than that, it overlooks the meaning of a personal device. Like Hitchcock, who is also a Catholic, Greene uses coincidence ritually and for a purpose. In his Mexican travel book, *The Lawless Roads*, he suggests that 'the magic element' in Christianity has always been minimized, and links the power of the unexpected to religion. This plea for the poetic truth of miracles, the devil cast out and the man raised from the dead as signs of a mysterious force behind the universe, runs through most of his novels. It provides a kind of spiritual jolt, equivalent in effect to the physical violence.

A quotation from Santayana prefaces *Stamboul Train*: 'Everything in nature is lyrical in its ideal essence; tragic in its fate, and comic in its existence.' Greene extracts from this a crucial sense of farce and absurdity lying behind even the most intense moments of danger. In *The Confidential Agent* D. thinks to himself that God can only be pictured as 'a joker'. In *The Comedians* the narrator says that only his sense of humour enables him to believe in Christ. We are all 'driven by an authoritative practical joker towards the extreme point of comedy'. Czinner in the early novel is the first of many characters to reflect how impossible it is to plan a future when intentions and results so seldom connect. As a final joke he welcomes death because it releases him from the problem.

Before *Stamboul Train* appeared, Greene asked a friend to find him a job in the English department of a university near Bangkok. 'His favourable reply came just too late to save me from this career of writing.' Astonished by a moderate popular success, he immediately mistrusted it and centred his next two novels on the tensions of failure. While writing *Stamboul Train* he dreamed that he'd been sent to prison for five years and woke up depressed by the idea that his wife would be over thirty when he'd finished his sentence. Out of the dream came *It's A Battlefield* (1934), in which a communist bus-driver waits to be hanged after he's been convicted of murdering a policeman. Since the crime hinged on a misunderstanding – Drover tried to protect his wife at a political demonstration – there is a case for reprieve. The wife and brother circulate a petition. A determined society hostess pressures the assistant commissioner. A journalist and a rich communist exploit the situation for their own ends. Concerned about public opinion, the government uses plain-clothes detectives to spy on the mood of London. It provides the novel's connecting link.

As the title implies, struggle and unrest are in the air. But Greene finds people preoccupied with fighting their own battles, isolated rather than united by despair. In a powerfully ironic scene, Drover's wife asks the policeman's widow to sign the reprieve petition, and a mutual sympathy springs up between two victims. After the moment of shared helplessness, they move apart again. Finally the only one to act is Drover's brother. The first of Greene's tormented, damned young men, Conrad tries to save his brother and at the same time betrays him by sleeping with his wife. Guilt and anxiety create a longing for violence. He fixes his rage on the assistant commissioner and decides to kill him. As he follows the stolid government official through the London streets, the story acquires a glazed and almost dreamlike tension. Then the joker's touch intervenes. The revolver contains only blanks, the would-be assassin is run over and killed by a car.

Here a novel spun off from a dream returns to a kind of dream, bitter and unexpected. For the rest, while the action is skilfully crosscut, most of its characters lack the definition of *Stamboul Train*. Only the outcast brother emerges in sudden depth, pointing the way to Raven in *A Gun for Sale* and Pinkie in *Brighton Rock*. A similar plan unfolds in *England Made Me* (1935), with its confused protesting figure murdered by the agent of a millionaire industrialist named Krogh. The setting is Stockholm, another battlefield. After *Stamboul Train* Greene began a novel about a girl in love with her fake spiritualist brother. Although he gave it up, emotional incest underlies *It's A Battlefield* – brother fixated on brother – and now emerges openly again. Kate holds on to her charming dishonest brother by getting him a job in the corporation of her far more dishonest lover. The casual trickster, shocked by Krogh's organized structure of fraud and murder, threatens to expose a corruption deeper than his own. The kinetic detail is sometimes masterly: the financier exiled in his fashionably abstract office building, Anthony exiled with his travelling bag packed with the souvenirs, photographs, old school ties and one good suit of the drifter's life. But Greene seems trapped between his own invented categories. The 'novel' about Kate and Anthony dissolves in dialogue of a strained unreal politeness, the 'entertainment' in melodrama that lacks surprise and excitement.

Both *It's A Battlefield* and *England Made Me* struggle to make the same central point. Their characters create violent events by performing violence on themselves. This is the way the world ends. Like Ambler, Greene fears the wasteland of his time and the signs of disintegration. But his religious sense, although still submerged most of the time, rejects the biological idea of an ape in velvet. In spite of everything, the prison chaplain in *It's A Battlefield* refuses to 'hand in a resignation to God'. Knowing the way the world ends, Greene begins to look for the way it began.

The shape of Africa, Greene has noticed, corresponds roughly to that of the human heart. His journey there is the first of several that will lead him beyond Europe, into countries

(Mexico, Vietnam, Haiti, South America) where primitive forms of life still exist. The primitive, like the child, knows the deepest and purest terror. Its secret lies in 'a quality of darkness', and Greene decides to search for it in Liberia, the first independent negro republic in Africa, established by freed immigrant slaves from the United States. It once called itself a Christian democracy, but successive governments tried to relieve the country's poverty by exporting forced labour. A few years before Greene arrived, a League of Nations committee had investigated Liberia as the centre of African slave trade. Since the journey 'represented a distrust of any future based on what we are', he chose a notoriously backward and squalid pocket of the world as if to find out whether its worst could possibly be worse than ours.

In *Journey Without Maps* (1936) Greene describes how he crossed Liberia on foot, from the Sierra Leone border to the Atlantic coast, and at the same time travelled back into himself. He finds that exploration, like psychoanalysis, means submitting yourself to the unconscious. The adventure stirs up memories of childhood, of Conrad's *Heart of Darkness* and Rider Haggard, and brings him close to the centre of unexplained cruelty and ancestral fear. After several weeks he reaches Monrovia, the capital city. Stunted and unfinished, offering a main street overgrown with grass, an abandoned palace, a waterfront lined with wooden huts, and telegraph poles which are only monuments to a defunct telephone system, its instant seediness strikes him as 'nearer the beginning'. It appeals because it represents a stage farther back in human development and provides a glimpse of what has been lost. Unlike the familiar mechanized desert, it escapes the curse of the new and the smart. Brutality appeals for a similar reason. It suggests a need for simplifying emotion and beginning to live again at a 'level below the cerebral'. In gangster novels, Greene infers, you find a nostalgia for uncensored emotional release. And when he sees an old half-witted native prisoner tied to a post and clubbed, or a child scream with terror at a masked devil dancer, he feels closer to 'the racial source', to instinct and even to happiness.

Returning to civilization, Greene illustrates his theory about the gangster novel by adapting its form to his own purpose.

142

In *A Gun for Sale* (1936; U.S. title *This Gun for Hire*), violence becomes the purest kind of self-expression and the killer recognizes his own primitive terror. By contrast, the threat of another major war only reflects society preparing to self-destruct as the result of its own thought and planning. Behind the scare headlines lies the power of the munitions manufacturer, whom governments encourage because he's good business. Ambler is making the same point at this time, but restricts himself to projecting a vast anonymous corporate force. Greene personifies it. Although only a minor character, Sir Marcus in *A Gun for Sale* seems far more dangerous than Krogh in *England Made Me*. He leaks supernatural evil like the man with gold teeth and rubber gloves in Greene's dream.

The battlefield opens up as Greene frames the action of a thriller in a double setting, the realistic backgrounds and then the intimations of demonic force and ancestral fear. He extends the technique in *Brighton Rock* (1938), *The Confidential Agent* (1939) and *The Ministry of Fear* (1943). This quartet of novels, with its sense of something increasingly monstrous behind the familiar English scene, is Greene's most powerful work in the first fifteen years of his life as a writer.

Murder didn't mean much to Raven. It was just a new job. You had to be careful. You had to use your brains. It was not a question of hatred . . .

Like its successors, *A Gun for Sale* swiftly establishes the painful isolation of its leading character. Raven's harelip is a psychic as well as a physical scar. He can kill with indifference because he's indifferent to life – 'Three minutes in a bed or against a wall, and then a lifetime for the one that's born.' His father was a criminal, hanged when Raven was a child. At about the same age as Greene when his nurse took him for a walk, he saw his mother cut her throat. He grew up in an orphanage and discovered cruelty. At thirty he has no friends, no girl, but can love a kitten because it doesn't know he's ugly. Yet, in his overcoat with the collar turned up, he looks like 'any other youngish man going home after his work'.

Raven's most recent work is the assassination of a Czech politician who believes in peace, on the orders of Sir Marcus who believes in war. It is the week before Christmas. The Czechs suspect the killer was an agent of the Yugoslav government, and after an exchange of ultimatums, nations line up on both sides. None of this concerns Raven. He never asked why they wanted him to do the job, he never met Sir Marcus, and touching off a war means nothing – 'There's always been a war for me.' But when Sir Marcus's middleman pays him off in marked stolen notes, he becomes hunter and hunted, a fugitive in search of revenge. Murder is unimportant but the double-cross outrages his sense of justice.

Now the authoritative practical joker shows his touch. Raven boards the midnight train from London to the Midlands town that Greene calls Nottwich. He suspects that Davis, the middleman, has boarded it. Mather, the detective in charge of Raven's case, is on the platform. He's not looking for the man who passed stolen notes, on whom he doesn't yet have a lead, but for his fiancée Anne. A chorus girl going to Nottwich to start rehearsals for a Christmas pantomime, Anne finds herself in the same compartment as Davis, a man of several names and interests and a backer of the pantomime. Mather misses Anne because Davis leans out of the window to buy chocolate from a platform vendor and blocks the view of her. Raven daren't make himself conspicuous on the train by looking for Davis, but in the dark early morning encounters Anne at the Nottwich station barrier. The police are now on his trail and he forces her to help him escape.

All of this stretches the improbable to the limits of the plausible – and beyond them, those who disapprove of the practice would say. But disapproval of the interventions of chance is a dull point of view, which even the quantum physicists now tell us they don't share. Leaving aside Greene's belief in 'the magic element' and the new scientific respect for the 'acausal connecting principle', these scenes create a tight, classic suspense. Excitement allows no time for thought because lives cross like telephone wires, the secret unconscious link more vital than any calculation. Eventually the detective feels 'a kind of relationship' between himself and Raven because he imagines that Anne has choosen to stay with Raven. But the real links are those he knows nothing about. Mather's brother committed suicide, so the criminal and the detective share a similar horror from the past. One case produced a violent outsider, and the other a solid conformist who works for the law because he needs the security of belonging to an

144

organization. They may be on opposite sides, yet their reactions often coincide. When Mather assumes that Anne has left him for Raven, he echoes Raven's instinctive fear of betrayal. When he says, 'It doesn't matter to me if there is a war,' he echoes Raven again. There's always been a war for Mather as well.

Finally the killer and not the detective becomes the agent of peace. Discovering Sir Marcus, Raven exposes the truth behind the political assassination. But it never occurs to him, since he cannot see beyond the desire for revenge. Christmas displays in store windows only make him think sardonically of 'the little bastard' in the vulgar plaster crib. He dies feeling totally betrayed. Anne, the first person he's ever trusted, gave him away to the police and confirmed his angry view of the world – 'People don't trouble to keep their word to me.' In an extraordinary passage Greene compares the pain of Raven's death to the pain of a woman in childbirth. The same cry of suffering begins and ends a life.

The urban landscape of *A Gun for Sale* looks like civilization's answer to the innocent seediness of Monrovia. Beneath layers of smoke and fog you can hardly tell dawn from night. A polluted river flows between banks of cement. A glue factory smells like bad fish. The old suburban villas and the new housing estates reflect the same corruption. While a solitary whore shivers under her umbrella, electric light bulbs above a department store spell out news of troop movements and precautions against gas raids. Raven turns up his coat collar not only to hide his disfigured lip but as a gesture of protection against the surrounding hatefulness. The day that he finally tracks down Sir Marcus coincides with a rehearsal for a gas alert, and the streets are full of masked monsters. Medical students reveal their latent fascism by using the occasion to play war games, and in a guarded suite at the top of Nottwich's newest building, Sir Marcus reads the tape prices.

The old industrialist, still deeply malevolent in spite of his sick and withered body, is a haunting creation. Sipping warm milk and hardly ever sleeping, he speaks in a faint whisper with the trace of a middle Europe accent, waits for the armament orders to increase, and congratulates himself on having lived through another day. He also provides the last and strangest of many underground links between the characters, for he grew up in the same orphanage as the politician whose death he commissioned. The memory of cracked bells and stone stairways lies behind the ancient capitalist and the socialist in the shabby apartment as well as behind Raven, who never escaped from the punishment cell. For his living victim, killing Sir Marcus is not enough. Raven's sense of outrage spills over to the unimportant Davis:

With despair and deliberation he shot his last chance of escape, plugged two bullets in where one would do, shooting the whole world in the person of stout moaning bleeding Mr Davis. And so he was. For a man's world is his life, and he was shooting that: his mother's suicide, the lone years in the home . . .

This remarkable scene foreshadows the despair of the young killer that Capote reproduced from life thirty years later and made into a contemporary type. *In Cold Blood* describes the life of Perry Smith, equally scarred and deprived, as 'an ugly and lonely progress toward one mirage and then another'. Like Raven he reached the desert and shot his own unbearable world.

Before the Czech politician, Raven had been hired to kill a racketeer called Kite. *Brighton Rock* refers several times to Kite's death – he was an enemy of Pinkie Brown, the adolescent gangster known as the Boy. The incidental link points to a deeper one, Pinkie as a development of Raven. Both are indifferent to the act of murder and traumatized by the horror of being born. His cheeks still downy but his eyes old and annihilatingly cruel, Pinkie remembers the nights he lay listening to his parents make love in the shared bedroom:

That was what happened to a man in the end: the stuffy room, the wakeful children, the Saturday night movements from the other bed. Was there no escape – anywhere – for anyone? It was worth murdering a world.

But Pinkie, unlike Raven, knows that he's damned. He believes in Catholicism because he believes in hell. Other people's pleasures (sex, drink, nature, friendship) become his pain. Security is the razor blade, the knuckleduster and the bottle of vitriol with which he can avenge his eternal unrepentance. A chilling early scene shows him winning a prize at the carnival shooting range. He carries off the doll with hair made of brown wool and begins unconsciously to mutilate it.

Against the Boy whose sense of sin has created the instant reflex of destruction, Greene sets the fortyish Ida Arnold with her enormous cheerful breasts and her contented belief that 'it's a good world'. The promiscuous earth-mother drinks cheap port and radiates a baseless optimism that Greene finds more appalling then even Pinkie's despair. Out for her usual good time on a Brighton weekend, she is picked up by Hale, a racetrack enemy already marked down by Pinkie as his next victim. When he's found dead, apparently of a heart attack, Ida doesn't believe the official verdict. She determines to solve the mystery, and *Brighton Rock* develops as a chase story that also becomes a contest between human and divine justice. Ida is obviously 'right' when she makes up her mind to pursue and expose Pinkie, but the Boy is 'evil' and therefore more spiritually alive. The puritan killer with his certainty of hell has a glimpse of eternity that sets him above the walking pleasure principle, with her comfortable permissiveness and childish belief in the Ouija board.

Ida summarizes Greene's disgust with the popular English scene, even more unlovely in raucous daylight than in the fog and darkness of *A Gun for Sale*. Hideous carnival prizes, cheap restaurants with greasy tablecloths, the fat girl with acne lolling in a deckchair, the corsage that hides a deformed breast, the rotting old woman hunched in an alley, the crooner spellbinding an audience on the pier and the guests whispering of money in the pretentious hotel, the blind street band and the commercial building with a child's coffin in the window next to the hairdresser's – *Brighton Rock* accumulates ugly detail to the point of horror. There is no relief, only the contrast of another kind of horror, the cruel closed world of the Boy and the waitress he pretends to love. When he marries Rose to stop her testifying against him in court, he only adds to his load of mortal sins. Emotionally starved, she can feed even on his contempt, and as a Catholic she responds to his thrilling mythology of damnation. It remains her only hope at the end, after Ida has frightened her into betraying Pinkie, but a priest refuses to encourage it. Catholics, he tells her, are more capable of evil than other people because they believe in the devil. This gives them first claim on the 'appalling strangeness' of the mercy of God.

Every organized religion argues its truth with some kind of comparative moral judgement. So Greene compares Ida and Pinkie, and judges them. Lined up against the final wall, they stand or fall in the spotlight of theology. Maybe Ida's good nature is really self-satisfaction – but to deny her a 'soul' because she doesn't live on the Catholic level of good and evil sounds like the religious equivalent of racial prejudice. Maybe Pinkie and Rose are on more than a trip of which today's counterpart would be the drug mysticism of Charles Manson and his followers – but when Greene tries to elevate them above ordinary criminals, they speak like puppets. Rose tells Pinkie that she wants to be in a state of grace before marrying him. 'The theological term lay oddly and pedantically on her tongue.' So it does, as ventriloquized as the Boy's reaction when he offers to buy Rose a present and she asks for a stick of Brighton rock:

. . . Only the devil, he thought, could have made her answer that. She was good, but he'd got her like you got God in the Eucharist – in the guts. God couldn't escape the evil mouth which chose to eat its own damnation.

Raven is unaware of his own mystery. Pinkie is a constant spiritual complainer. Between *A Gun for Sale* and *Brighton Rock* Greene has apparently discovered that to accept Christianity is to embrace suffering. Pinkie has to absorb the full shock of it, veering between terror and admiration of his church. It splinters the character and breaks through the chosen framework of suspense. The pain has a murderous intensity but finally dissolves in its own acid. The Boy, 'always ready for more death', says that he once thought of becoming a priest to shut out the horror of the world, and in a seizure of disgust beats on the window with his hands. Here Greene seems to be tearing at him as Pinkie himself tortured the doll. The word 'horror' recurs in *Brighton Rock* like a static buzz in the head.

When the Boy died, he was 'whipped away into zero', tossed out of existence by an invisible hand. He joined the other young fugitives of the thirties, Raven shot in the back,

148

Anthony drowned, Conrad Drover crushed under a car. The protagonists of *The Confidential Agent* and *The Ministry of Fear* are middle-aged reflective men licking the wounds of the past. At the age of thirty-five Greene not only begins to build his stories around men older than himself, incipient burnt-out cases, but gets under the skin of their consciousness and adopts their point of view. The change occurs within a year and suggests that the personal crisis behind *Brighton Rock* has taken a heavy toll.

But if youth has lost, middle age seems better equipped for the battlefield. D. in *The Confidential Agent* is the first of Greene's protagonists to survive, and in his later work the survival rate is about fifty per cent. Fear and danger now offer a chance of self-renewal. 'Wherever D. was, there was a war.' This time, instead of trying to murder a whole world, he reluctantly defends it. Morally he sees very little to choose between his government and the rebels, but you have to decide on a line of action and live with it, even if it turns out to be wrong. When no ideology can be wholly trusted, you can only trust yourself. Through D., Greene is clearly drawing an analogy between himself and Catholicism. Religious belief, after all, is no less melodramatic than political belief. As many people have killed and betrayed for both.

On the boat that brings D. to England – it is fog and night again – he encounters L., the rebel agent with same mission. Both men are on their way to negotiate a coal deal with Lord Benditch, the mine-owner. 'Separated by different initial letters, a great many deaths', they separate again after a moment of silent confrontation. D., whose wife was shot by the rebels and who is haunted by the memory of being buried under rubble after an air raid, the fur of a dead cat pressed against his mouth, carries death around inside himself. L., the inbred and treacherous art collector, works for the rebels because he thinks they're going to win and they promise him life. Yet the death inside D. is more vital than the corrupt life inside L. Greene would choose the same initial for himself.

After passing through customs D. gets into conversation with a girl who offers him a lift to London in her car. Behind the second coincidental meeting lies the practical joker's hand, for Rose is Lord Benditch's daughter. She is also the novel's one unconvincing character, with a schoolgirl arrogance that recalls obstinately well-bred British film heroines of the time. (It is curious that Greene, who began reviewing movies for *The Spectator* in 1935, often expressed a dislike for the type. He mocks Madeleine Carroll as a 'colonial visitor', then writes a Madeleine Carroll part. The girl from Hitchcock's version of *The 39 Steps*, which he didn't much care for either, is given a drinking problem and a father complex.) Fortunately she has a minor role and remains a minor flaw. The momentum of the opening recovers when the car stops at a roadhouse and D. steps into a world of sinister grotesques. This is England, technically at peace. At first it looks like another planet whose people are almost recognizable as human beings. Then he realizes the power of disguise. The only difference between peace and war is that in England violence and corruption remain concealed, so you can still behave as if you're living in the best of all possible worlds. Camouflaged in the subtly eccentric crowd, danger is hard to locate. While the monocled manager is only an aggressive fool, the wall-eyed chauffeur turns out to be one of L.'s agents and tries to steal D.'s wallet in the washroom.

The tension is built on D.'s attempts to sort out appearance and reality. The beggar wearing a bowler hat in the London street is another enemy agent, but the inquisitive Indian at the seedy hotel is just mildly insane. At the international language centre where D. has to meet a contact, the manager pads down the corridor on rubber-soled shoes like a spy – but only to make sure the rules are observed and the pupils speak Entrenationo from the first lesson. Then Lord Benditch's rigidly correct manservant is shown working for L. He rifles D.'s overcoat and steals his credentials while D. tries to make a deal with Benditch and his aristocratic partners, one of whom dozes in an armchair. Since there is no trust anywhere, even D.'s own contacts – the language teacher, the hotel manageress, the embassy secretary – may secretly have gone over to L.'s side. None of this surprises D. The man who evades danger and violence only in sleep can still feel, after being robbed and beaten up, that on the whole he's had a successful day. He can even start to make love to Rose in a basement room with the dead double agent staring blindly from the couch.

The incongruities and reversals have a sardonic humour,

and D.'s acceptance of them adds an undercurrent of dream. It grows stronger in the crucial section at the Midlands coalfield, when D. tries to argue the manager out of sending coal to L.'s forces. Arriving at dawn in a landscape that suggests a huge rubbish heap, he seems to cross a frontier that leads beyond 'the rim of the turning world'. Ravaged hillsides, tilting black chimneys and piles of slag remind him of the desolation after an air raid. Letting go, as much as war, can make a ruined world – which, like a ruined man, can still be raised from the dead. Cocks crow as an ugly dawn breaks. A gang of delinquent boys with a leader nicknamed Crikey helps D. escape from the police. Out of tune voices singing a hymn in the chapel haunt the empty street in the rain. Although D. no longer believes in God, he cannot escape providence. The religious overtones here are like the echo of an unheard sound. There is no theological argument, only a poetic suggestiveness. It creates one of the most powerful phantasmagoric episodes in Greene's work.

The tone of *The Confidential Agent* lies in its abrupt changes of tone. Everything contains its opposite. Providence is mysteriously kind to D. and horrifyingly cruel to Else, the fourteen-year-old girl who works at his hotel. Her brief wretched life points to 'the guilt which clings to all of us without our knowing it'. A child who was surely right to cry in the tenement before she knew what the dark concealed, Else has developed a self-protective cunning but can still respond innocently to kindness. Because D. is kind, she helps him. The hotel manageress, another double agent, pushes her out of a high window. This death has a numbing brutality, while the death of the frightened treacherous language teacher is almost comic. He becomes the corpse in whose presence D., long telescoped into himself by the habit of fear, recovers his sexual drive. Caught between the grisly and the ironic, D. wonders about 'reconciling irreconcilables' and approaches the mystery that all Greene's later novels try to resolve. Like *The Confidential Agent*, the most dynamic of them – *The Ministry of Fear, The Quiet American, The Comedians, The Honorary Consul* – work subtly within and against the conventions of melodrama. They offer the surface excitement of a strong central situation, a romantic relationship, a happy end. But when suspense becomes a metaphor for human uncertainty,

151

there is no real escape from it. To love and survive is to exchange one danger for another. *The Confidential Agent* opens and closes on a dark night. D. and Rose return to his country on a boat. Although never identified, the country can only be Spain, and D.'s cause will soon be lost. 'You'll be dead very soon,' Rose tells him, and he doesn't argue. Any ending this side of death is premature.

Four years separate *The Ministry of Fear* from *The Confidential Agent*. In the interval Greene travelled to Mexico, produced a book of impressions and a novel about it, *The Power and the Glory*. A year after the Second World War broke out, he joined the intelligence service of the Foreign Office, and the frustrated amateur agent of the 1920s became a professional. At MI5 he worked under Kim Philby, the double agent who would later defect to Russia. The two men liked and admired each other. In his autobiography, this Vidocq-like figure in Greene's life confessed that he was influenced by D.'s remark in *The Confidential Agent* on the necessity of choosing a side and remaining loyal to it no matter what happens. Greene, in his introduction to the autobiography, compared Philby the unswerving Stalinist to a 'kindly Catholic' during the Inquisition. Unshocked by the idea of betraying one's country, he comments that there are far more important kinds of treason.

The title of an article that Greene wrote in 1940 reflects his feeling about the war. It is called *At Home*. Anticipating the mood of *The Ministry of Fear*, he notes that 'violence comes to us so easily because it was so long expected. . . . The world we lived in could not have ended any other way.' As the bombs fall over London he sees in retrospect how the 1930s demanded violence. They were like a room in a dream where the dreamer knows something is about to happen, and we recognize this atmosphere of expected disintegration in *A Gun for Sale* and *The Confidential Agent*. As well as ruined buildings and craters in the earth, there is a personal wasteland now. Already in *The Confidential Agent* D.'s wife has died, and in *The Ministry of Fear* Arthur Rowe has killed his wife to save her (or himself) from the pain of cancer. The connected situations suggest that Greene knows his own marriage is approaching death.

He writes *The Ministry of Fear* far away from London and the blitz, transferred by MI5 to Freetown, Sierra Leone. Anonymous as D., 59200 lives alone in a small house on the edge of the city. His professional attitude towards espionage is ironic, and among his rejected schemes for collecting information is to open a brothel and lure enemy agents there. A double sense of isolation hangs over the new novel begun in the spare night hours. The intelligence officer is exiled on a remote African coast, vultures hovering over nearby marshland and rats swinging on the curtains of his bedroom windows. The writer remembers the shattered London streets, a house sliced in half, pavements strewn with broken glass, a grand piano sticking through the hole in a blasted wall. The sense of exile and the feeling that in a bombed city life has become 'what it ought to be' translate into a series of hallucinating effects. Another tired, haunted protagonist, Rowe still wonders whether he poisoned his wife out of 'mercy to her or to me' and is obsessed by the thought that pity represents the easy way out, selfishness in disguise. In a looking-glass world, all virtues are illusions. 'Courage smashed a cathedral, endurance lets a city starve, pity kills. . . .' Walking through a bombed street, Rowe feels himself to be part of the general destruction. In his encounter with criminals, he comes to recognize the criminality within himself.

Wandering into a charity bazaar, he wins a cake that he was not supposed to win. It contains a microfilm of military secrets, and a German agent is soon on his trial. Hunchbacked and crippled with polio, Poole typifies the malignant weirdness of the enemy forces in this novel, and in his battle against them Rowe begins to feel as if he's controlled 'by some agency with a surrealist imagination'. In a chapter called 'Between Sleeping and Waking' he has an imaginary dialogue with his dead mother on the lawn of her country house, and tries to connect the logical past with the irrational future:

'It sounds like a thriller, doesn't it, but the thrillers are like life – more like life than you are, this lawn, your sandwiches, that pine. You used to laugh at the books Miss Savage read – about spies, and murders, and violence, and wild motor-car chases, but, dear, that's real life: it's what we've all made of the world since you died.'

On the dissolving frontier between reality and dream, Rowe

learns that while an insect can at least hide under a stone to escape being trampled, a human being can no longer run for cover. Hilfe, the charming fanatic Austrian refugee working for a charity organization that masks a Nazi espionage network, tells him that criminals as a separate class have ceased to exist. They are everywhere now, and a war is not the only battlefield on which people are paid to kill each other. Murder has become a job: the politician and the bank manager, the psychiatrist and the (Protestant) minister may all be revealed as killers in search of greater position and power. The danger of the room in the dream has spread to every room. When the lights go up after a spiritualist séance, a man at the table has been murdered. Rowe suffers amnesia after a bomb explosion and wakes up in a private asylum run by a distinguished psychiatrist who is really another German agent, more disturbed than any of his patients. Rowe's life is now as fragmented as the bombed city with its rubble and scars and boarded windows. In another extraordinary chapter, 'Bits and Pieces', he lies in the twilight zone, grappling with his ambiguous past and the dangerous present. Like D. in the mining town he's at the end of his rope, and in a setting equally touched with fantasy moves through corridors of returning memory and free association towards a new wholeness. Before the accident he fell in love with Hilfe's sister, Anna, who tried to make him shed the weight of guilt. Having seen a great many killings of which none was a mercy killing, she told him that she preferred the weakness of being unable to endure someone else's pain to the strength of 'the people who don't care', who can bear other people's pain endlessly. Now loss of memory succeeds where argument failed. Lighter on account of many lapsed habits and fears, an Arthur Rowe 'next door to his own youth' escapes from the asylum and helps the police round up the spy ring. In a final confrontation, Hilfe becomes as demonic in his cool handsome way as the hunchbacked Poole. Cruelly filling in the last important memory gap, he reveals that Rowe poisoned his wife. With a powerful imaginative stroke, Greene makes this coincide with the distant sound of a bomb exploding, and Rowe can only reflect how many things will have to be destroyed before peace comes again.

Another inverted romantic ending describes Rowe and Anna

beginning an 'ordinary' life together in a world of continuing danger. Rowe knows that Anna hopes he will never remember about the mercy killing, and to make her happy he pretends that he's still forgotten it. Watching each other like enemies, always afraid of being found out, the lovers dissolve into another kind of shadow-land where peace will never really come again. 'If one loved, one feared.' The Ministry of Fear begins as a technique of blackmail and intimidation created by fascism. It ends by infiltrating the atmosphere of everyday lives.

This stunning novel maintains a suspense as grippingly implausible as that of Hitchcock's *North by Northwest*, its surrealism open where Hitchcock's is concealed. In an echo-chamber world, Greene's preoccupations return through long corridors, shattered streets, empty rooms. Entering the bazaar, Rowe not only stumbles into a nightmarish adventure but is deceived by the call of innocence and the promise of child-hood memories about to be revived. It seems to offer an escape from the horrors of his adult life, then produces horrors worse than any he has experienced. 'Pacing round the railings he came to his doom. . . .' The microfilm hidden in the prize cake is like the poison in the flowers of Greene's dream. When Rowe wins it, dream starts to compete with reality and the novel mixes the irrational and the inevitable, the precise and the imprecise. Like a dream it is peopled with apparitions rather than characters: Poole the monstrous dwarf, the coy spiritualist lady with the masculine voice in the crumbling Victorian house, the corrupt psychiatrist with his beautiful white hair and noble profile, the detective who suggests an incongruous reincarnation of Sherlock Holmes. Hilfe and his sister, with their mutual dependence and intimate antagonisms, recall Kate and Anthony in *England Made Me*. Greene's thumbnail sketch technique, more sharply developed than in his earlier novels, gives them a kind of minimal definition, slight yet complete. Anna is a deliberately fragile creation with an aura of wish-fulfilment – not only for Rowe but perhaps for Greene himself, for she will reappear with the same name, nationality and elusive sadness in *The Third Man*. The green baize door recurs, this time separating Rowe from the asylum sick bay and its secrets. The asylum itself begins as a false refuge, like the bazaar, but when Rowe opens the door he walks into another nightmare. Before the murder at the spiritualist séance, Greene summons another favourite image, the cupboard door that the terrified child knew would open of its own accord.

A good night, Greene says in his *Congo Journal*, is a night with only one bad dream. He has often reproduced his dreams in his novels, and on the journey to Sierra Leone at the end of 1941, to begin his life as 59200, he had a nightmare that combined violence and fatality in a way that looks forward to the continuous doomsday surrealism of *The Ministry of Fear*:

A friend accidentally draws a breadknife across his throat and cuts it. He lifts up the flap of flesh to see how serious it is. Taking him to hospital I see a woman in a car knock down a small boy of my son's age at the kerb and then she walked on him accidentally. The skin is wrinkled up exposing the red raw apple cheek.

In the novel Greene compares the effect of regular dreaming to religious discipline. Repeated words, like dreams, form a habit and 'a kind of unnoticed sediment at the bottom of the mind'. One day you find yourself acting on the belief you never thought you had. In the same way the dreamer begins to recognize his life from his dreams. Bombs fall in answer to an unconscious demand for violence. Murderers are dirt cheap because murder has become respectable. When Rowe escapes from the asylum, he's forgotten the crime he committed and yet still feels like a criminal. It explains his calm, his readiness for 'the horror of returning life', when Hilfe reveals what he did. Perhaps, too, Greene's friendship with Philby left another 'unnoticed sediment', for the emphasis in *The Ministry of Fear* on political treason in familiar establishment circles prefigures the defection of Philby and others to Russia after the war. In any case, most of the dreams in this novel seem prophetic. Thirty years later the idea of a Ministry of Fear induces only a shock of recognition. Governments that card-index potential enemies, espionage by wire-tapping, the act of terrorism at the airport or school, kidnapping and murder for profit – they are all the result of delayed expectation, of life again becoming 'what it ought to be'.

Cycles in Greene's work overlap. *The Ministry of Fear* ends a cycle that began with *Stamboul Train*, but in 1938 Greene began another when he travelled to Mexico, commissioned to write a book on the repression of the Catholic church by President Calles's government. *The Lawless Roads* (1939; U.S. title *Another Mexico*) goes far beyond its subject, and like *Journey Without Maps* records a personal exploration, a search for 'a quality of darkness' that ends this time in disappointment. Greene's Mexico is a land of vultures and sinister decay, patient sadness and 'pistol-shot violence'. The closeness to a racial source that he felt in Liberia is absent, since he spent most of his time in a swampy isolated region with a few locked crumbling churches and no Indians. In any case, the Aztec legacy repelled him, pyramids and temples suggesting something inhuman and vaguely evil.

Since he felt tired and homesick and succumbed to the usual tropical infection, he admits this may have been a dysenteric view. But it appears in *The Power and the Glory* (1940), which takes place in the same ghostly Mexico, haunted by poverty and persecution and death. Like D. making his contacts in *The Confidential Agent*, an unnamed priest continues to give the sacraments in secret. Equally on the run, he is never sure whether to expect shelter or betrayal. He is also a coward and an alcoholic, and beneath the story of his pursuit and eventual capture lies Greene's concern with salvation for 'the half-hearted and the corrupt'. Shocked out of half-heartedness only as he faces the firing squad, the priest has a flash of revelation and thinks it would have been just as easy to become a saint as a failure. It's difficult not to feel that he deceives himself, for his belief lacks any touch of ecstasy. He clings to it because he's terrified of losing it, and seems to project fear and self-humiliation on the faithful when he recommends them to pray for more suffering. His truest moment, and the novel's best scene, occurs when he's thrown into prison and finds himself in a world of stench and criminal darkness. The shadow of an angrily pious woman asks him to stop two other shadows making love on the floor. He refuses, preferring desperate passion to self-righteousness.

The only thing that mitigated Greene's dislike of Mexico was a sense of living 'under the shadow of religion – of God and the Devil'. Feeling no human sympathy for a people or a place, he couldn't create it. In *The Lawless Roads* the problem doesn't exist, since he was an outsider reacting to a climate

157

of hate and dismay. The novel seems theoretical, the personal impressions have an intense physical vitality.

Like a tropical disease that subsides and then flares up again, the tormented Catholic recurs over the next twenty years in *The Heart of the Matter* (1948) and *The End of the Affair* (1951), then burns itself out in *A Burnt-Out Case* (1961). The first two novels are concerned with adulterous love affairs. Scobie relieves the pain of guilt by suicide. Neither Sarah nor Bendrix are believers at the beginning of their affair, but guilt converts them. After they separate, Sarah dies and Bendrix settles into bitterness and isolation. The adultery quotient presumably stems from the break-up of Greene's own marriage, the guilt quotient again produces a desire to suffer rather than to love, an exchange of sad grey dialogue or a despairing orgasm on a wooden floor. And when Querry the architect and burnt-out case loses his faith, he loses his sense of vocation and sexual drive as well. Before being shot by a mistakenly jealous husband, he has found an image of the world in a leper colony in the Congo and seen the mutilated agonizing in the terminal disease of hope.

A prolonged circular battle with the same problem is inevitably depleting. The exhausting and exhausted cycle reflects a trap set by the author for himself. If the will to believe produces only anger and death, the will has surely been misdirected.

But a kind of salvation is waiting, slower and more reluctant than D.'s in *The Confidential Agent* when he feels like a ruined man in a ruined world. After *The Heart of the Matter*, Greene's subconscious seems to have been at work when he jotted down on the back of an envelope an idea for a new novel, about a man raised from the dead. The narrator attends the funeral of a friend and is astonished to see him walking down a London street a week later. When Alexander Korda commissioned him to write a movie story about the four-power occupation of Vienna, Greene used the idea to create a basic thriller situation. He returns to the device of his most powerful earlier work, the human and physical uncertainty of suspense, the urgent contemporary setting. *The Third Man* was published in 1950, a year after the movie itself appeared.

As Greene points out in his introduction, the story was not written to be read. The finished film is the vital product, Carol Reed's direction a vital part of it. Writer and director collaborated on revisions to the story, all of them improvements except for an over-extended chase scene through the sewers at the climax. This director's cadenza was Reed's mistake, minor in comparison with the insights he brought, the edgy atmosphere and cutting, actors perfectly cast and handled, the ironic use of a zither accompaniment, the imaginative reversal of Greene's ending. But the material itself, though slight, remains unmistably Greene's.

Harry Lime has offered his old friend Martins a job on the International Relief Agency in Vienna. When Martins arrives in the city, he learns that Lime has just been run over and killed by a car. He attends Lime's funeral. He meets and falls in love with Lime's former girl-friend, Anna. He discovers that Lime trafficked in penicillin and diluted it to increase his profits. Then he encounters Lime himself in a deserted street at night. Suspense continues on a characteristic double level: the mystery of Lime and his false death, the dilemma of Martins trapped between friendship and moral antagonism. After seeing photographs of children killed or mentally destroyed by Lime's penicillin, Martins betrays him to the police. The act of conscience leads to the death of his best friend. He loses Anna, and feels like a criminal.

In one of the most effective scene, Martins and Lime are sitting up above the world on the Great Wheel at the Prater. Martins asks Lime if he's ever visited a hospital and seen his victims. Lime finds the idea melodramatic, then looks down at the people below the turning wheel:

'Would you really feel any pity if one of those dots stopped moving – for ever? If I said you can have twenty thousand pounds for every dot that stops, would you really, old man, tell me to keep my money – without hesitation?'

With his schoolboy's criminal pride, Lime sees himself as the most honest person in a corrupt society. Immaturity makes him at once vulnerable and dangerous. Greene develops this idea with Pyle in *The Quiet American*, along with other elements that detonate like a delayed charge.

The Quiet American (1955) begins a new cycle that includes

159

The Comedians (1966) and *The Honorary Consul* (1973). Like *The Third Man*, each novel centres on an act of topical violence – of war, of dictatorship and attempted revolution, of kidnapping with a political motive. The enemy-friends and the girl in the middle reappear. Suspense begins with physical danger, then extends to a deeper level, the choice of betraying a friend or a conviction. The Minstry of Fear continues to operate. You succumb to its reminders of death and loneliness, or you escape by not being able to love and becoming one of 'the people who don't care'. In technique the novels look backward and forward. Greene found exciting variations in the hunted-hunter formula that began with *A Gun for Sale*. Now he refines the balance between melodrama and self-examination. In *The Ministry of Fear*, Rowe is shocked by what the world has made of itself since his mother died – 'thrillers are like life, more than you are.' Since that time, pursuit and murder, the bomb explosion and the killing of hostages have become part of the texture of the day. Life imitating the thriller is no longer a shock, any more than reality imitating dream or violence coexisting with farce. Plot and atmosphere are stripped of hallucination, images of death surprise by their coolness. After the raid on the Vietnamese village the mother and child are 'very clearly dead', and the boy lies 'like an embryo in the womb with his little bony knees drawn up'. The suicide in the empty swimming pool looks like 'a middle-aged foetus ready dressed for burial in his neat grey suit'. The Indian's body outside the *barrio* hut suggests 'a bundle of old clothes thrown to one side, sodden with the night's rain'.

A meeting with Greene in 1958 is described by Robert Craft in his *Stravinsky*. Brief and precise, his sketch evokes the mood of these novels. He notes the 'sad, wise, fanatical' features, sagged with preoccupation, and the eyes that are still unnervingly, implacably blue. They have seen a great deal and known the worst. So have Fowler and Brown and Plarr, protagonists who abandon their origins and live in exile – as Greene himself has lived in the south of France for many years. Memories of a lost childhood still exist for them, but less intensely than for Raven or Pinkie or Arthur Rowe. They have found a relationship with a woman, and it seems more than coincidence that they choose to be at home in places

160

where the brothel is an open institution. In *Congo Journal* Greene mentions a brothel scene in a novel about Brazil, *La Forêt Veuve*. Its author despises people who despise whores. In his view a whore is a *Dame Amie*, the highest compliment one can pay a woman. Greene's later protagonists have found their *Dames Amies*: a professional prostitute in *The Quiet American* and *The Honorary Consul*, a woman accustomed to betraying her husband in *The Comedians*.

Fowler and Brown and Plarr are aware of failure and drift in their lives, but they refuse despair. Again it seems more than coincidence that none of them seriously believe in God. Fowler and Plarr are agnostics, Brown a lapsed Catholic who plays with the idea of God as a practical joker. (In *The Heart of the Matter* and *The End of the Affair*, God's performance is altogether different: the great plaintiff, intent on spiritual damages.) In a preface to *The Comedians*, told like *The Quiet American* in the first person, Greene disclaims identity with his narrator. But a writer can assume a mask as revealing as the face in his autobiography. While absence of religious belief may still create a prison, the non-believer is permitted to see believers in another kind of prison.

In *The Honorary Consul* the priest who has turned revolutionary describes his relationship with the church as 'a separation by mutual consent, not a divorce'. He feels no hate, only regret for an early period of happiness that failed to last. Although the church makes rules that simply don't apply to the majority of human cases, he still considers that he belongs to it. 'The only way we can leave the Church is to die . . .' Yet the rage of *Brighton Rock* and the agonized hatred of *The End of the Affair* have vanished. The atmosphere of this later cycle is extraordinarily relaxed, a major reason for its breadth and power. As the worst of all possible worlds becomes an accepted fact, Greene's protagonists move closer towards reconciling irreconcilables. They know that the most natural death is the violent death, and death in itself a means of escape.

When Greene first went to Vietnam in 1950 he was hoping only for an antidote to boredom, but he found a country and a situation 'that held you as a smell does'. He interviewed Ho Chi Minh and reported on the war between the French and the rebels for the London *Sunday Times*. The year of his arrival coincided with the idea of intervention by a 'third force' that was neither communist nor tainted with colonialism. It resulted in the beginning of U.S. military and economic aid to Saigon. *The Quiet American* is Greene's reaction. One of his shortest novels, almost as concentrated as a Simenon, it took over three years to write. Perhaps it owes some of its lucidity and tension to the fact that Greene smoked opium during his time in south-east Asia, and like Wilkie Collins found that it quickened the wits and tranquillized the nerves.

The novel is structured like a detective story. The opening reveals that Alden Pyle, a young American official in Saigon, has been murdered. We don't know by whom or why. Fowler, the narrator, seems to be holding something back. In fact there are things he doesn't know as well as things he conceals. Interrogated by the police, comparing their facts with his own memories, Fowler begins to see his motives more clearly. As the story moves fluently between past and present, the dead haunt the living. For a long time Fowler has insisted that he is only a reporter who tells what he sees, but the experience with Pyle has led to the necessity of involvement. 'We all get involved in a moment of emotion, and then we cannot get out.'

Fowler is an ageing disappointed man who comes to terms with exile in Saigon because he likes the country and because he has Phuong. 'Invisible like peace', the graceful childlike prostitute resembles the effect of the opium pipes she prepares. She would like to get married, because marriage represents security, but Fowler's wife, an Anglo-Catholic living in England, will not agree to a divorce. (An offstage character, the two letters that she writes to Fowler create a more human and complex person than the centre-stage portrait of Scobie's wife in *The Heart of the Matter*.) While Fowler knows that a prostitute is always on the market for a better offer, he has caught something of the attitude of primitive people that Greene defines in *Congo Journal*: 'Life is a moment. This is their form of eternity.' Phuong acts as Fowler's form of eternity until Pyle falls in love with her and proposes marriage.

The quiet high-minded American not only disrupts Fowler's personal life, but as a representative of the 'third force' makes him re-examine his indifference to politics. 'I never knew a man who had better motives for all the trouble he caused . . .' Just as Pyle's 'love' for Phuong would reduce her to one more plastic housewife in the American 'gadget-world', so his attitude goes no deeper than the idea of making the world safe for democracy and keeping south-east Asia safe from the communists. Substituting textbook slogans for experience, he never understands the shallowness of his ideals. Surrounded by dead bodies in the middle of a war, he never notices their wounds. Innocence as great as this arouses protective feelings, while in fact the world needs protection from it. When it attempts to impose its delusions by force, it becomes 'a form of insanity'. Pyle connives with a group that he fails to recognize as shabby terrorists, and they mistime a bomb explosion in the centre of Saigon. The only victims are the genuinely innocent.

For its clairvoyance about the future mistakes of American foreign policy, the novel was accused of anti-Americanism. Greene observes Pyle with mortal accuracy, yet the portrait is not completely unsympathetic. Like the sandwiches he prefers, Pyle's ideas are packaged, ignorance wrapped in romantic cellophane. If only he'd stayed home and followed the baseball games instead of reading books with titles like *The Challenge to Democracy* and *The Role of the West* no harm would have been done. But the man obtuse enough to ask Fowler to translate his proposal of marriage to Phuong also believes that terrorists can help democracy because they're anti-Red. On the personal level Fowler can't help liking Pyle for his terrible puzzled honesty. The point of no return is reached only when he sees it leading to more bloodshed. 'Sooner or later,' a Vietnamese remarks, 'one has to take sides. If one is to remain human.' The warning unavoidable moment echoes through Greene's work, a reminder of the cupboard door slowly opening in the childhood dream. The taking of sides also involves a betrayal. In Fowler's case it involves delivering Pyle into the hands of an assassin.

Ironically, Fowler is just as flawed as Pyle in many ways. Selfish and often malicious, he lies both to Phuong and to Pyle when he tells them his wife has agreed to a divorce. But at least he understands the waste and terror of war, the crying in the dark. He remains precariously and regretfully

163

human because his own fear of death alerts him to the surrounding graveyard, the canal filled with floating bodies, the mother and child in the ditch, the fragmented baby and the legless torso still twitching after the explosion in the square.

The Comedians is one of Greene's longest novels, its more expansive manner due to its narrator. Brown is a mellower version of Fowler, his background more fully developed and his life following the same basic pattern: exile, a *Dame Amie,* a refusal to be committed, and then 'that dangerous journey which we all have to take before the end'. There is the same wry affection for the seedy and exotic, although the Caribbean setting has a darker tone. Behind Vietnam lay the gentleness of Buddhism, but Haiti is shadowed by voodoo. Duvalier the dictator seems like a reincarnation of Baron Samedi, the sinister ritual figure who robs graveyards and enslaves the dead as zombies. Brown has no illusions about this 'shabby land of terror', yet feels at home in it. Many years ago he was a convinced Catholic and saw life as a very serious affair. Now that he views God as a practical joker and refuses the idea of tragedy, he is a comedian who plays a part rather than expose himself to beliefs and causes that always end in death. (His background, incidentally, is the point of departure for Greene's next novel, *Travels With My Aunt.* The illegitimate son of a heroically adventurous mother, he has inherited the hotel above Port-au-Prince where she ended her days with a negro lover.) His affair with the wife of a South American diplomat reflects a flight from boredom rather than a need to love. He views adultery, like espionage, as a secret adventure. It entertains him because of the furtive thrill of making love in a car at night and the constant fear of discovery.

Brown passes his first important test of non-involvement when a secretly anti-Duvalier government official cuts his wrists in the hotel's empty swimming pool at night. By hiding his friend's body in the hills, he hopes to dissociate himself from the whole business. He knows and sympathizes with a group of young revolutionaries, but keeps his distance. Like Fowler he doesn't value his own life highly but is still afraid of death. Greene's ironic touch declares itself in the choice of an agent to penetrate the barrier. Left cold by idealism, Brown gradually finds himself drawn to an adventurer who goes by the name of Jones, a small dapper creature with preposterous tales of exploits during the Second World War. He has the breeziness of Harry Lime and the ambiguous innocence of Pyle. Like both of them, this schoolboy has never grown up. The instinctive liar and swindler retains a childish dream of owning a hotel and a golf course in some travel brochure Caribbean paradise. Arriving in Haiti with a letter of official introduction, he finds like so many others that the contact in question has fallen from Duvalier's favour. Cheerfully resilient, he survives being thrown into jail and beaten up, then manages all the same to interest the government in a fraudulent business scheme. Having heard and believed his stories of war service, the revolutionaries approach him to train their army in the mountains. The comedian is tempted by a new part and the promise of acting out his fantasies. More than this, he unconsciously seizes a chance of self-renewal. Brown senses it, open to the same chance in spite of defending himself against it for years. The brotherhood of comedians leads towards a genuine involvement.

The episodes that follow mix excitement and absurdity on Greene's highest level. Moments of extreme comedy occur without diminishing the atmosphere of fear and brutality that once again refers back to childhood nightmares 'when something in a cupboard prepares to come out'. When the police grow suspicious, Brown helps Jones to escape to the South American embassy, disguised in grotesque improvised drag. Martha and her husband offer him political refuge, but Brown soon became jealous, mistakenly convinced that his mistress and his new friend are having an affair. In spite and because of his jealousy, he risks his life to drive Jones into the mountains at night to link up with the revolutionaries. Obliged to flee the country, he lands penniless in Santa Domingo and takes a job as assistant to an undertaker.

Through reversals and failures and escapes, irreconcilables again try to reconcile. Brown loses Martha, his hotel, his exile's working corner in life, and hears a priest at Jones's funeral remark that it's better to be wrong with the violent than 'right with the cold and the craven'. While the revolution fails, Jones's death has proved him capable of loyalty. An old friend in Haiti, long committed to overthrowing Duvalier and now in danger of his life, writes to Brown:

165

'Catholics and Communists have committed great crimes, but at least they have not stood aside, like an established society, and been indifferent. I would rather have blood on my hands than water like Pilate . . . If you have abandoned one faith, do not abandon all faith. There is always an alternative to the faith we lose. Or is it the same faith under another mask?'

For Greene himself the question seems to be loaded, for he answers it in *The Honorary Consul*: 'The only way we can leave the Church is to die.' But for Brown it remains open and troubling. In a dream he asks Jones why he died, and the adventurer tells him, 'It's in my part, old man, it's in my part.' Brown's part has been to live in a country of darkness and terror and find a kind of happiness there because it mirrors his own fears and frustrations. Now that he's escaped he realizes Haiti is not an exceptional place, only 'a small slice of everyday life taken at random'. His temptation is to revert to the comedian's role, accepting the bitter farce of his new profession and making his modest contribution to the need for burying the world's dead. At the end of *The Quiet American*, Pyle has been murdered and Fowler's wife agrees after all to a divorce. Everything has gone right for him in a way, but Fowler is left with a desperate wish for someone to whom he can say he's sorry. Everything has gone wrong for Brown and he is left with a desperate wish that he hadn't postponed the involvement and the dangerous journey until it was too late. A Jesuit education has saddled him with a conscience that refuses to stay entirely quiet, and the habit of fear has taught him tricks to quiet it. As usual, Greene allows the suspense to continue after the story is over.

In *The Honorary Consul* the journey is less than twenty yards, from the door of the *barrio* hut to the point along the mud track at which the paratroopers open fire. Up to this point the novel has alternated between past and present, like *The Quiet American*, but without revealing in advance which of the two enemy-friends is going to die. In fact Plarr's death reverses the pattern. After the two other novels, it seems likely that the consul himself is doomed. Perhaps another reference to the great joker should have been taken as a warning. His spirit presides over the action, and Plarr's death seems in retrospect the final twist.

166

The son of an English revolutionary imprisoned for many years in Paraguay, Dr Plarr practises in a small Argentine town near the border of the two countries. A group of revolutionaries plans to kidnap a visiting American ambassador and use him to bargain for the release of a dozen political prisoners, including Plarr's father. The doctor agrees to help to the extent of providing them with information about the ambassador's itinerary, but the terrorists mistake one Cadillac for another and kidnap the British honorary consul instead. Charley Fortnum is a man of no importance, not even an official diplomat. He has married a girl from the local brothel, and is one of the few people in the town unaware that Plarr is having an affair with her.

This time the mixture of tension and farce begins with the basic situation. Its development is subtle but relentless. The revolutionaries only discover their mistake when their captive falls ill and they summon Plarr to treat him. They refuse to believe that Fortnum is totally unimportant, and go ahead with the plan. Because of his complicity, Plarr in a sense becomes their prisoner as well. He is unable to prevent Fortnum from discovering the part he has played: the affair with Clara, the fact that he and not Fortnum has fathered the child soon to be born. Plarr himself has been equally cheated, for his father really died in prison a year ago and the revolutionaries kept it from him in order to secure his help.

As in *Stamboul Train*, a famous novelist acts as chorus to a series of betrayals. The link extends to their names, Savory and Saavedra, and to the combined impatience and respect they arouse. The South American writes violent melancholy works full of symbols and *machismo*, and tells Plarr that the situation of the honorary consul would make a poor novel because 'nothing dates more quickly than the contemporary'. Only timelessness brings importance, and the true novelist must stand at a distance from his subject. On the other hand, he can sum up Fortnum's predicament:

'As I see it, Señor Fortnum is a simple man – not very wise or intelligent – and suddenly he finds himself close to violent death. Perhaps he has never even thought of death before. It is a situation in which such a man either succumbs to fear or he grows in stature.'

Plarr has never particularly liked Fortnum, a good-natured

and boring drunk apt to become maudlin about his wife and his lapsed Catholicism. Lying on a blanketed coffin in the slum hut on the edge of the jungle, he somehow organizes his confusion and fulfils Saavedra's prophecy about growing in stature. In Plarr's eyes he becomes admirable because he genuinely loves Clara. 'I know how to fuck,' the doctor realizes. 'I don't know how to love.' Nor, unlike the revolutionaries committed to violence, does he know how to believe in anything. His physical and spiritual isolation increases with the suspense outside. Refusing to bargain for Fortnum's release and indifferent to his danger, the government orders police and paratroopers to close in on the hut. When Plarr breaks out to appeal to them, he is trying at last to break out from himself.

The kidnappers include a poet and a renegade priest who has married and turned to political activism. The priest had once wanted to be a lawyer and the poet thought of farming, but injustice moves too quickly and they find the professions of peace too slow. While the poet is proud of his criminal status, Leon has moments of self-doubt. In a fine terse scene he prays for the man he expects to kill, and the prospective victim comforts him. *The Power and the Glory* theorized the conflict between religion and politics through its arguments between a priest and a socialist lieutenant. In *The Honorary Consul* the conflict exists within a single character and has much more personal intensity. But the only flaw in a gripping novel, perhaps Greene's richest work, is a tendency to labour the point. When Leon talks about the archbishop sitting down to dinner with the general, he touches a raw contemporary nerve. When he complains about the God who allows Jews to be sent to the gas ovens, he touches cliché.

The novel ends on a firmer note of reconciliation than either *The Comedians* or *The Quiet American*. Fortnum goes back to his wife, the girl in whom Plarr has noted the whore's intriguing quality of somehow remaining a stranger. ('Her body has been scrawled over by so many men you can never decipher your own signature there.') When she shrugs off Plarr's death, Fortnum knows she is lying. But he goes beyond the moment in *The Ministry of Fear* of two people bound together by secret mistrust. He feels closer to Clara than ever before, because he knows he's capable of loving the child of a man who died for him.

As *The Honorary Consul* opens, Plarr stands watching the port on the river. It is the kind of evening when 'some mysterious combination of failing light and the smell of an unrecognized plant brings back to some men the sense of childhood and future hope and to others the sense of something which has been lost and nearly forgotten'. As it ends, the personal balance-sheet seems to divide evenly for the first time between the sense of loss and of hope. When Greene looks down from his home on what he calls the Côte d'Ordure, he can watch the inhabitants of Antibes turning a garden of magnolias and palms into a garbage dump. In another twenty years the Riviera will have moved to one terminal state or the other, appealing seediness or total mechanized pollution. Like Greene's own life it remains suspended between opposites.

In the early *Stamboul Train*, Czinner the exiled revolutionary can never entirely shake off his early Catholicism. Whichever side he takes, he feels 'damned by his faithfulness'. More than forty years later Greene is a residual Catholic drawn to socialist causes and saddened by the deaths of Allende and Che Guevara. The seventies as much as the thirties seem to demand violence. Greene began by exploring a relatively narrow spectrum of crime, the tormented solitary taking his revenge on the world. Later he showed peaceful men like D. and Rowe becoming reluctantly involved with violence and a general atmosphere of destruction. Finally the doctor, the poet and the priest in effect justify murder: better to have blood on your hands than to deny your convictions. For Ambler this is only the ape changing into another velvet suit, but for Greene conflict brings a man closer to God. 'He made us in His image,' says Leon, 'and so our evil is His evil too. How could I love God if He were not like me? Divided like me. Tempted like me.'

Raven the killer was also an instrument of peace. Pyle the innocent was a kind of killer. The idea of the double agent has obsessed Greene since he was cast in the role at school. Like Raven at the orphanage he begins by knowing how the hunted feel. Slipping back to the croquet lawn or the orchard, he still returns in his mind to 'the horror and the fascination' of the other side. Caught in a border zone of uncertainty, he continues to look for the secret exit. The Catholic refuses to be damned by faithfulness and hopes for salvation in disloyalty. The novelist compares himself to a spy, watching and listening and overhearing, and salutes the example of Philby.

'I'd like to change commitments every day of the year,' he said recently. 'In a communist society I would be against communism. In a capitalist society I would be called pro-communist.' Once again he echoes the early discovery that belief needs betrayal to prove its strength. It is belief in betrayal that shapes the novels with their succession of fugitives on the run between one country and another, their violence that offers 'the great chance of death', their recurrent images of a door opening on a secret, of a frontier crossed and recrossed, of the ancestral fear and the central darkness in which you can either lose yourself for ever or find a way of beginning again.

FIVE

Night Vision

INTERVIEWER: . . . I often hear people ask about the violence in modern fiction. I'm all for it, but I'd like to ask why you write of it.
SIMENON: We are accustomed to see people driven to their limit.
                                            Interview with Georges Simenon,
                                            The *Paris Review*

As a child he saw his country and his parents driven to their limit. The Germans occupied Belgium in 1914. An atmosphere of concealed violence occupied his family, creating the same kind of pressure as a strong wind that blows day after day and fills the air with brittle dust and haze. Simenon's father worked for an insurance company in the ugly industrial town of Liège. Since he had a weak heart the company refused to insure its own employee. He kept his condition a secret, and his wife found something mysterious and exasperating in his detachment and his refusal to behave like a man interested in success. It increased her terror of poverty, and the devout Catholic plunged into the role of family martyr-saviour, taking in lodgers (and cheating them), persuading a Jesuit school to educate her son at reduced fees because she wanted him to become a priest, ruining her own health in a desperate attempt to put away enough money to start a bakery business. Simenon was nineteen when his father died and the truth came out. His verdict on the situation appears in *Pedigree* (1948), a book conceived as autobiography and then recast as autobiographical fiction.

Accused of failure and weakness during so much of his life, the father has discovered the strength of tranquillity. The threat of death is even transformed into a kind of blessing that extends his capacity for happiness. The mother complains that he has 'no antennae' but lacks them herself, since a hunger for security never allows her to look beyond appearances. As misunderstanding drives each of them to the limits of patience and anxiety, the son feels a terrible atmosphere of non-communication and is unable to account for it. The mystery sends him into helpless rages and its solution leaves him with a desire to escape from a world suddenly revealed as false and cruel, judging without perceiving, equating respectability with material success.

In his notebooks that he kept during the early sixties, Simenon recalls the 'Religion and Morality with capitals' that afflicted his adolescence, and explains that he turned his back on them because they turned their backs on reality. 'The naked man' recurs as his favourite image of reality. Moral conventions, fantasies about God and the devil, are ways of clothing someone with artificial fears. Reality strips him bare, alone with his basic fear of himself.

He begins to explore this reality while writing pulp fantasies, serial novels and short stories for newspapers. It is 1923. A year after his father's death he has married a painter, Regina Renchon, and escaped to Paris. He is twenty. He agrees to give precedence to his wife's career, leaving her free to paint what she likes while he writes only for money, disguising himself under various pseudonyms, most often as Georges Sim. The sacrifice is also a convenience. Sim feels that all he knows of life comes from two cities, Liège and Paris, and it's not enough to make him Simenon. Discovering a facility for inventing plots, he mass-produces at a fantastic pace, writing a novel in a couple of days and a short story in a morning.

Behind this intensity he recognizes an inherited fear, his mother's dread of poverty. One part of himself remains attached to middle-class values, another encourages him to escape into different lives. Human curiosity is bound up with fascination for the opposite of middle-class existence, the world of rejects and outcasts.

At sixteen, as an apprentice reporter for the *Gazette de Liège*, he already felt its pull. Walking home at night, he often passed houses drably respectable from the outside, with curtains not fully drawn across their street-level windows. But instead of a glimpse of family life and an aspidistra in a brass urn, a dim light revealed a girl sitting in a chair. At the sound of approaching footsteps, she always looked up. The young reporter always moved on, since two women supplied him with regular sexual satisfaction at the time. Several weeks later, he stopped. A black prostitute waited in the chair that night and the sight of negro flesh aroused the desire for a new experience.

172

Another distraction from provincial life: getting drunk once a week with a group of young writers and painters who called themselves La Caque (The Keg). Believers in alcohol, anarchism and their own genius, they idealized the poet of criminals, François Villon. In a disreputable section of town, professional criminals hung out in cafés – but only Simenon among the group felt impelled to move from the abstract to the real, sitting by himself and watching them at close quarters. When he followed them through the streets they became suspicious, yet somehow he escaped physical attack.

In Paris, since his wife needs models, it entertains Simenon to look for them in lowlife bars and dance halls where most of the girls have recently arrived from the country to take up prostitution. Again he risks danger, for the pimps are violently jealous and he's seen one of them slit a girl's throat. It also entertains him to make casual love in streets and alleys around Montmartre at night, and for a while to have an affair with a married woman. Sometimes this is carried on in her own house while the unsuspecting husband, busy in another room, makes small talk through the half-open door.

Exhausting this kind of anticonformism after two years, he feels the need for wider discoveries. By 1925 he's made enough money to buy a small boat and sets out to explore France, particularly the countryside and seacoast, about which he knows nothing. He chooses to travel by canal and river because highways and railroads offer only the front door view, and he prefers to take places by surprise. Accompanied on the trip by his wife, a maid and a dog, he gets up early each morning to finish the daily quota of fifty pages before noon. Returning to Paris, he goes to Normandy and lives on a farm like a peasant for several months, then moves south to the little Mediterranean island of Porquerolles, where he lives like a fisherman. The pattern of exploration is repeated in his sexual adventures. He continues to prefer prostitutes, but no longer for reasons of novelty or danger. Lust, like farming or fishing or horseback riding, is a necessary and natural means of self-renewal that professionals can satisfy with a minimum of pretension. (This habit creates problems with his first wife, but the second will allow him complete freedom.) By 1929 he's written more than a thousand stories and novels and stored up a knowledge of everyday life in France that he feels ready to use.

In the view from canal and river he has located the truly extraordinary. It lies in the so-called ordinary that never ceases to alarm and surprise him. Like the life of the sea that he discovered as a fisherman, it reveals a perpetual offensive and defensive motion: *'Innate, indispensable cruelty.'*

Buying a second and larger boat, he sails to an estuary in Holland and becomes Simenon. He works on wine – about three bottles a day – and produces eight Maigret novels within a year, having previously arranged with his publisher to launch them as a series. Because he wants to reach the largest possible audience, he also convinces the publisher to bring them out at half the usual paperback price, functionally printed on cheap yellow paper. An instant success in France, they are praised by Janet Flanner in her 'Letter from Paris' to *The New Yorker* and translated into English within a year. By 1932 several have been filmed and Simenon is a celebrity – another life into which he escapes with the same unrelenting energy and speed that he brings to his novels. He buys a spacious apartment in Paris and has it decorated in fashionable thirties *moderne*, rents a château near Orléans, joins the Yacht Club, employs a liveried chauffeur, gambles at Monte Carlo, wears the best English clothes and a pearl in his necktie. Three years later he's acquired a house on Porquerolles and built another near La Rochelle on the Bay of Biscay. For publicity, he even agrees to start writing a Maigret in a glass cage.

Having researched France, there remains the world. Until the Second World War Simenon travels almost everywhere, throughout Europe and most of Africa, the United States, Russia, Lapland, Egypt, India, Tahiti, Australia. He moves back and forth across the equator below Panama, Singapore and the Ivory Coast. In the same period he produces another sixty novels. T. S. Eliot becomes a Maigret fan, Cocteau and Gide praise the 'other' Simenon that begins in 1933 with *Les Gens d'en Face* (*The Window over the Way*). None of the conventional problems of success seems to bother him. Later he will remember that he always knew where he was going, even if at first he didn't know how to get there. The technique he discovers is to become a client of experience, which he buys as it were wholesale. Using money as a passport and success as a visa, he penetrates the world of bankers, doctors, gangsters, society people, politicians, landowners, lawyers, police commissioners. 'I take everything from life,' he tells a journalist. Joining many groups while giving total allegiance to none, he breaks into an environment as easily as he breaks out of it. The more he explores his own freedom, the more he's struck by other people's lack of it. Most of them exist in a kind of prison, another image that recurs in varying forms throughout his work. Their lives confirm the rule that circumstance and background erode the individual, while Simenon's own life attempts to refute it. Submitting to a vast load of experience, he finds himself increasingly detached from conventional morality.

One of his most caustic and disturbing novels of the thirties, *Chez Krull*, takes place in a French town near the German frontier. A German family has settled there, become naturalized, but still provokes hostility from the French. A young visitor tells his cousins that they made the mistake of not being more 'frankly honest' or more 'frankly dishonest'. When you settle among strangers, don't copy their ways unless you can do it really well, or they'll despise you. Otherwise be calmly different and keep to yourself. Half-heartedness is the great betrayer. Here, of course, Simenon uses a racial issue to discuss the problem of existing as a minority of one and getting away with it. He gets away with it personally by copying people with the conviction acquired from inside knowledge. Writing novels is a process of moving closer to the bone each time, what he calls 'becoming' his central character. Like the mystic who prepares for concentration by fasting or going to the desert, Simenon needs his own order and discipline to set the mechanism in motion. His desert is the anonymous security of middle-class life. So he lives as a secret anarchist, operating within society and obeying its rules while inhabiting the psyches of outlaws and murderers.

At sixty, having 'become' so many of them, he's also become the complete family man, living with his second wife and their three children in Switzerland. He builds a house with twenty-six rooms on a large estate outside the quiet and firmly middle-class town of Lausanne. The household is run with a peculiarly Swiss precision, at once comfortable and isolated. The silhouette that Simenon presents to the public, on a book jacket or in a magazine feature – the pipe, discreet conservative clothes, homburg hat and bow-tie in winter, panama and golf

175

jacket in summer – looks as anonymous and remote in its way as Conan Doyle's. But the eyes meet the camera eye with a veiled complicity. They suggest the dreamer of multiple lives and the man who describes his profession as 'a vocation of unhappiness', coloured by anxiety and the need to reach his limit. His characters pursue a similar vocation, reaching their limit by committing an act of violence instead of a novel. When something triggers the shipping clerk or doctor or student into killing, another kind of secret anarchist is revealed.

In his notebooks Simenon confesses that while he's freed himself of the twin superstitions of established religion and morality, he is still haunted by the fear of poverty and failure that surrounded him in childhood. Something of it lies behind the ravenous method of work and the construction of entirely different surroundings for himself. To this extent the novelist and his characters share the naked common ground of fear, and years of living together have exposed the impulses that link creation and destruction. One day in 1960 he reads a medical report on murderers that stresses their tendency to resemble the rest of us. 'I have tried to make it understood,' he adds as a footnote, 'that there are no criminals.' He might have added that getting away with murder is perhaps a less difficult problem than getting away with not murdering.

For almost as long as I can remember, I have felt an anguish over spoiled lives, which made me invent and describe, when I was fourteen, maybe in 1917, the profession of 'restorer of destinies', a sort of Maigret as doctor, psychiatrist etc., a kind of consulting God-the-Father...

Simenon's notebooks suggest a parallel with Conan Doyle and Sherlock Holmes. Things have to be set right. But Maigret and Holmes start from opposing positions, professional and amateur. The state-employed detective obeys orders to gather information that will condemn an individual to imprisonment or death. Wilkie Collins didn't overlook the inherent nastiness of this idea, only a few years after Scotland Yard came into existence, in his portrait of Sergeant Cuff. Unlike the later technocrats, Cuff feels guilty about his talent. The amateur obeys a personal code and accepts a case in response to a human appeal. Holmes is a licensed outsider, respected enough to flout or make use of authority as it suits him. An outsider without a licence, Marlowe sees authority as an enemy. Unlike the police, neither of them makes innocent people feel afraid.

In the Maigret novels, Simenon approaches the professional detective as a phenomenon. He holds no brief for or against, and refuses to judge, just as Maigret refuses to judge others until his later years, when he becomes occasionally fractious. The point of view is biological, a study of someone who decides to join the police force, who discovers powers of intuition that make him famous, then gradually feels the pressures of his chosen life. The novels hinge on the fact that Maigret finds himself up against a contradiction. Since he can only solve a case when he 'understands' the criminal, which means imagining how he feels, he has a natural sympathy for the man whom society pays him to capture. A deductive virtuoso like Holmes exercises his genius by analysing facts, but in the early *Tête d'un Homme* (1931, translated as *A Battle of Nerves*), Maigret declares his principle of 'moral proof'. The final evidence lies in character, revealed by a sudden act of empathy. Yet to understand is not to forgive but to arrest.

The murderer's identity may be disclosed halfway through a story without loss of suspense, because his psyche is more important. The real element of surprise is the human shock. After the motive has been decoded or the moment of self-betrayal engineered, Maigret confronts Simenon's 'naked man'.

Since he sees the world outside his novels as an artificial creation of politics, Simenon never 'dates' his fiction. Only a few scattered internal clues locate the action in the 1930s or later. Only a light handful of his 214 books acknowledges the Second World War. A private theatre of fear and greed and anger exists within its own time continuum, and history is what happens in people's minds every day. But Maigret himself can be dated specifically, since Simenon tells us when he was born (in 1877) and when he was promoted to his first case (in 1913). He must have reached the retirement age around 1942, although Simenon continues to write about him until the early seventies. As Simenon has admitted, Maigret could never have functioned in contemporary Paris. Born thirty years later, he would certainly have resigned in protest against corruption and the new methods. Towards the end of his career he already feels the climate changing, and doesn't like it.

Yet if Maigret himself belongs to the past, his criminal arena remains undated. A different kind of detective in Paris today would encounter many of the same murderers. Many of them could also be the protagonist of a non-Maigret novel, and sometimes you feel a direct emotional overlap. *Les Scrupules de Maigret* (1951) begins with a man telling the inspector that his wife is trying to poison him. It is immediately followed by *Dimanche*, a non-Maigret about a man who decides to poison his wife. Both tales share a climate of sexual duplicity and domestic hatred, at its most intensely concentrated in *Dimanche*. Simenon has pointed out that a Maigret often resembles a sketch for the painting to follow. The detective himself also seems like a first sketch for a self-portrait – or, put another way, like a transitional device for Simenon the detective of life when he feels ready to move from potboilers to reality.

Like his creator, Maigret changes his life after his father dies unexpectedly, abandoning his medical studies to join the Paris police. He comes from a family that has to struggle against poverty – his father managed several farms on a country estate – and marries in his early twenties. He lives an outwardly conventional middle-class life in a suburban apartment. He rises from the ranks of street and vice squad duty as Simenon rose from the apprenticeship of pulp fiction. Even before he becomes famous his professional methods are unorthodox, and he seems driven by a private intensity. During his first case he develops an ability to escape into the lives of others, 'to put himself inside everybody's mind'. Like Simenon writing a novel he works against time, absorbing a new atmosphere and unfamiliar set of characters and yet reaching a solution as quickly as possible. Simenon begins a novel with a series of routines, card-indexing characters, making street maps and outlining events on the back of a manila envelope. Maigret begins a case by taking statements, consulting reports, making notes. Then he waits for the key moment, the start of an imaginative process by which the abstract turns into something human and complex. Like Simenon he is irritated by theorists. Examining magistrates oppress him with their middle-class attitudes and sermonizing, psychiatrists lack 'physical intimacy with the criminal world'. Alcohol and withdrawal into oneself are much more stimulating. Maigret constantly nips on the job, white wine at one café and calvados at another. And as Simenon becomes a total recluse during his ten days' stretch on a novel, ignoring the telephone and hanging a 'Do Not Disturb' sign outside his study door, Maigret takes to his bed to sweat out a problem alone.

Maigret also inherits Simenon's 'anguish over spoiled lives'. As an adolescent he felt that many people around him were at odds with themselves, playing a losing game and mutely asking for help. He dreamed the profession of 'mender of destinies' and later wonders whether he joined the police force by accident or fate. During his first case he asks, 'Aren't police-men sometimes actual menders of destinies?' Twenty years later, when they begin to seem more like mindless instruments of the state, he begins to doubt his early idealism. In *Maigret et le Voleur Paresseux* (1961, translated as *Maigret and the Lazy Burglar*), there are moments when he feels like a personal anachronism in an impersonal age:

The world was changing, Paris was changing, everything was chang-ing – men and methods alike. At times retirement seemed a bugbear, but wouldn't it save him from starting to feel lost in a world he no longer understood?

His private evolution is a vital part of the cycle. Between 1931 and 1934 Simenon wrote about twenty Maigrets. Their plots are notably complicated and Maigret himself seems a relatively simple character, a big slow man in a bowler hat who plays his hunches and a few unorthodox tricks. Between 1935 and 1949 only nine Maigrets appear, low-profile and rather perfunctory. Simenon is preoccupied with other work. Since 1949 he's produced another fifty, and the later Maigret reveals more of himself as he becomes more emotionally involved with his cases. His view of the world darkens. He feels the exhaustion of prolonged contact with criminal life. He is famous but suspects younger colleagues of secretly dismissing him as old hat. He looks back nostalgically to childhood and looks forward to the dreaded release of retirement.

The first Maigrets are the first Simenons, and they establish a personal technique of extreme compression, tersely loaded paragraphs ranging from two to ten lines, laconic and frag-mented dialogue. Sim once submitted a few stories to Colette, then fiction editor of *Le Matin*. She found them promising but 'too literary'. The advice made a strong impression. From the moment Sim becomes Simenon he creates a very sparse kind of prose, matter-of-fact and yet immediately suggestive. (Only the good translations, which are rare, convey it in English.) The images are sometimes striking and sometimes conventional, but always exact. The physical world – a street, a house, a path by a canal, the weather – is implied with a functional precision. At the same time it is full of atmosphere and essence. The rain and the hour of the day and the quality of a face are never decorative. They carry a psychological charge. Simenon often describes Maigret as 'scratching' and 'ferreting' and 'sniffing' around. His own sense-reactions work in the same way, scenting the detail that makes the moment and clinches the impression.

In *La Tête d'un Homme* Maigret investigates the murder of a rich widow and her maid. Making routine inquiries at a restaurant, he sees the reflection of a redheaded man in a mirror:

Two light eyes under heavy brows, a smile, such a faint smile, yet full of sarcasm.

As if the eyes told too much, the lids dropped immediately. But not quickly enough, and the inspector couldn't help feeling this sarcastic smile had been meant for him.

He files the image away, but remembers it later as the first secret gesture of a particular kind of murderer, compelled to boast and to seek attention. In *M. Gallet Décédé* (1931, translated as *Maigret Stonewalled*), the detective is unable to connect the face in a dead man's photograph with anything that he's learned about his life. He puzzles over a thin-lipped yet unusually wide mouth that seems 'almost to slice the face in two'. The instinct leads him to expose a physical duality. The body identified as M. Gallet, commercial traveller, is really the body of the Comte de St Hilaire. Years ago Gallet bought his title off a penniless young aristocrat, and escaped from middle-class life to become St Hilaire and eventually inherit a legacy. The real St Hilaire, deprived of his identity, fell into a series of dreary middle-class traps and finally escaped by committing suicide. The mystery ends as an ironic social fable. Technically innocent of any crime and officially dead, Gallet is left free to enjoy his St Hilaire fantasy. In *L'Affaire Saint-*

Fiacre (1931, translated as *Maigret Goes Home*), the detective remembers the *comtesse* from his boyhood as 'a tall, slim, melancholy woman glimpsed from a distance in the park'. Returning to the village where he was born, he finds a grotesque emaciated corpse slumped across the aisle of a church. The image of collapse also signals the end of a great family. Uncovering its descent into vindictiveness and greed, Maigret confronts the ruins of his childhood world.

Each case is like a journey into a new country, with its own topography and habits: the brilliantly destructive egomaniac in Paris, the cunning little businessman in the suburban wasteland, the crumbling aristocracy in the country village. In *La Danseuse du Gai-Moulin* (1931, translated as *Maigret at the Gai-Moulin*), Maigret travels to Liège for his first encounter with alienated youth and the perverseness of the adolescent rich. In *Le Fou de Bergerac* (1932, translated as *The Madman of Bergerac*) he enters the world of a terrifying psychopathic murderer who sticks women through the heart with a huge needle. These five novels show Simenon at his most convincingly bizarre and Maigret reacting to different human experiences, saddened by his brush with the rich and privileged, amused by the cunning little businessman, shocked by the young. There remains the problem of the explanation scene. Adventurous in every other way, Simenon falls back on the artificial monologue, the criminal confessing or Maigret denouncing.

The exception, and the true masterpiece of the period, is *La Nuit du Carrefour* (1931, translated as *Maigret at the Crossroads*). Empty and isolated as a de Chirico landscape, the setting is a crossroads surrounded by flat countryside, with only three buildings nearby: a garage, an ugly suburban villa, an old country house screened by trees. The garage proprietor, the plump self-important insurance agent and his wife, the Danish brother and sister in the old house, seem to have little contact with one another. But Maigret sniffs and ferrets out the secret links between members of a diamond and cocaine smuggling gang. The most brilliant scenes are centred on the old house. The sound of a tango played on the phonograph drifts across parkland. Inside, brother and sister (who turn out to be man and wife) live in a mixture of luxury and filth. The man has a cool, elegant manner and a glass eye. The bored wilting girl wears a long low-cut velvet dress that slips occasionally to reveal a scarred breast. The climax moves into surrealism, with Maigret discovering the girl and the insurance agent fistfighting at dusk at the bottom of a dry well. They are hauled up on pulleys, the girl still in her long dress and blotched with green moss. In spite of her frailty, she's blacked her opponent's eye and dislocated his jaw. Violent and absurd, the tone of the novel prefigures Polanski's movie *Cul de Sac*. So does the extraordinary adaptation made in 1932 by Jean Renoir, with Simenon collaborating on the script.

The point of departure for Maigret in his later years is a journey from Paris to the island of Porquerolles. In *Mon Ami Maigret* (1949, translated as *My Friend Maigret*), an old tramp who claimed to know him has been brutally murdered, and the detective moves from his usual setting of a city in the rain to the Mediterranean of garlic and mimosa. The islanders greet him like a movie star. He is accompanied by an inspector from Scotland Yard who wants to study his methods. Maigret's apparent lack of them provides some ironic commentaries on the gulf between intuition and textbook technique. For much of the story his mood is genial. He runs across a woman whose destiny he helped to mend in the past, and approves her new career as the madam of a brothel in Nice. Then, as he confronts the solution, the tone darkens.

The young criminals, an unsuccessful writer and a failed artist, have a touch of Leopold and Loeb. Their racket, which the tramp discovers by chance, is forged paintings. As well as making money, they enjoy revenging themselves on society by swindling an art museum or a rich old woman, faking van Goghs as an act of protest. Obliged to murder, they deliberately choose to be vicious about it, then analyse their reactions. Faced with lives that he finds too strange and threatening to enter, Maigret becomes violent and abusive. In his earlier days he dismissed the perverse adolescent murderer of the Gai-Moulin as insane. But the combination of dissent and sadism is an experience he cannot absorb or classify, only rage against. This kind of crime is like a bomb thrown at the *status quo*. For all the experience he acquires and the illusions he loses, Maigret remains at heart the child of a conservative country upbringing.

For the rest of his career Maigret will seldom be driven so

close to his imaginative limits, but anxiety often pricks at the surface and shows in the dark pouches under his eyes. He complains of police work slowed down by bureaucrats while criminals become 'skilled technicians'. He drinks more heavily. He dreads having to testify in court, finding trials more and more like 'last rites', abstract and pompous. Central heating has been installed in his office, but he despises it and retains the old black stove for its human warmth. When it finally gives out and has to be taken away, the moment turns into a funeral for time past.

The later cases often suggest earlier ones more grimly replayed. In *Maigret a Peur* (1966, translated as *Maigret Afraid*), the situation echoes the Saint-Fiacre affair, but the landowning aristocracy survives now only as a cankered relic, resented by villagers and hated by its own servants. Maigret can no longer feel nostalgia for a dying life, only read the angry social handwriting on the wall. In *Maigret et les Témoins Recalcitrants* (1959, translated as *Maigret and the Reluctant Witnesses*), the atmosphere is reminiscent of *La Nuit du Carrefour*, but more seedy and degraded. A member of a family that manufactures biscuits has been murdered. The biscuits, which Maigret remembers from his childhood as tasting like cardboard, no longer sell well. The family no longer feels or lives well, floundering in debt and dust and bitterness. Interrogations become like stripping the clothes off ugly people. In *Maigret et la Vieille Dame* (1951, translated as *Maigret and the Old Lady*), he flies into a rage again. The elegant and benign widow in her house by the sea seems to be living an ideal retired life. She charms Maigret so completely that he feels betrayed when he discovers the greed and cruelty that leads her to murder for money. Sometimes he pauses to wash his face and hands during these cases, as if afraid of contamination. In *Les Témoins Recalcitrants* he looks at his face in the bathroom mirror and almost sticks out his tongue:

The glass distorted things slightly, of course. All the same, when he came back from the Quai de la Gare, the chief-inspector felt his face had become not unlike the faces of the people living in that weird house.

Other stories develop earlier themes of the psychopathic killer and the criminal like M. Gallet trying to break out of middle-class solitude. In *Maigret Tend un Piège* (1955, translated as *Maigret Sets a Trap*), the architect who stabs five women to death in the streets of Montmartre is really killing his possessive wife and mother each time. In *Le Voleur Paresseux*, the thief who breaks into other people's houses feels that he's breaking into their lives. He watches a man asleep with a kind of aching curiosity before making off with his jewellery on a bedside table. In all these novels the explanation scene is much more skilfully integrated than before and the backgrounds vibrate with detail. They give a continuous sense of other crimes going on at the same time – a body fished out of the Seine or discovered in an empty room with the same regularity as train whistles pierce the air or church bells ring for mass. Reporters and informers haunt the corridors of the Quai des Orfèvres. In a glass-panelled room near Maigret's office, people subpoenaed for testimony wait to be called, sitting under photographs of policemen killed on duty.

The whole cycle reaches its highest level with three novels based on sexually motivated crimes involving a husband, a wife and a lover. Here, as so often in his work, Simenon uses the situation to make one of his essential points: the victim is as guilty as his murderer, and, by extension, the murderer ends as his own victim. *Maigret et le Corps sans Tête* (1955, translated as *Maigret and the Headless Corpse*) begins with a man's arm being fished out of a Paris canal at dawn. A diver retrieves other fragments of the body, but the head remains missing. Maigret centres his interrogation on a nearby bar. The owner has recently disappeared, but Mme Calas insists that her husband often goes off without a word. He means nothing to her dead or alive, anyway. Maigret becomes fascinated by the woman's total lack of emotional response. A heavy secret drinker and sexually promiscuous, alcohol has no more effect on her than casually obliging a lover on the kitchen table. Nothing seems to get through to her – except, as Maigret finally discovers, her husband's attempt to cheat her out of an inheritance. This drove her into partnership with a young lover, and after he killed Calas she helped to dismember his body as indifferently as she might have cut up a rabbit. Submitting to arrest as if she expected it, she asks Maigret to find someone to look after her cat.

In *Maigret aux Assises* (1960, translated as *Maigret in*

Court) the detective has to testify at the trial of a picture-framer accused of murdering his aunt and her child. The magistrates, as usual not looking beyond facts, believe Meurant guilty. Maigret, as usual looking beyond them, believes him innocent. But to make his case, he has to reveal that Meurant's wife has been consistently unfaithful. Acquitted, Meurant goes back to his wife and apparently forgives her. In fact the potential murderer inside him has been released. Obsessed with jealousy, he tracks down his wife's current lover and shoots him, then submits to arrest with the same indifference as Mme Calas. Maigret returns to court to testify against the man he never thought capable of violence.

In *Maigret et le Client du Samedi* (1962, translated as *Maigret and the Saturday Caller*), a building contractor with a harelip tells Maigret that he wants to kill his wife. The detective persuades him to at least think it over. A few days later he calls at the house and finds only Planchon's wife living there, with a lover. She insists that her husband disappeared without a word. Stonewalled again, Maigret eventually unravels the truth. For months Planchon had accepted the most extreme humiliation, sleeping downstairs while his wife and her lover occupied his bed, drinking himself into a stupor, even signing away control of his business. The man who told Maigret that he wanted to kill really wanted to be killed.

Criminal and victim alike choose their own paths. Planchon preferred to lose his life rather than his wife. Mme Calas waited for Calas to cross her threshold of tolerance, then did what she had to do. Found innocent after his first trial, Meurant obeyed a secret guilt mechanism, went back to his wife and reached the same point as Mme Calas. Inevitably Maigret remembers his early impressions of people at odds with themselves and playing a losing game. And Mme Maigret, the discreet background figure who hardly ever questions her husband about his work, senses his new mood when he comes home at the end of a case:

> She had a confused feeling that he'd gone a long way away, that he needed the habit of everyday life again and the company of men who could restore his confidence.

Maigret wonders if he joined the police force by accident, or if he subconsciously recognized a personal destiny. Many of

Simenon's protagonists share the same feeling about the quotient of accident and destiny in their lives. They search the past for some important overlooked moment that might explain their curious dread of a hidden threat in the future. *Une Vie Comme Neuve* begins by pinpointing this secret unease in the life of an obscure accountant: 'He had expected a disaster for so long – and a disaster that would happen at precisely such a moment – that he felt no terror and so to speak no surprise.' *L'Ours en Peluche* begins with a successful doctor waking up from a dream. He tries but fails to remember it, and is disturbed because he knows it held the key to his present anxiety. In any case the expected and the unexpected have the same result. The only difference lies in the degree of shock. (Perhaps it's the only difference between accident and destiny.) For Kees Popinga in *L'Homme qui regardait passer les trains* there are no premonitions. He would have laughed at the idea of his photograph being featured in newspapers all over Europe, with captions about a dangerous murderer. Alain Poitaud in *La Prison* has no advance warning that it will take 'only a few hours, perhaps only a few minutes', for him to change from one man into another. Finally the same question recurs: which was the real Popinga, the real Poitaud, the real accountant, the real doctor, the man before or after the change?

The mystery of reversal is found in men of widely differing circumstances. They may live in Paris or the tropics, the small town or the remote countryside. When Simenon set out to explore France and then the world, he was looking for universal and not local colour, for a private theatre independent of place as well as time. Personal background and heredity exert a very limited influence in his novels. A general psychic environment is the deciding factor. Growing up in Liège among people who worshipped respectability, Simenon was later astonished to find that no more powerful collective attitude exists anywhere. It has replaced religion as the fantasy most difficult to escape. Like the displaced family in *Chez Krull*, the individual has the choice of losing himself in the respectable crowd or of staying aloof. Either decision may land him on the common ground of fear. If he compromises, his relationships and his profession are dictated by duty. Concealing his failures for fear of disappointing other people, he never comes to terms with them. His idea of success is society's, not his own. If he rebels, he risks another kind of pressure and another kind of unreality. The outsider provokes mistrust or envy, and begins to feel a lack of human connections. Both paths can lead to a point of no return, and the point that concerns Simenon is murder.

In a world where the dividing line between accident and destiny is unclear, murderer and victim become interchangeable roles. 'If you admit the murderer as a criminal type,' Emile reflects in *Dimanche*, 'you must also suppose there is a type of natural victim.' The corpse is as responsible as the killer. More than fifty of the non-Maigret novels create variations on this theme. They begin with what Simenon has described as an almost geometrical problem. 'I have such a man, such a woman, in such surroundings. What can happen to them to oblige them to go to their limit?' When the limit involves death, murder or being murdered becomes the fine art of self-revelation.

Simenon's métier is the sustained close-up, and his most compelling novels centre on a single character and his reactions. Using a wider angle lens to frame a group, most often a family, he dilutes his effects. His most impressive group is the sum of his individuals. Some of these individuals are also avatars. They develop on parallel lines throughout his novels, and end at different points. One avatar reaches a final stage, then disappears. Others continue to evolve. Like figures in a mosaic, each is complete in himself, yet forms part of another section and eventually of a whole design.

In his first important non-Maigret, years before Camus, Simenon introduces the idea of the outsider. *Les Gens d'en Face* (1933, translated as *The Window over the Way*) contains his first portrait of the alienated man faced with a mysterious human barrier:

... Every time he had tried to live, to do what he had always called living, he had come up against a brick wall.

It left him as inert, perhaps even more inert, than the people around him. He didn't necessarily want this. But it was so easy. You made no effort. You carried your solitude around with you ...

Adil Bey, Turkish consul in the Soviet port of Batum, only moves beyond emotional neutrality when he discovers that someone has been trying to poison him. Up to this point, like the hero of Hitchcock's *Rear Window,* his best hours have been spent watching the apartment across the street, which he can see from his office window. Three people inhabit this little communist cell: Adil Bey's secretary, her brother (a local OGPU official) and his wife. Although attracted to his secretary, Adil Bey finds her belief in the new Russia absurd. He tries to demolish it by insisting on the horrors of secret police, monolithic bureaucracy, endless food shortages. He boasts about the relative comfort of his own country. Then he starts to feel physically ill, and remembers that his predecessor died of poisoning.

An extraordinary confrontation with his secretary provides the turning point in both their lives. Accusing her of trying to poison him, Adil Bey admits that he taunted her because he was afraid of falling in love. Sonia admits that she put arsenic in his food, just as she poisoned the previous consul, because her need to believe in something was being cruelly undermined. They insult each other and weep. Then Sonia confesses that she loved Adil Bey even while she wanted to kill him. They plan to escape to Turkey together, but the OGPU arrests her and Adil Bey leaves Batum alone. Surprised by his absence of grief, he looks through his cabin porthole and is relieved to face an empty sea instead of a troubling window over the way. No longer menaced, he can return to his emotional vacuum.

For Adil Bey the world is a series of rooms with 'each person in his corner'. This compact and sinister episode from his life marks Simenon's own point of imaginative departure. Like Russia, his protagonists move obstinately towards isolation. A new political ideal is only another method of imprisoning people in fear. Never questioning a belief that drives her to murder, Sonia accepts a communal society no more liberating than Adil Bey's solitude. In the end both are equally victims, and the turning point turns back on itself.

In *Chez Krull* (1939) the outsider is still cornered, but shows signs of aggression. He moves into somebody else's corner, commits an act of psychological murder, retires again. Hans is a young German who arrives to stay with relatives living in a French town near the frontier. A girl is raped and murdered. Suspicion falls on Joseph, his clumsy repressed cousin. The local dislike of foreigners intensifies dangerously. For the Krulls, the threat of mob violence is a terrifying reality, but for Hans it becomes an absurd spectacle that exposes their fears and failures. His face betrays 'a constant gleam of amusement, like the reflected morning light, the clean rinsed sky . . .'. He seduces Joseph's virgin sister and enjoys the knowledge that his cousin watches with appalled fascination through a keyhole. He pretends to doubt Joseph's innocence and hints to the Krulls that his cousin has the attributes of a potential murderer. When the family barricades itself in the house and the old deaf grandfather commits suicide, Hans moves on. At the moment of leaving he feels a curious twinge of panic and guilt, and wonders whether his role is to play 'the Stranger, the cause of all the evils in the world'.

Although the question remains unanswered, Simenon makes it clear that Hans is capable of playing many roles. He invents a fantasy background for himself as a political refugee. He has a trick of adapting to people's moods, and uses it to control them. He imagines himself as Joseph, comparing his own strength to his cousin's weakness. Joseph complains of feeling different from other people and unloved by his neighbours. Hans recognizes the same feeling in himself, but has no desire to join the crowd and be loved. He chooses to stay behind a brick wall, equating difference with superiority. Proud of having discovered the girl's body in the canal and delighted by the shock it causes, he's fascinated by murder but too intelligent to commit it. He disrupts and humiliates the living instead. People often call this kind of man 'a killer'.

La Veuve Couderc (1942, translated as *Ticket of Leave*) takes the outsider a stage further, across the threshold of violence. A powerful opening paragraph frames his isolation:

A man walking. On a three-mile stretch of road with the shadow of a bare tree slanting across it every ten yards, a solitary man loping from one shadow to the next. As it was almost noon, and the sun neared its highest point, an absurdly foreshortened shadow – his own – glided ahead of him.

Jean is a rich man's son who remains a spoilt child. He falls for a stupid girl with expensive tastes and steals from his father to buy her presents. When his father cuts him off, he robs and murders a man. His lawyer manages to suppress the evidence of robbery and Jean gets only five years for manslaughter. On his release from jail, a middle-aged widow takes him in as handyman and lover. In her own way this simple blowsy peasant is as much of a child as Jean. She quarrels endlessly with her dead husband's family over a few cows and a plot of land. Her ancient father-in-law lives in a daze of satyriasis, and she takes him to bed from time to time as if giving an old dog a bone. For Jean her little farm becomes a kind of playground in which he can amuse himself and feel no ties or responsibilities. He likes Tati well enough, but she exists on the same level as her pigs and rabbits, part of a life without claims or shadows.

Days like this are always numbered, and Jean becomes obsessed with a girl living across the canal. Meeting her secretly and deceiving Tati, he moves back into adulthood, the profession for which he's never been suited. In *Chez Krull*, Hans wonders whether his destiny is to cause evil. Jean knows that his destiny is to betray. He begins to think about the past again, and the sentence of death cheated like Tati. The widow falls ill and he nurses her dutifully while remaining indifferent to her pain, slipping out at night to meet Felicie. When Tati grows suspicious, has a pathetic outburst of jealousy and begs him not to leave her, he cracks her skull with a hammer and then suffocates her.

The murder is Simenon at his purest. Tati is only a pretext. Jean directs his real anger against an adult world in which he finds it impossible to live. After the terrible act of violence he imagines himself walking along the empty road again, following his shadow, then falls asleep like a child. The police wake him, and he can only say, 'Don't hit me . . . I'm tired.' For the widow, Felice is equally a pretext. Her real jealousy comes from a fear that Jean's childhood is being stolen. If he loses it, she'll lose him. The rescuer is at heart a jailer who provokes her own murder. A newspaper report would reduce the anecdote to an ageing woman brutally slain by her young lover, an ex-convict. Simenon's report finds far more in the cliché than meets the eye. He sees the collision of two lives without exits, violence the only possible way of escape. At first there seems a kind of innocence in two lonely people coming together, then solitude reveals its other face, an absolute and ruthless despair. Simenon strips each layer off the situation without a single moral nudge or literary gesture. *La Veuve Couderc* is a masterpiece written in an anti-masterpiece style.

'He was alone. So much the better . . .' This is Frank's reaction to almost everything that happens to him in *La Neige était Sale* (1948, translated as *The Stain on the Snow*). Simenon's final and most overwhelming account of the totally estranged and aggressive man is set in an unnamed European country occupied by enemy forces. There is no specific reference to the Second World War. In the opening scene Frank stabs an enemy officer as he walks home through the snow at night. The murder has nothing to do with patriotism. It is a gratuitous destructive act that the nineteen-year-old boy describes to himself as 'losing his virginity'. Others follow. He seduces a sad and timid girl who's fallen in love with him, then arranges for a friend to rape her. He takes part in a robbery and kills an old woman. The second murder feels more important than the first, somehow inevitable, a sign that he's on the way to his 'ultimate limit'. Reaching a point of private horror that separates him from everyone – his gangster friends, his mother who runs a brothel and whom he hates, the prostitutes he bullies and enjoys – he doesn't try to resist arrest. The police take him to a prison that was formerly a school, an eerie no man's land of mazelike corridors, small windows, doors with mysterious inscriptions, uniformed bureaucrats. Every day he is interrogated by an official whom he thinks of as 'the old gentleman', mild and fumbling on the surface, tireless and cunning beneath it.

At first he seems trapped like Kafka's K. in mysterious and arbitrary procedures. Then he realizes that the authorities suspect him of belonging to the political underground. Personal nihilism is beyond the imagination of this grimly brutal regime, and the old gentleman believes that Frank will eventually break down and name names. Once Frank understands this, he has no desire to save himself. He knows that he's 'in for it' anyway, and his whole life seems to have led up to this moment. He drops false clues and promises evidence that never materializes. The sessions with the old gentleman become a game that he mustn't be allowed to win too quickly. The longer Frank holds out, the richer his preparation for death:

It was strange. Frank had spent much of his life, much the greater part of it, in an almost personal hatred of destiny. He'd sought it out, wanting to challenge it, come to grips with it.

And now, suddenly, after he'd stopped thinking about it, destiny made him a gift.

The old gentleman is the bearer of this gift, providing Frank's life with a last act of unhoped for excitement. The last act is also one of Simenon's most daringly protracted climaxes, delaying violence instead of allowing it to explode. The cruelty that Frank has shown towards other people now turns on himself. It becomes not exactly noble, but pitilessly honest. Shuttling between pride and atonement, he takes the centre of a bleakly spotlit stage. He bears nobody a grudge and feels sorry for nobody, himself included. The ancient chain-smoking interrogator seems at times almost a father-figure, at times more coldblooded than a fish. Most important of all, he is *necessary*. 'Everyone had his own old gentleman . . .' As the duel continues, Frank ceases to fear the prospect of torture. He's been too much of a torturer himself. He loses all sense of time because 'it didn't matter how long something lasted. It only mattered that it should exist.' He will know instinctively when to throw in his hand, to confess to the old gentleman that he's been using the situation to come to terms with his crime, which has nothing to do with politics and concerns only himself.

They beat him up a few times, then lead him across the snow to face a firing squad. Three other men wait there to be shot. He feels curious about them and peers at their faces in the early morning darkness, moving briefly outside himself at the last moment, not completely alone.

The occupied country of *La Neige était Sale* is a metaphor for the world as these haunted outsiders see it. Adil Bey's Batum and Frank's unnamed city are both in police states, but a police state can be imposed from below as well as from above. Hans in *Chez Krull* feels that he's living 'in a foreign country' and Jean in *La Veuve Couderc* that he's being 'swallowed up by another world'. Simenon implies that in the present stage of evolution the fear of displacement is common to all. Only its intensity separates his characters from 'ordinary' people. The exile's eye has the clearest vision of a closed aggressive structure in which vicious neighbours and greedy peasants occupy a lower point on the same human scale as commissars and autocrats.

In his notebooks Simenon writes that 'man has lost his purity, which, if I were pushed to the wall, I might finally call an animal one'. He adds that he prefers the cruelty of purity to the cruelty that succeeded it, conscious and studied. Here at least he agrees with Greene, even though his dislike for 'so-called problems of conscience' keeps them generally apart. In another note on the similarity of behaviour between novelists and their characters, he suggests that Dostoyevsky is the proto-type of the people he describes, and that Greene creates a novel from what he considers his guilt and unworthiness. He says nothing about himself, but the man who makes his house in Switzerland a fortress against the world and a private indepen-dent country, seems closest to the fears of his outsiders.

Was there any serious reason behind his anxiety? No. Nothing extraordinary had happened. No threat was hanging over him . . . Anyway, the feeling was not strictly anxiety, and he could never have said exactly when it took possession of him, this anguish and unrest that seemed the result of an imperceptible loss of equilibrium.

In *Le Coup de Lune* (1933, translated as *Tropic Moon*), Joseph Timar arrives on a boat from France at Libreville, the capital of Gabon. In the 1930s this country on the west equatorial coast of Africa was still a French protectorate. Timar finds himself suddenly abandoned on an empty quay, surrounded by the total blackness of an African night. It is not the immediate situation that affects him, but the image of solitude it implies.

Another avatar, he has no idea where he really is. Nothing is quite real or clear. On the surface he may be satisfied with his place in society, or at least not seriously frustrated by it. He may be single or married, and his age can vary from twenty-three to fifty. For no apparent reason he has moments of emotional vertigo. Events will justify the warning.

The job that Timar has been promised by a French company fails to materialize, and he's stranded in a seedy tropic hotel. The drift of its life corresponds to his own. Subconsciously ready for disaster, he falls for the owner, a lenient and sensual Frenchwoman called Adèle. They get married, and she takes him on a long journey upriver through the jungle to a plantation that she intends to buy. He gradually discovers that Adèle's casual good nature and easy sexuality disguise a life based on murder and fraud. But the African 'quality of darkness' overwhelms him. He starts to drink heavily, contracts fever, sinks into an indifferent passive role. When they return to Libreville, a young native is on trial for the murder Adèle committed. The judge is Adèle's lover, the proceedings a colonial parody of justice. Timar watches in a daze of fever and alcohol and recovers for an instant to denounce his wife. Then he retreats into stupor. On the boat back to France he has his first attack of 'moonstroke', talking to himself in an attempt to erase the journey upriver, Adèle's disintegration, France, Africa itself. Africa proves the hardest to forget, and he repeats for fifteen minutes, 'There is no Africa', until everything dissolves into a kind of non-existence.

The novel's texture is exceptionally dark and oppressive, black instead of Simenon's usual grey. Yet for all its power the colour is not strictly local. The primitive background exists for Adèle to stain with her ordinary universal greed, and the same drama of murderer-into-victim recurs. Equatorial heat and jungle contribute to Timar's collapse, but the collapse had begun before he arrived. After his job falls through, he feels homesick and thinks about returning to France. Then he looks at a boat in the harbour and has no desire to leave, even though he's bored. 'He had a need to feel listless and disgusted . . .' Passivity has its own will, and Simenon finds a subtly predestined quality in Timar's transition from a vaguely hopeful, vaguely uneasy young man on a dark and empty quay to the moonstruck figure telling himself that nothing ever happened.

The circumstances are entirely different but the state of unresolved drift remains the same for Lhomond in *Les Témoins* (1955, *The Witnesses*). A middle-aged judge in a French provincial town, he has allowed himself to be tyrannized for years by an invalid wife. An upcoming murder trial fills him with sudden anxiety. (A trial in Simenon's novels is always a social autopsy as well. It divides everyone into accusers and accused.) At first Lhomond tells himself he's caught the flu, but as the trial proceeds he feels a mysterious sympathy with the man accused of murdering his wife. The issue is not the prisoner's guilt or innocence, but the way his situation releases Lhomond's terrible hatred of his own wife. The judge recognizes his affinity with the accused, and the pattern extends to witnesses, lawyers, jurymen. The prisoner's background happens to be squalid, but as Simenon reveals a network of secretly crossed lives, several people with murder in their hearts are on the respectable side of the fence. As in *Chez Krull* the murder remains unsolved but its mystery lodges in a number of lives.

After the prisoner's acquittal, Lhomond murmurs to himself, 'I wonder . . .' He looks at the man in the dock, and the sense of complicity becomes mutual:

Lhomond was fascinated and couldn't take his eyes off him; he had the impression of something mocking, almost pitying, in the smile so obviously directed at him . . .

Then he returns home to learn that his wife has just died, and with a guilty sense of relief congratulates himself on his innocence. Ironic and virtuoso, *Les Témoins* offers yet another twist. With no one to hate, Lhomond feels the panic of loneliness and resolves to marry again.

Both *Dimanche* (1959, *Sunday*) and *La Chambre Bleue* (1964, *The Blue Room*) are also constructed like perfect traps. But the plot mechanisms show more than ingenuity. They are bait for the unwary and a reminder that emotional drifters create their own pitfalls. Emile in *Dimanche* decides to poison his wife. He *thinks* it's because he's fallen deeply in love with a maid working at their hotel, but as he plans the murder he becomes infatuated with crime as a secret gesture of self-liberation. Too engrossed with the details of his skill to notice Berthe's suspicions, he's unable to prevent himself being tricked. His wife suddenly invites the girl to lunch in the hotel dining-room and hands her the plate of arsenic risotto. Simenon finishes the story in less than a page, but packs it with a series of appalling reversals. Naturally Emile's first reaction is panic. Then, as he realizes he must either give himself away or let the girl die in a couple of hours, he feels no emotion at all. 'She belonged to the past . . .' His wife reminds him that he wanted to go to a football match that afternoon, and the casual remark is a signal that she's in charge of the whole situation:

She would see to everything. It was better that way. When he came back, it would all be over.

195

Nothing would have changed very much, anyway, since they'd never stopped sleeping in the same bedroom.

Rather than admit that Emile wanted to kill her, Berthe will arrange for the crime to look like an accident. She has also eliminated a rival. Emile will continue to wish he didn't belong to her, and to wonder where he really belongs, while the memory and hope of a bloody Sunday gradually recedes.

In *La Chambre Bleue*, emotional indecision is even more cruelly baited. Tony and Andrée, both married, are having an affair. On his side there is only physical passion, but on hers a total devouring love. When he hesitates to get a divorce, Andrée executes a double murder by poison – his wife, her husband. Their affair is revealed and Tony fails to convince the police or the court that he wasn't implicated. Both are sentenced to life imprisonment. Throughout the novel, which moves with intricate skill between past and present, Tony is haunted by a question that Andrée asked him: 'Wouldn't you like to spend the rest of your life with me?' To please her, he answered casually, 'Of course.' At the end of the trial, with a mesmerizing smile of 'love triumphant', she reminds him of it.

Andrée is the most spectacularly decisive woman to take charge of an undecided man, invading him with an orgiastic possessiveness. Berthe rules by frigid shrewdness, Lhomond's wife by the power of being bedridden, and Adèle by the power of sex. The captive nature seeks out the most suitable captor, but although the weak need the strong, the strong destroy their pride. The end for the strong is control, whatever the means. The end of the weak is rebellion, however long they hesitate. It is another no exit situation, like the outsider's solitary despair, that almost inevitably dissolves in violence. Lhomond only escapes because his wife dies from natural causes and removes a temptation. In one of his most extraordinary novels, *L'Homme au Petit Chien* (1964, *The Man with the Little Dog*), Simenon uses a completely subjective approach to this kind of struggle. He achieves the paradox of a Chekhovian story, as the title implies, about a murderer.

Felix Allard is an ageing recluse who lives in a poor quarter of Paris with his mongrel dog, and works in a second-hand bookstore. He has been contemplating suicide for some time. He begins keeping a notebook, a mixture of reminiscence and observation through which he hopes vaguely to save himself. The facts of his life emerge indirectly, not always in chronological order. He mentions that he committed a murder, and later that the victim was his wife's lover, but implies that the crime was not sexual. His character builds up in the same jigsaw-puzzle way, melancholy, ironic, self-deprecating. An intelligent parasite has improvised his life from failure to failure, never admitting the truth to himself. The girl he marries is deceptively modest and compliant. Since he needs her desperately, his instinct is to be possessive, but her own instinct for false respectability and material success proves much stronger. She finally pushes him to a business speculation that ends in collapse. He kills her lover after finding them together and the judge sentences him to a few years' imprisonment for *crime passionel*. But Allard's real motive has nothing to do with jealousy. He overheard the lover call him a conceited failure:

There behind the door, I knew that I'd just heard the truth. I had got it, as they say, straight between the eyes.
Only, he had no right to speak it. He had no right to rob me of my dignity and my self-respect. Nobody has the right to do that . . .

Written down years after the event, the truth seems less unbearable. Allard flushes his barbiturates down the toilet and takes his dog out for a walk in the rain. He is run over by a bus and killed.

Simenon's best work, with its combination of suspense and inevitability, and its engraved bleakness, always makes a poetic effect. *L'Homme au Petit Chien* is rare in superimposing a kind of watercolour charm, tender as well as acid. It is keyed to an autumnal account of the loneliness and mystery of a failed life on the fringes of an indifferent city. Allard's encounters with other people create a community of the afflicted: a pair of hideously crippled lovers, the ancient bookstore proprietress as reclusive as himself, with her dyed hair, sharp intuitions and erotica sold under the counter. 'We all steal lives, or pieces of lives,' Allard reflects, 'to feed our own lives.' The man who drove him to violence stole his life, not his wife. When Allard comes out of prison, he can only centre his affections on a dog. Rescued from the pound, it is sent back there after Allard's death, a stray like its owner.

197

La Prison (1968, *The Prison*) ends this cyle with a return to the baited plot and the device of a murder setting off guilt mechanisms in someone who didn't commit it. Alain Poitaud edits a slick illustrated weekly and is part of the fashion aristocracy of Paris. His wife shoots her sister, confesses, but obstinately refuses to discuss the motive. She also refuses to have anything more to do with her husband. Stunned as much by her rejection as by her crime, Poitaud begins to search for a clue. He ends with a total indictment of his own life. Simenon's portrait of the swinging pacesetting scene makes *La Prison* one of his rare 'contemporary' stories. As Poitaud loses his cool, Simenon's own cool becomes more incisive and deadly. The inner mystery is not why Jacqueline shot her sister but why her action is going to kill Poitaud as well, stripping him naked and exposing him as a man of imaginary feelings.

The hollow man, his freedom as false as respectability, is finally mirrored in his own glossy weekly with its 'in depth' pretensions. Choosing a particular sycamore tree into which to crash his expensive sports car, Poitaud remains an image-maker even at the moment of suicide. Like Allard, he has to admit that he's 'blank as an empty page'. The same moment of blankness confronts Emile in *Dimanche* when he can feel nothing about the girl he's accidentally poisoned, and Tony in *La Chambre Bleue* when he's unable to be honest with his wife or his lover. For criminal or victim, violence in these novels fills an empty space.

The psychotic, of course, is an outsider who doesn't realize it. As a serial or mass murderer he recurs in several Maigrets and in a gripping minor novel called *Les Fantômes du Chapelier* (1949, *The Hatter's Ghosts*). Simenon's recurring point is that a man displaced from reality, however wild and unconnected his actions may appear, follows a rigid interior logic. The hatter feels impelled to explain this by writing anonymous letters to a newspaper: 'No, sir, there is no madman. Don't talk about things you don't understand.' The inhabitants of La Rochelle are terrified by a series of murders that seem completely unrelated, the hatter performs a necessary task. After killing his hateful invalid wife and burying her body in the cellar, he behaves as if she's still alive and too depressed, as usual, to see anybody. Then he realizes he has to cover his tracks by murdering a few people who always visit her on Christmas Eve. The ending carries a curious echo of Jean in *La Veuve Couderc*. Having discharged what he calls his final responsibility, Labbe goes to sleep and wakes up to find the police in his room: 'Don't hit me. I'm coming . . .'

Simenon had written his central work on this subject more than ten years earlier. *L'Homme qui regardait passer les Trains* (1938, *The Man Who Watched the Trains Go By*) is the first of those definitive, completely astonishing novels that mark certain peaks in his career, like *La Neige était Sale, L'Homme au Petit Chien* and a few others yet to be discussed. Kees Popinga, an apparently phlegmatic Dutchman, is forty years old, head clerk of a shipping company, husband and father, good amateur chess player. The company goes bankrupt overnight, and the Popinga who walks out of his house next morning is now only disguised as a respectable member of society. In Amsterdam he beats and strangles a woman who refuses to go to bed with him. Reaching Paris in a state of mild exhilaration, he finds himself front-page news. This is gratifying as well, except that the newspapers refer to him as a madman. He spends his days writing anonymous corrective letters to editors, breaking off to eliminate another woman who offends him. After reading an interview with his wife, who claims that Popinga must have gone out of his mind, he composes his longest reproof.

This letter contains the heart of the novel. Popinga insists that he only began to be a 'normal' man *after* his first murder. The model employee and family man was a fraud, indifferent to wife, children and responsibilities. The 'real' Popinga is alive and well after discovering a little late in life that 'nobody obeys the law if he can help it.' As for the future, there may or may not be more crimes. Popinga considers himself essentially peaceful, but warns that if the world continues its conspiracy, he will stop at nothing to defend himself.

When the police finally catch up with him, Popinga is declared insane. Committed to a state asylum, he plans to write his memoirs but gets no further than a title: *The Truth about the Kees Popinga Case*. Then he comments to the psychiatrist, 'There really isn't any truth about it, is there?' The paranoid killer looks in the mirror and sees the image of a completely ordinary person victimized for deciding 'to live as he thinks fit,

199

without bothering about conventions or laws'. Tired of making the same point over and over, he prefers now to spend most of his time asleep. Simenon implies that Popinga the murderous anarchist is certainly more 'real' than the man in a conventional mask who found a guilty release in watching express trains go by. Allowing Popinga to end up happier than he began, he prefigures a favourite idea of the sixties, that madness is the safest state in society as it exists. Popinga is only an extreme example of a familiar experience:

'I have put up with forty years of boredom. For forty years I lived like the hungry urchin who flattens his nose against a teashop window and watches other people eat cake. Now I know that cakes are there for anyone with guts enough to go and get them.'

Simenon describes the violence inside Popinga in his most chillingly neutral style, and yet arrives at a subtle distortion of reality. The effect is like watching a movie in which the camera remains slightly tilted throughout. An almost imperceptible shift in viewpoint changes the ordinary into the fiercely grotesque.

Routine according to Simenon is a set of habits that people create and accept in order to reassure themselves. To follow standard procedures, to embark on the 'right' career or marriage, is a way of feeling solidarity with the rest of the world. But when it fails to satisfy, it becomes a trap for the solidarity of prisoners instead of free agents. The premonitions begin, twinges of anxiety that are really a longing for surprise or even disaster, any form of rescue. Conscious unease distinguishes the ordinary man of habit from Popinga or the hatter of La Rochelle. Released by accident, the paranoiac tries to dominate the world that enslaved him and never notices the transition. The break from the past seems completely natural, the world his enemy for failing to understand it. But the 'normal' person maps his own struggle. A new choice is also a new danger, and he wonders if he can handle it.

In *L'Homme de Londres* (1934, translated as *Newhaven-Dieppe*), Maloin is the avatar of the ordinary prisoner, immediately recognizable by his cage. A night-shift signalman enclosed in a box above the railway lines along the Dieppe quayside, he spends hours of his life in a kind of working isolation ward. The night when the unexpected occurs finds him in a bad humour which he fails to diagnose as a premonition. From his box he watches passengers disembarking from a ship. Two men remain on deck. A struggle begins. One of them throws a small suitcase overboard. A moment later, the other kills him, then leaves the ship.

Instinctively, Maloin neither calls for help nor reports the incident. He retrieves the suitcase instead and finds it packed with English banknotes. Gripped by a criminal impulse that he can't sustain, he hides the case and tries to decide what to do next. He behaves strangely and guiltily enough to arouse the suspicions of the man from London, the murderer searching for the case, and ends by accidentally killing him. Exchanging the signal-box cell for the prison cell, he lies on his narrow bed and thinks about the dead Englishman. Once again, two lives seem interchangeable. Each has his wife and family, the same kind of house overlooking the English Channel from the cliffs of Dieppe and Newhaven. Each is a victim of the same mysterious force of circumstance, 'the kind that occurs every day: sometimes it's an accident, sometimes a shipwreck, sometimes a crime'. The man from London murdered for money and ended as a victim without money. Maloin tried and failed to become a thief and found himself an involuntary murderer. Both men had the opportunity to break out from an imprisoning routine, and fumbled it. Accident reveals the destiny of failure.

In *Lettre à Mon Juge* (1947, translated as *Act of Passion*), a middle-aged doctor writes a long letter to explain another kind of failure. Sentenced to death for strangling his mistress, Alavoine chooses the judge as his confessor. The son of a brutal alcoholic peasant tells how he escaped from his origins to become a small-town professional, then over the years fell unsuspectingly into all the middle-class traps, and had to escape again. A cold and arrogant wife kept him in a cage where he felt like a schoolboy afraid of his teacher. He rebels at last by leaving her for an archetypal opposite, promiscuous, coarse, good-natured and gold-toothed. But behind the compulsive liar and whore, Alavoine sees a child in need of a protector. This, of course, becomes his role. When it fails, he blames what he calls 'the Other', the Martine whose impulses overwhelm both of them. The only end to this fatally plausible obsession is to

201

kill 'the Other', and free the Martine he loves, the innocent creature who loves him too. As he strangles her, he even deludes himself that Martine was 'encouraging' him, telling him 'that she willed it, that she had always foreseen this moment, *that it was the only way out*'.

The power of this novel is based on a favourite Simenon paradox. In spite of his extraordinary life, Alavoine remains an almost pathetically ordinary man. The frustrated romantic disowns convention, but never realizes the convention of his romanticism. When Martine torments him, he blames 'the Other', but 'the Other' is really any human experience that he cannot accept. To idealize is finally to kill. The world will never come up to Alavoine's touchingly simple expectations, and to underline the point he kills himself in prison after finishing the letter.

Elie, the murderer of *Crime Impuni* (1954, translated as *Account Unsettled*), inhabits the cage of the unloved. Plain, awkward, intelligent without humour, he makes himself unlovable by anticipating rejection. Most of the novel takes place at a rooming house in Liège in the late twenties, a setting drawn intact from personal memory. When another student takes a room there and quickly establishes himself as the star boarder, the situation becomes reminiscent of Hans and Joseph in *Chez Krull*. Both are foreigners, a circumstance that only adds to Elie's sense of exile but allows Michel to prove his adaptability. Michel's easy charm masks a cold nature, but the landlady's daughter falls for it, and Elie watches through a keyhole while they make love. Projecting all his disappointment and frustration on Michel, he finds something criminal in the other's happiness, and when the idea of 'crime' leads to the idea of 'punishment', everything becomes clear and simple. He shoots Michel in the face on a deserted bridge at night, and takes a train for Germany.

The scene switches abruptly to Arizona, about twenty-five years later. Elie is now a night porter at a hotel in a town grown up around a mine. The mine is about to change ownership, and a businessman from New York arrives with his entourage. Elie immediately recognizes Michel, but cannot be sure of Michel's reaction, since the face is almost motionless after plastic surgery and the voice sounds 'like water boiling'. The final scenes lead up to one of Simenon's most cruel and perfect surprises. Indifferent as ever to Elie, and too successful to care about revenge, Michel ignores him completely. Elie relives his old frustrations, with the difference this time that he doesn't want to punish Michel but to be punished by him. Rejected even as a victim, he can only shoot Michel again and make sure he kills him.

Jealous or humble, Elie remains the excluded failure. Thumbed down by Michel the popular student, successful lover, rich and powerful businessman, he is driven to violence to gain attention. In his mind it becomes 'a question of justice':

If he didn't do something about it, Michel would go on being happy. The moment such a thing became possible, the world no longer had any meaning and a life like Elie's was a kind of monstrosity.

A bid for attention also lies behind Professor Chabot's violence at the climax of *L'Ours en Peluche* (1960, *Teddy Bear*), even though from the outside his life looks like a prescription for success. A gynaecologist with an expensive private clinic, a wife and children, and a secretary with whom he's having an affair, he is still haunted by a sense of inner failure. Unable at first to define it, he thinks about suicide. To other people he reveals nothing more than the usual signs of overwork. He begins to take a sardonic pleasure in being misunderstood. It reinforces his feeling that an invisible transparent cover surrounds him wherever he goes, and no one can penetrate it. Rather like Emile in *Dimanche* falling in love with his crime, he is drawn to the idea of suicide in terms of theatre and imagines the effect it will create. In an electrifying last scene he surprises his mistress with a lover and suddenly realizes there's no need to kill himself:

Chabot raised the gun, hesitated, not about firing it, but about which target to aim for. The barrel pointed first at one, then at the other. His mind was perfectly clear. It was a long time since he'd felt so lucid.

He could kill them both, but then no one would be left as a witness...

Preferring Viviane for this role, Chabot empties the barrel into her lover's body. The performance is complete. He has found a way to make a sacrificial protest and yet survive as his own star witness. Now people are bound to ask how he really feels, to give him the personal attention he craves instead of taking him for granted as a self-sufficient man. He feels almost eager for the police to arrive.

Short even for Simenon, and daringly understated, *L'Ours en Peluche* focuses on one man during one day, although it shifts between memory and speculation in Chabot's mind. A fable about the 'inexplicable' crime that turns out to be chillingly simple, it belongs on Simenon's upper range. Sometimes, it suggests, a man gets killed by pure accident even though the gun has been aimed at his body. For Chabot is not in the least jealous. He has no apparent 'reason' to kill himself or anyone else. But the only way to break his infallible success-image is to create a disaster. The final angle of the revolver is as coincidental as the winning number in roulette.

Three other exceptional novels connect with *L'Ours en Peluche* in their analysis of solitary lives trying to break out of a routine. In *Une Vie Comme Neuve* (1951, *A New Lease of Life*) and *Le Chat* (1967, *The Cat*), violence remains in the wings. The bachelor accountant of the earlier work is drowning in monotony. He comes up for a breath of air by embezzling petty cash and following his weekly visit to a prostitute with a visit to the confessional. His premonitions of disaster are confirmed when he's run over by a car, but a freak of circumstance turns accident into opportunity. A season in hospital becomes a transition from one world to another, and he emerges with a better job and an amiable affectionate wife. Then he begins to miss the habit of frustration. Again with no 'reason', he slips back into the old round of guilt – the prostitute and the confessional – and creates a climate of unresolved domestic hatred. This hatred is the starting point of *Le Chat,* in which two people have remarried in middle age out of loneliness, and find loneliness side by side even more desperate. They strike at each other through their pets. Believing that Marguerite has poisoned his cat, Emile mutilates her parrot. Refeathered and stuffed, it returns to its cage as a grisly silent comment on a silent marriage, for after this episode the two antagonists never speak to each other. Communication is reduced to an exchange of cryptically insulting notes. Then Marguerite dies and Emile has to endure the bereavement of a lost hate. Its anguish brings on a heart attack.

204

Chabot in *L'Ours en Peluche* substitutes murder for suicide. Dudon in *Une Vie Comme Neuve* substitutes guilt for pleasure. Emile substitutes hate for love. The appalling protagonist of *La Cage de Verre* (1971, *The Glass Cage*) combines all three substitutions. Like many of Simenon's later novels, beginning with *L'Ours en Peluche,* its stripped and microscopic style creates the impression of a continuous present. From this claustrophobic angle, the past is memory and regret, and the future a hope of emotional jailbreak. Emile of *La Cage de Verre* spends his working life as a printer's proof-reader in a glass-walled booth, and his life outside it equally segregated from the human race. Embedded in routine like Simenon's other middle-class solitaries, Emile is different because he doesn't resent it. What he resents is any interference with it. The world beyond his cage is peopled by Them, hostile or contemptible. He marries for the convenience of having someone to cook his meals. Finding a woman lonely enough to accept him, he discourages any attempt at intimacy. Forced to listen to his sister's domestic problems, he grows impatient and remote. When her husband commits suicide he cannot summon a trace of pity. Migraine headaches eventually compel him to see a doctor, who probes his refusal to feel. Emile admits with his usual dryness:

'There are moments when I hate the whole world.'
'Why?'
'Because . . .'
He did not go on with his sentence.
'Because what?'
He muttered almost inaudibly:
'What difference is there between you and other people?'
'I don't know.'
'Are you jealous?'
'No.'
'Is your wife unfaithful to you?'
'I'd be surprised if she were. She'd have difficulty finding a lover.'
The doctor did not press him further.

Finally a new neighbour puts her head inside his cage, a silly compulsive flirt whose attraction Emile is reluctant to admit and unable to explain. She suggests a secret meeting, then tells him it was a joke. Emile returns home feeling oddly pleased

205

that for once he has a piece of news to tell his wife: 'You know, I've killed her ...'

Without the trigger of this petty deception, Emile would probably have killed his wife. He bore her no personal grudge, but sooner or later she would have disturbed his equilibrium. (She almost did so once by persuading him to take a holiday for the first time. He had terrible headaches.) Aware since childhood that he is the kind of person who arouses uneasy curiosity, but never love, Emile looks for a sanctuary against Them and finds his cage. So long as They keep their distance, he keeps his painful equilibrium, but when Lina foolishly disturbs it she embodies Them, the promise he avoids because he dreads the humiliation of seeing it broken.

Grey on grey, spare and unsparing in its portrait of a man who feels that he was born under a curse of misunderstanding and isolation, *La Cage de Verre* prefigures Simenon's decision to give up writing novels a year later. Soon after finishing it, the dizzy spells from which he's been suffering for some time grow longer and more severe. He enters a clinic for treatment. Emile's headaches suggest a parallel to the spells, just as his glass cage reflects the process of 'depersonalizing' himself, as Simenon has called it, in writing a novel. In the *Paris Review* interview in 1953 he was already describing the strain induced by his method of writing, of total entry into another person's skin. It became almost unbearable after a week – 'one of the reasons my novels are so short'. Before starting each novel he would have a medical check-up, and sometimes the doctor would suggest that he rationed himself to only two more novels for the next six months. In the Maigrets written during the sixties, the detective thinks increasingly about retirement and his wife has an instinct that he needs the reassurance of 'everyday life'. During the same period, Simenon also begins keeping his notebooks, originally not intended for publication but appearing in 1970 as *Quand j'étais vieux* (*When I Was Old*). One note speaks for many: 'Novel finished. I re-enter life.' A few years later, when the final decision has been made, he speaks of a deliverance, of 'returning to my own body, into my own life'.

Another reccurring theme of the notebooks is family life as an essential sanctuary. Simenon even implies that the bachelor or bohemian artist is somehow 'incomplete'. Yet his novels

206

show people crippled by domestic hatreds. Chabot in *L'Ours en Peluche* feels totally estranged from his children. *Novembre* (1969, *November*), an ominous minor work of the period, contains a particularly dark view of the family unit: Laure only begins to feel close to her mother after discovering she's committed a murder. Simenon's personal affection for his family seems also an affection for the *idea* of it, for its quality of reassurance. In spite of his novels, the 'normal' can be desirable.

Yet by the time he abandons his profession, this private universe has fallen apart. Simenon writes that his second wife, who managed all his business affairs, was the only woman for whom he felt total love, unique closeness as well as physical attraction. During the sixties she had a series of nervous crises terminating in a crucial breakdown. The ex-novelist became a solitary man after all, selling the great house and estate – newspaper advertisements stressed that it would make an excellent international corporation centre – and moving to an apartment in Lausanne.

Perhaps Simenon was born with an affinity for exile, the father from Brittany, the mother from the Walloon French-speaking minority of Belgium, the Germans occupying Liège when he was eleven, the father's death, the severed maternal cord when he moved to Paris at twenty, the intense exploration of other countries and lives, and a second term of German occupation. In 1945 he broke out of his environment again to live in the United States for ten years, where he also broke the habit of heavy drinking and began to write on tea, then coffee. The decision to settle in Switzerland, with its established community of exiles, completes a pattern of what he's called 'reality making way for new reality'. In his notebooks he suggests that a man has more than one past, and his life is a series of them.

In spite of so many arrivals and departures, no break occurs in the continuum of the novels themselves. By the middle 1930s Simenon has fixed his sights on a kind of silent counter-culture. When he writes, 'There are no criminals', he proposes crime as the individual expression of a universal discontent, the act of violence that breaks the long period of quiet pressure. Until the gun is fired and the knife drawn, the counterculture passes as part of the ordinary culture, for Simenon's murderers and suicides are clerks, small businessmen, railway workers, doctors, struggling students, housewives, secretaries, hatters, building contractors. Very occasionally they rise as high as a sucessful magazine editor or surgeon. Whatever their situation, material gain is the least of their motives. On the contrary, they are trying to articulate their hostility to the present stage of material evolution. The human mechanism reacts most violently to a threat, and Simenon's counterculture reacts to the threat of a huge expanding society that overwhelms the individual. Yet being an individual is not a question of being different from other people. Most of these protagonists want to be 'ordinary', but find it impossible when the ordinary has been levelled down to its most negative aspects – frustration, exclusion, insignificance. They need a sense of community, but not the community of disappointment.

Simenon has spoken of all his characters as 'brothers', which explains why in the long view they sometimes seem to blur into one another. This is really a symptom of their individuality, not its opposite. As members of a silent counterculture, their circumstances and reactions obviously overlap. At the moment of killing or being killed, each one becomes unique. Through Sherlock Holmes, Conan Doyle found a way to 'remove the roofs', as he expressed it, and reveal a criminal pattern of coincidence, design and cross-purposes. Simenon's novels create the same effect over a period of forty years in the twentieth century. It begins with Adil Bey leaving Batum after falling in love with a woman who tried to poison him, while Timar on board another ship hallucinates himself out of Africa and the memory of a criminal wife. Then Maloin hides the suitcase filled with stolen money and sets a course that will end in involuntary murder, Popinga finds himself as a paranoid killer, Hans discovers the girl's body in the canal, Jean cracks the skull of the widow Couderc. Paris in the sixties contains several people who could have passed each other in the street: Allard living alone with his dog and thinking about suicide, Poitaud the magazine editor moving unconsciously closer to it, Chabot at the last moment committing murder instead, Emile and Marguerite at their long silent war after the death of cat and parrot. In the provinces, Emile sleeps side by side with the wife he tried to poison and Andrée makes sure that Tony will never escape her by landing them both in prison. The flow of violence recalls that perpetual offensive and defensive motion that Simenon found in the life of the sea.

If every murderer is also a victim who feels cheated out of his place in life, his actual victim seems to personify the forces that cheat him. In *Crime Impuni* the existence of a happy man becomes unforgivable to an unhappy one, in *La Veuve Couderc* the emotional demands of Tati strike at Jean's lost capacity to feel, in *Lettre à Mon Juge* 'the Other' Martine destroys Alavoine's idea of love as total fulfilment, in *L'Homme au Petit Chien* his wife's lover forces Allard to recognize a lifetime of failure. In his notebooks Simenon writes that 'everyone struggles so hard to exist', and in his novels he shows the other side of the struggle, the need to destroy. His characters never seem more brotherly than when they break with the past and echo each other's idea of murder as 'the only way out'.

In a novel called *Les Anneaux de Bicêtre* (1963, translated as *The Patient*), a man goes into hospital and begins to review his life. Ten years later, in a clinic in Lausanne, Simenon does the same thing. The fictional patient is a rather disappointing character. Unlike Simenon's more passionate creations, he gets no further than a hope of somehow patching his life together. But the novelist patient behaves like one of his fictional 'brothers' when they commit a murder and also murder the past. By the time he leaves the clinic, Simenon has found 'the only way out' for himself. He murders his past as a novelist by declaring that his novels mean nothing to him any more. With a further imaginative replay, he breaks into yet another new environment. 'The naked man' he now confronts, directly and in private, is himself.

SIX
A Private Eye

The realist in murder writes of a world in which gangsters can
rule nations and almost rule cities, in which hotels and apartment
houses and celebrated restaurants are owned by men who made
their money out of brothels, in which a screen star can be the finger
man for a mob, and the nice man down the hall is a boss of the
numbers racket; a world . . . where no man can walk down a dark
street in safety because law and order are things we talk about but
refrain from practising.

Law e order is key element is
A Christie common good is theme
throughout.

Raymond Chandler,
The Simple Art of Murder

In 1919, when he was thirty-one, an unmarried American of
no fixed address or career arrived in California with his
mother. They had lived together since he was seven, mainly in
London, and only the First World War had separated them
for any notable length of time. In this year of his life he had a
trunk full of good clothes but practically no money, and spoke
with a British accent that, as he later remembered, 'you could
cut with a baseball bat'. Although he liked to dress elegantly,
there was no hint of personal glitter. His manner was shy and
gentle, he had written a few sentimental poems and read a
great many books. An inch under six feet tall, he looked like
a taller and leaner Scott Fitzgerald, who was also Irish on his
mother's side, believed his creativity came from his maternal
genes, and found the rich extraordinarily fascinating.

This Side of Paradise appeared while Raymond Chandler's
creativity lay buried, and the admirer of Henry James and
Flaubert began working on an apricot ranch for twenty cents
an hour. He graduated to stringing tennis rackets for a sporting
goods company at $12.50 a week, then decided to become a
businessman in spite of his dislike for the life. He completed
a three-year book-keeping course in six weeks, and within a
few years had promoted himself to the directorship of several
independent oil corporations around Los Angeles. They were
small but surprisingly rich, like many enterprises during this
time of national boom. In 1924 his mother died, but at thirty-
six Chandler was still reluctant to cut the umbilical cord. A

210

few weeks later he married Pearl Cecily Bowen, aged fifty-three, to whom he remained faithful until (and perhaps after) her death thirty years later. By then, of course, the quiet man who loved cats and idealized his motherly wife had become famous as the creator of Philip Marlowe, a private detective at war with a society based on murder and corruption and sex as part of the grift.

He had been born in 1888 in Chicago. His father was a civil engineer and his mother came from a wealthy Anglo-Irish family. They divorced when Chandler was seven. His mother took him to London, to live with her own mother, and he never saw his father again. He arrived in London in the middle of the Sherlock Holmes decade, grew up in a household run by two women, and became a day pupil at Dulwich College, 'not quite on a level with Eton and Harrow from a social point of view, but very good educationally'. He left it at seventeen, having discovered an affinity for Latin and Greek and an ambition to write. His mother, on the advice of an uncle, persuaded him to join the civil service, but he found it intolerable after six months. Going off to live by himself on very little money in Bloomsbury, he started writing poetry and had a poem accepted by *Chambers' Journal*. He never kept a copy of it, but remembered later that it might have gone over well if recited by Margaret O'Brien. Other magazines published a few more poems and some book reviews, but Chandler was beginning to feel displaced in England. He prised a reluctant consent from his mother and a reluctant loan from his uncle, and landed in San Francisco in 1912. Accepting whatever work he could find, including a job at a British bank, he joined the first Canadian Expeditionary Force on the outbreak of war in 1914. This was partly because he still felt like a man without a country and preferred the idea of a British uniform, and partly because the Canadian government paid a dependant's allowance which he could send to his mother.

She joined him in Los Angeles when he decided to go there after the war, living long enough to see the start of his business career. When the Depression came and the oil companies went bankrupt, his wife saw the end of it. She seemed fragile, but Chandler described her later as 'a terrific fighter'. At the age of almost sixty she was apparently unfazed when her third

211

husband began driving up and down the Pacific coast, on the surface in search of a job, underneath it in search of himself. She didn't object when he finally announced that he'd spent a lot of his time reading pulp magazines and wanted to try his hand at writing that kind of fiction.

Chandler's only previous attempt at fiction had been 'a Henry James pastiche' written shortly after the war and allowed to gather dust, like his literary ambitions, when the *Atlantic Monthly* rejected it. He was now sparked by the stories appearing in *Black Mask*, a pulp founded in 1920 by H. L. Mencken and George Jean Nathan to underwrite the losses on their *Smart Set*. The pace, realism and violence of its early stories was a reaction against the trend of the popular American crime novel, heavily influenced by British puzzle-makers and epitomized during the twenties by S. S. Van Dine. (His amateur detective Philo Vance was educated at Oxford and wore a monocle.) *Black Mask* began by launching the work of Carroll John Daly, whose Race Williams was the first tough private eye in fiction, speakeasy language replacing allusions to Cellini and the four hundred. It continued with the early stories of Dashiell Hammett, featuring an overweight sleuth known as the Continental Op. When Joseph Thompson Shaw took over as editor in 1926, it moved beyond the other pulps to acquire an underground reputation in its own right. Shaw had ideas for developing the genre. In a preface to the first number with his name on the masthead, he announced that the deductive story inspired by Poe had reached a dead end because it lacked emotional tension. The new crime stories must centre on 'character and the problems inherent in human behaviour over crime solution'. He found new writers, including Horace McCoy and Erle Stanley Gardner. He found new readers, including Hemingway, who acknowledged the gritty laconic approach to violence in *The Killers*.

When Chandler first read the *Black Mask* stories, he felt they generated 'the smell of fear'. Many years later he recalled his first impression of characters who 'lived in a world gone wrong . . . The law was something to be manipulated for profit and power. The streets were dark with something more than night.' This was partly a feat of imaginative projection.

Hammett, a former Pinkerton detective and the most gifted of these early writers, was cynical about a cynical world. His stories and novels had a cold documentary skill, and identified policemen and politicos as members of the criminal class. But fear is the one quality they fail to generate. They are too monotonously terse and knowing for that. Hemingway found subtle inner rhythms and tensions in the apparently colloquial sentence, but Hammett's prose only xeroxed the effect of a man talking out of the side of his mouth. Even *The Maltese Falcon,* first published as a serial in *Black Mask,* reads disappointingly today. It has a classic plot and Hammett's ripest characters, especially 'the fat man', one of the most exuberant derivatives of Wilkie Collins's Fosco. Yet it lacks the allure of genuine style that John Huston brought to his movie adaptation. Gardner's first stories are less expert than Hammett's, but have more intensity and shock, the primitive 'unputdownable' element on which Chandler fastened from the start: 'When in doubt, have a man come through a door with a gun in his hand. This could get to be pretty silly, but somehow it didn't matter.' The detective is a catalyst of improbability, and the writer who draws back from it will be happier in another environment.

Black Mask was the catalyst of another improbability. It released the imagination of a private diffident exile, on the threshold of middle age, who sought the protection of women much older than himself. The man without a country suddenly embraced a fiercely alien country, full of youth and danger and brutality. But the outsider often reacts more sharply and deviously to many things that the native son takes for granted. Chandler's decision to settle in Los Angeles coincided with the rise of organized crime in the United States. After prohibition created gangland, the rival syndicates moved from bootlegging into drug smuggling, gambling, prostitution, labour unions, local politics. They even penetrated oil companies, so perhaps Chandler had some first-hand knowledge of them. By 1930 the interstate gang known as The Syndicate had begun to employ professional killers (Murder, Inc.) and to pioneer murder as big business. The pulp stories were the first fiction to recognize escalating crime, although in *Echoes of the Jazz Age* Scott Fitzgerald noted 'the dark maw of violence' into which so many of his contemporaries had vanished, and which he prefigured in *The Great Gatsby,* with its suggestion of wealth as the secret partner of illegality.

In southern California, the outlook for such a partnership was grand-scale and almost hallucinatory. Los Angeles had a major Depression-proof industry, the movies, and movie wealth lay superimposed on the older millions of land and oil. As a background for the novelist it was equally rich, although none had yet taken advantage of it. A mainly immigrant accumulation of people and power was occurring in a vast boom town spread out between an ocean and a desert. A sense of lonely space and prehistory haunted its machinery of ambition and dreams. Authority and crime soon interacted like movies and life, at the same exorbitant pitch. 'This is a big town now,' Marlowe says in *The Big Sleep* (1939). 'Some very tough people have checked in here. The penalty of growth.' The full penalty of growth only became apparent thirty-five years later, when the president of the United States, born and educated in Los Angeles County, resigned in order to evade multiple criminal charges on which fifteen of his appointees had already been indicted. *The Big Sleep* was no sudden illumination, but the development of a process that began in Chandler's earliest stories. They plant the clues that the novels follow up, and no other American writer of the period remained as faithful to his previsions.

The invention of Marlowe makes it clear that Chandler was shocked into them. Although not called Marlowe until *The Big Sleep,* the same character exists in the pulp stories, a private eye narrator who is sometimes anonymous and sometimes goes under the name of Dalmas or Carmady. Like Chandler, Marlowe communicates only fragmented details of his background – he was born in Santa Rosa, near San Francisco, an only child, parents dead – and feels emotionally exiled from it. All the years of his pre-Los Angeles past seem to belong to another person. Asked why Marlowe came to southern California, Chandler said only that 'eventually most people do, though not all of them remain.' Like Chandler again, Marlowe started by working for a corporation. After finding the ethics of the district attorney's office in Los Angeles incompatible with his own, he left to set up as a private investigator. The ethics in question, Chandler makes clear, are personal and not social. The world of pay-offs, blackmail and murder happens to offend his basic nature and arouse an instinct for revolt. Theories about corruption don't interest him, only the chance to fight it. Honesty isolates him from a great many people, policemen and lawyers and public officials as well as mobsters, and from the prospect of making much money. It even isolates him from sex, except between cases, since he refuses the bribe so frequently offered by the willing desirable women he encounters. His emotional ancestry stems partly from the thirties, for the idea of the lone crusader already existed in western movies and was soon to infiltrate comedies like Capra's *Mr Deeds Goes to Town*. But Marlowe's tone of voice, pungent and melancholy, is entirely new. In his shabby dusty office without a secretary and his commonplace bachelor apartment where he makes coffee, ponders chess problems and is woken by the phone ringing in the middle of the night, he seems bounded by transience and solitude, a permanent stranger in the city that he'll probably never leave.

Recognizing the element of fantasy in Marlowe, Chandler once pointed out that at least he was 'an exaggeration of the possible'. From the start he had a deliberate touch of burlesque, like the world in which he operated. The American good guy to the nth degree, at once puritan and romantic, is fighting American evil to the nth degree, greed for money and power. Within this simple imaginative structure Chandler creates his own baroque, cruel and ironic melodrama. But however extravagant the surface, there is always something alarmingly ordinary beneath it. The sum of Marlowe's adventures is a collision with everyday corrupt life at a particular time and place. As the private eye becomes Chandler's private eye, he echoes Holmes and Maigret in explaining personal beliefs and anxieties as well as solving a case. Hammett's Sam Spade, only a few notches above the general level of everyday corruption, provides only minimal relief from it. A more 'realistic' character, he reveals much less about the life around him. Marlowe's rude and drop-out independence makes him the complete investigator, framing a world in the perspective of his hostility towards it. Chandler believed, like Simenon, that contemporary history was not a matter of politics or religion. He saw it as 'the marriage of an idealist to a gangster and how their home life and children turned out', and he invented Marlowe to keep an endangered loner's eye on it. He had to invent Marlowe because he didn't exist, and there seemed no one else around to do the job.

It took Chandler almost five months to write his first story, *Blackmailers Don't Shoot*, which *Black Mask* published in 1933. Always a slow worker ('I am a fellow who writes 30,000 words to turn in five'), he averaged three stories a year until his first novel appeared in 1939. Aware that plotting didn't come easily to him, he seldom discarded his best situations, which reappear in *The Big Sleep, Farewell, My Lovely* and *The Lady in the Lake*. These three novels follow a similar plan of using various scenes and characters from the early stories, linking two or three of them together. New material is added, most of the old material rewritten and expanded and given a different emphasis, but an occasional short passage recurs almost intact. Even the later novels contain echoes of the stories of the thirties – a sentence, an image, a fragment of a scene. Los Angeles appears in all of the stories and Marlowe, under different names or no name at all, in most of them. Rugged and flip, mistrustful of cops and blondes, he often has a curious sense of private letdown at the end of a case – 'I felt tired and old and not much use to anybody', he signs off after exposing *The Killer in the Rain*. Written to formula, punctuated by the man who suddenly comes through the door with a gun in his hand, the stories still reveal glimpses of an original novelist in the making and the gusto of self-discovery. Two of the best stand by themselves, since Chandler never went back to them for his novels, and both hinge on the search for a pearl necklace. In *Red Wind* (1938) it turns out to be false, and the symbol of a false love. In *Goldfish* (1936) the single stones are genuine, hidden in the bellies of tropical fish. *Red Wind* creates its edgy atmosphere in the opening paragraph:

There was a desert wind blowing that night. It was one of those hot dry Santa Anas that come down through the mountain passes and curl your hair and make your nerves jump and your skin itch. On nights like that every booze party ends in a fight. Meek little wives feel the edge of the carving knife and study their husbands' necks...

The wind underlines the violence of the action, then dies down for a quick moody ending. Dalmas sits on a rock overlooking the Pacific, the air suddenly cool and languid, but the landscape behind him scorched and blackened. Seagulls swoop after the worthless imitation pearls as he drops them one by one into the water.

Goldfish moves from Los Angeles to the wild north-western coast, with Carmady and a group of criminal fanatics on the trail of the stolen Leander pearls. It is obviously inspired by *The Maltese Falcon*, but the isolated setting – 'the last outpost of the coast, the farthest west a man could go and still be on the mainland of the United States' – has its own power. The characters are Chandler's most striking early creations, especially the pretty girl with a cold voice and an obsessive brutality, and the dismal old couple in the cliff house, its main room lined with fish tanks:

> There were long slim fish like golden darts and Japanese Veiltails with fantastic trailing tails, and X-ray fish as transparent as colored glass, tiny guppies half an inch long, calico popeyes spotted like a bride's apron, and big lumbering Chinese Moors with telescope eyes, froglike faces and unnecessary fins, waddling through the green water like fat men going to lunch.

These moments have the authentic Chandler overtone, at once casual and strange. As a whole the stories are unavoidably thin in texture, yet in their quick fragmented way they explore a variety of backgrounds. Like a sketchbook of Los Angeles, they contrast sleazy beach cities or downtown areas with rich exotic houses in remote foothills, they indicate the haunting presence of desert and ocean and power behind the scenes – the mayor controlled by a gambling syndicate, the police chief linked to shysters. In the same way, Chandler allows Carmady-Dalmas to catch his breath for a personal reaction, romantic in his twinge of pity for the woman deceived about the pearls in *Red Wind*, puritan in his wary over-reaction to homosexuals (the pornography merchant of *Killer in the Rain* who reappears in *The Big Sleep*, the blackmailer of *Mandarin's Jade* who reappears in *Farewell, My Lovely*). The rich, the sexually unconventional and the official machinery of law and order arouse his suspicion and animosity, the helpless or betrayed his protectiveness. Yet he retains a kind of amused existential loyalty towards his clients. No matter how aberrant, they pay him $25 a day plus expenses, and their interests come first

217

unless he discovers they are criminal as well. Recognizing a world beyond his own prejudices and affections, he divides it very simply into two classes, his clients and the others.

Another detective element underlies these stories. Chandler is investigating the American language as a foreigner. In the *Black Mask* style, harsh and colloquial, he finds a blueprint for conveying a life of sensation and instinct rather than thought. While it can quickly invent its own clichés, it makes the literary English on which he's been brought up seem over-refined. He discards it as completely as Gertrude Stein when she wrote *Three Lives* a quarter of a century earlier. Her guidelines then were 'beginning again' and 'the continuous present', and not by coincidence she later became interested in mystery stories. In an interview transcribed in 1945 but not published until 1962 in the *UCLAN Review,* she recalled her reasons. She defined her technique of the continuous present as a moment to moment insistence on things as they actually happen, and saw how it could be developed in the novel of 'one man's way of doing a thing'. This approach to the mystery story is surprisingly close to Chandler's when he writes of 'the very determined individual' who makes justice happen against all the odds, and of a narrative in which the immediate scene 'outranked the plot in the sense that a good plot was one which made good scenes'.

Chandler's primal remoteness from Los Angeles allowed him to look at it in a way that no one had done before. With his allegiance to 'revered' Henry James and his Flaubert-like concern for words, he could also look at a new language with the same creative astonishment. He saw a break with the past in the focus on instant physical response and the assimilation of slang to heighten it. Since his territory was violence, and the impact of the unexpected, and one man's way of reacting to it, he naturally looked for one man's way of writing about it as well.

At the age of fifty Chandler began the process of what he called 'cannibalizing' his earlier work and produced his first novel, *The Big Sleep*. As the stolen pearls in *Goldfish* were hidden by slitting open fish bellies and suturing them afterwards, the dramatic stitches here are expertly sewn. All the material seems to be organically related. Combining stories with widely

218

differing backgrounds, Chandler creates a human linkwork and joins together apparently disconnected lives. The terraced mansion in the foothills, stiff with wealth and family portraits, leads to the disguised pornography store on Hollywood Boulevard. The exclusive gambling club down the coast with its Mexican orchestra and crystal chandeliers leads to the shabby suburban garage apartment where the gangster's wife hides out. *The Big Sleep* announces Chandler's favourite mystery pattern, the secret alliances between wealth and the underworld.

It opens on an October morning 'with the sun not shining and the look of hard wet rain'. Philip Marlowe, wearing a powder-blue suit and black brogues, is 'calling on four million dollars' in the person of a retired general. A stained-glass panel in the hallway makes a casual sardonic reference to the private detective as crusader: a knight in dark armour is trying to rescue a naked lady tied to a tree. General Sternwood made his millions out of oil, and can see the pumps still working in the city below his windows, but he is now sick, near death, and seems to exist 'largely on heat, like a newborn spider'. The interview takes place in a steamy greenhouse, like an indoor tropical forest. The old man has sent for Marlowe because his younger daughter is being blackmailed and the husband of his older daughter has disappeared after a month of marriage. The trail leads through pornography and gambling syndicates to several violent deaths and the discovery that the younger sister murdered her brother-in-law. The psychotic Carmen giggles and sucks her thumb and wets her pants after firing a gun; her rough and greedy sister is a compulsive gambler. Though frequently naked, rich ladies are more likely to tie their men to trees, and the knight himself is in need of rescue.

Chandler's portrait of the west-coast business aristocracy blisters while it chills, but he reserves a subtle touch of sympathy for the ancient general, his life slipping away and his millions gradually eroded by daughters and racketeers. Along with the gambling syndicate and city hall, the Sternwood family represents power in a community where a police record usually means that you don't know the right people, and where the chief of the Missing Persons Bureau tells Marlowe that he's 'as honest as you could expect a man to be in a world where it's out of style'. The novel is at times overwritten – 'I sure did run the similes into the ground,' Chandler commented later – but has a propulsive force and a completely original blend of violence and melancholy brightness. The episode with the gangster's wife, Silver-Wig, is the first example of one of Chandler's favourite and most telling devices. Marlowe wakes up in a strange place after having been knocked unconscious and wonders if he's not hallucinating: 'It seemed there was a woman and she was sitting near a lamp, which was where she belonged, in a good light . . .' He asks her, 'What time is it?' She looks at her watch and answers, 'Ten-seventeen. You have a date?' The moment typifies Chandler's dialogue, at once ironic and a precise diagram of character. Many atmospheric touches have the same throwaway exactness, like the description of the elder daughter's bedroom, 'A screen star's boudoir, a place of charm and seduction, artificial as a wooden leg.' The end strikes a note of almost lyrical disgust:

> What did it matter where you lay once you were dead? In a dirty sump or in a marble tower on top of a high hill? You were dead, you were sleeping the big sleep, you were not bothered by things like that. Oil and water were the same as wind and air to you. You just slept the big sleep, not caring about the nastiness of how you died or where you fell. Me, I was part of the nastiness now . . .

Late in 1943 Chandler began a period of screenwriting in Hollywood, during which he produced no other fiction. Before that, he followed *The Big Sleep* with three more novels, of which *Farewell, My Lovely* (1940) is his first masterpiece, *The Lady in the Lake* (1944) not far below it in quality, and *The High Window* (1942) an intervening disappointment. All of them are dominated by portraits of a deadly female of the American species, combing the power-drive of one Sternwood sister with the psychosis of the other. However promiscuous, they remain faithful to their love of money. 'There's no such thing as too much money,' Marlowe realizes in *Farewell, My Lovely*, and it seems to haunt the whole city, its light and architecture, exorcized only at land's end by the Pacific:

> We curved through the bright mile or two of the Strip, past the antique shops with famous screen names on them, past the windows full of point lace and ancient pewter, past the gleaming new night clubs with famous chefs and equally famous gambling rooms, run by polished graduates of the Purple Gang, past the Georgian-Colonial vogue, now old hat, past the handsome modernistic build-

ings in which the Hollywood flesh-peddlers never stop talking money, past a drive-in lunch which somehow didn't belong, even though the girls wore white silk blouses and drum majorettes' shakos and nothing below the hips but glazed kid Hessian boots. Past all of this and down a wide smooth curve to the bridle path of Beverly Hills and lights to the south, all colours of the spectrum and crystal clear in an evening without fog, past the shadowed mansions up on the hills to the north, past Beverly Hills altogether and up into the twisting foothill boulevard and the sudden cool dusk and the drift of wind from the sea.

In *Farewell, My Lovely* the *femme fatale* with the dollar-sign heart began as Velma Valento, an ambitious redheaded singer in a fifth-rate downtown Los Angeles club and the girl-friend of a huge simple-minded bank robber. Several years later she's become Mrs Lewin Lockridge Grayle, a flintily gracious blonde with a made-over voice and a sad adoring elderly husband worth $20,000,000. Money not only talks but kills talk. When Malloy ('about as inconspicuous as a tarantula on a slice of angel food') gets out of jail and starts looking for his Velma, she connives with the police to keep him drugged in a private sanatorium. When he escapes and tracks her down, she kills him and returns to her origins as a black-haired singer in a Baltimore club. The rise and fall of Velma emerges indirectly, since the novel begins with Marlowe engaged by a client who gets murdered and whose case seems to have nothing to do with an obscure singer and an ex-convict. Mrs Grayle first appears as a rich and coolly erotic lady who claims to have been robbed of a jade necklace. Her previous identity and her habit of killing when cornered are revealed only in the last few pages, like a two-sided mirror suddenly turned around to catch a new reflection.

Farewell, My Lovely replaces the fast episodic manner of *The Big Sleep* with a jigsaw structure, equally rapid and complex but firmer. Between his first meeting with Velma as Mrs Grayle and his final encounter with Mrs Grayle as Velma, Marlowe only knows that he's at the centre of a violent puzzle. Repeating his device of disconnected pieces that gradually fit together, Chandler explores more rites and mysteries of a city unlike any other. The same stained visiting card links a cunning drunken old woman in a downtown slum to a perfumed blackmailer in an elegant house overlooking the ocean. His murder becomes a bridge to the walled and silent Grayle estate with its chiming doorbells, butlers and rugs 'as thin as silk and as old as Aesop's aunt'. Mrs Grayle leads to the fake psychic and his filthy Indian medium living in exotic grandeur in the foothills, who lead to the dingy sanatorium where Marlowe is imprisoned and drugged like Malloy. Its corridors connect to a beach city with a corrupt police chief and a 'hot dishonest light', then to a gambling ship off the coast run by smooth gangsters in dinner jackets. The transitions have a kind of dream logic, climaxed when Marlowe wakes with a drug hangover in the sanatorium and hallucinates thin lines of smoke apparently hanging in the air of a cell-like room with barred windows. Every character and background is realized with an abrupt and stunning insight; the effects never over-reach themselves, the circuit in Marlowe's words is 'dark and full of blood'.

Although he mistrusts her from the start, Marlowe is fascinated by Mrs Grayle and the sexual tension she generates. It only ceases to work at the moment he's ready to expose her, when she suddenly looks 'like a woman who would have been dangerous a hundred years ago'. Throughout the story Marlowe has the alternative of a 'nice girl' who's attracted to him, but the experience only convinces him, as he tells Detective-Lieutenant Randall, that nice girls are not his type:

'I like smooth shiny girls, hard-boiled and loaded with sin.'
'They take you to the cleaners,' Randall said indifferently.
'Sure. Where else have I ever been? . . .'

Velma Grayle almost takes Marlowe to the cleaners when she tries to kill him, yet he continues to think about her with a touch of nostalgia. The novel leaves him walking out of City Hall after her death, on a cool clear day. 'You could see a long way – but not as far as Velma had gone.' It emphasizes his ambivalence towards the rich and corrupt, enemies who point to his failure in the world's eyes. Marlowe wears loneliness and a monthly income of maybe $400 like the badges of an honest man, but knows the allure of the other side.

The strongest feature of *The High Window* is its portrait of a hefty matriarch who likes to dress in silk and lace but speaks in a baritone voice and belches while drinking port. The novel begins when she summons Marlowe to retrieve a valuable stolen coin, and ends when he discovers that she murdered her husband to collect his life insurance. Apart from this mercenary dragon and some patches of atmosphere, the story has a rather mechanical feel. *The Lady in the Lake* makes a totally opposite effect, its mystery based on a cunning and oblique method of character exposition. Engaged by Derace Kingsley to find his missing wife, Marlowe follows the trail of a woman who supposedly ran off with her lover. Along the way he encounters dead ends and dead bodies, one of them belonging to the lover, and comes to suspect that Crystal Kingsley is a killer. But her motive remains as baffling as his failure to locate her. A reversal similar to the climax of *Farewell, My Lovely* provides an ironic solution, and the suspected killer is really the victim.

The first body, the lady in the lake with her face bloated and disfigured after lying for a month beneath an underwater flooring, has been wrongly identified. She is the rich and careless woman for whom Marlowe has been searching, murdered by a broke and desperate one. Alive, Crystal Kingsley seemed to make no sense. Dead, she becomes as logical as her killer's motive. Greedy for money and a place in the sun, the triple murderess emerges as a failed Velma. Prepared to use sex, blackmail and murder in the relatively modest pursuit of thousands rather than millions, she nets only a series of disappointments. In a last bid to recoup, she assumes the identity of her well-to-do victim. Chandler never approaches this character directly, only through reflected images. During most of the novel Muriel Chess is believed to be dead, the actions she performs attributed to another person. Marlowe confronts her twice without knowing it, since she's in disguise both times. The third time, he confronts her literally stripped naked, just after he's recovered from a blow on the head. Coming to in an apartment room, smelling 'like dead toads', he realizes a bottle of gin has been poured down his throat while he was unconscious, then looks across to the naked body on the pulldown bed, belly clawed and tongue bulging out of its mouth.

Up to this point, a sequence of bizarre deaths and a mysterious portrait by indirection create the kind of suspense at which Chandler is unequalled – the 'what the hell went on, rather than who done it' kind, as he once described it. But the murder of Muriel Chess leaves Marlowe with the task of exposing a second murderer. It diffuses the remaining movement and leads to an overlong explanation scene. There is a compelling hatred behind Chandler's study of a California cop, the criminal wearing the uniform of authority, but it seems to belong to another story. In fact it does, imperfectly welded to two other early novelettes which supply the basic material of *The Lady in the Lake*.

But even when the narrative falters, the jaunty bitter eye for detail persists. Investigating California Middletown instead of gangsters and the super-rich, Marlowe finds an equally reckless appetite for violence. He moves through a gaudy folksy mountain resort and a series of suburban settings littered with brisk character vignettes and sudden visual intelligence. He even pauses to sniff the elevator with 'an elderly perfume in it, like three widows drinking tea'.

Five years after *The Big Sleep* Marlowe has become conscious of his reputation as an insubmissive American. He makes a new client immediately aware of it:

'I don't like your manner,' Kingsley said in a voice you could have cracked a brazil nut on.
'That's all right,' I said. 'I'm not selling it.'

But after playing up to his role in public, he studies himself in his private mirror:

I brushed my hair and looked at the grey in it. There was getting to be plenty of grey. The face under the hair had a sick look. I didn't like the face at all.

As the private eye grows more defiantly solitary, the moments of social clairvoyance intensify. This 1944 novel sketches a doctor who gets rich by turning his nervous and depressed patients into amphetamine addicts. It compares police business to politics, noting that 'it asks for the highest type of men, and there's nothing in it to attract the highest type of men'. And from a brief season in jail, Marlowe takes away an unforgettable impression of his jailer:

I'm a cop, brother, I'm tough, watch your step, brother, or we'll fix you up so you'll crawl on your hands and knees, brother, snap out of it, brother, let's get a load of the truth, brother, let's go, and let's not forget we're tough guys, we're cops, and we do what we like with punks like you.

Chandler's Hollywood experience began when he collaborated

with Billy Wilder and Charles Brackett on the screenplay of *Double Indemnity* (1944). In retrospect it seemed 'an agonizing experience', but it remains his most successful movie work. James M. Cain's novel is set in Chandler territory, with its Los Angeles background and its story of a suburban housewife who seduces an insurance agent into murdering her husband after he takes out a new policy. Chandler's personal touch appears in the reworking of the central character. In Cain's novel the wife is a rather fascinating hypocrite, with a wispy fragile manner that conceals an obstinate greed. Chandler makes her into a pitiless drugstore *femme fatale,* sexual and predatory, sister to Velma Valento and Muriel Chess.

After contributing to a weeper (*And Now Tomorrow*) and a ghost story (*The Unseen*), Chandler did some preliminary work on the adaptation of *The Lady in the Lake.* It is the only movie of one of his novels with which he has even a marginal connection. Like Greene and Ambler, he witnessed most of them reduced to mediocrity. *The Big Sleep* at least had Bogart (the only effective Marlowe), and at the time (1946) Chandler approved the atmosphere of cryptic sadism in its opening scenes; but today it seems badly hobbled by censorship.

Two original screenplays followed. When he saw *The Blue Dahlia,* poorly directed and with new dialogue added, Chandler disowned most of it. When the studio decided not to produce *Playback*, he left Hollywood and brought a house in La Jolla, seventy miles down the coast, where he lived with his wife from the end of 1946 until her death. In 1950 he returned for two months to work on the first draft of a screenplay for Hitchcock, *Strangers on a Train.* Then Hitchcock assigned the project to another writer. The most interesting aspect of this aborted collaboration is Chandler's attitude to a story that he found ingenious but empty. Whatever he may have failed to do, he searched for a more substantial premise. His working notes on the script suggest an approach that the movie eventually adopted, but fumbled: 'If you shake hands with a maniac, you may have sold your soul to the devil.'

In general Chandler seems to have found the Hollywood experience wasteful and depleting. Soon after seeing *The Blue Dahlia* he wrote to hs friend Erle Stanley Gardner that he was trying to 'get over a case of complete exhaustion', and also published an article called *Writers in Hollywood* which describes the movie capital as 'a degraded community whose idealism is even largely fake'. He complains that the writer has too little control over his own work and mourns his failure to find a professional relationship with 'the few people in Hollywood whose purpose is to make the best pictures possible within the limitations of a popular art'. It seems probable that Chandler, like many exceptionally gifted novelists, disliked the collaborative process. While he understands the director's precedence, he can't help resenting it. Hitchcock remembers Chandler's reaction when he suggested a way of dramatizing a scene in *Strangers on a Train*: 'Well, if you can puzzle it out, what do you need me for?'

Of the several articles written during his Hollywood years, *The Simple Art of Murder* (1944) is Chandler's most important. A testament of belief in the art of the mystery story, it also contains his famous soliloquy on Marlowe, 'a complete man and a common man and yet an unusual man'. His destiny, Chandler writes, is to challenge a botched and violent civilization: 'Down these mean streets a man must go who is not himself mean, who is neither tarnished nor afraid.' This paragraph, so often quoted to the virtual exclusion of the rest, makes Marlowe seem a much simpler amd more idealized character than he appears in the novels themselves. For Chandler also mentions Marlowe's 'lively sense of the grotesque', his 'rude wit' that stamps him as a man of his age, his loneliness and pride. In any case the soliloquy is a digression in an article basically concerned to protest against the escapism of the formal detective story.

The Simple Art of Murder is a manifesto on the need to locate the mystery novel in the actual dishonest world. It must be centred on 'movement, intrigue, cross purposes, and the gradual elucidation of character'. Any powerful theme, Chandler suggests, can provoke a powerful performance – just as there are no dull subjects, only dull minds. He defines his own theme as 'murder, which is a frustration of the individual and hence a frustration of the race'. This central section not only shows Chandler the crime-artist discussing the possibilities that his own novels realize. It is the confession of an ironic moralist made at a time of personal unhappiness. The over-emphasis elsewhere on Marlowe's 'honour' reflects Chandler's feeling that Hollywood had betrayed him. He couldn't be the hero of

226

this particular adventure, and compensated for it by insisting that Marlowe could always be a hero, could be 'everything'. There was a further reason for unhappiness. Chandler wrote *The Simple Art of Murder* after he'd begun work on a novel that was to cause him the greatest problems of his career, abandoned and started again over a period of four years. The temporary nature of his Marlowe-worship was underlined when *The Little Sister* finally appeared in 1949. The detective is in his most anti-heroic mood.

Ten years after *The Big Sleep*, Marlowe charges his clients $40 a day instead of $25. The cost of living rises, but its style declines. The haunted city has grown shabby at the edges, and there are elements in *The Little Sister* that seem like warnings of the years ahead: the angry teenage junkie, the movie starlet who kills her gangster lover, the graft specialists surrounding the studio executive and the agent who tapes all the conversations in his office, the cops frozen into cruelty by a civilization that holds no meaning for them, since all they see of it is 'the failures, the dirt, the dregs, the aberrations and the disgust'. Marlowe shares the disgust. Alone in his office trying to swat a bluebottle fly, alone in his car driving back to a Los Angeles with the musty smell of an abandoned house, he feels that he's living in a 'cold half-lit world where always the wrong thing happens and never the right'. The landscape that he saw in *Farewell, My Lovely* has lost it strangeness and excitement:

I drove on past the gaudy neons and the false fronts behind them, the sleazy hamburger joints that look like palaces under the colors, the circular drive-ins as gay as circuses with the chipper hard-eyed carhops, the brilliant counters, and the sweaty greasy kitchens that would have poisoned a toad.

The story went through several shifts of emphasis in writing and rewriting. Its point of departure was always Orfamay Quest, the smalltown girl from Kansas who turns up in Hollywood to ask Marlowe to find her missing brother; but as Chandler developed the action he seems to have become equally interested in the rising star involved with a gangster, and the absurd yet dangerous Dolores Gonzales, who confuses life with the B movies in which she plays small parts. A Hollywood in subliminal decline still casts a powerful spell over most of the characters, as they try to live out fantasies of rags to riches, of glamorous gangsters, of wild romantic passion. With her pseudo-Mexican manner, her black jodhpurs and scarlet scarves, Dolores talks about herself as if reciting lines from her last south-of-the-border cheapie: 'I must have men, amigo. But the man I loved is dead. I killed him. That man I would not share.' Her madness is outrageous, yet she passes for sane. Stabbed by her ex-husband, she dies with 'the dim ghost of a provocative smile' on her lips, playing out her role to the end and apparently pleased with it.

This sinister burlesque, one of Chandler's most electrifying creations, finally unbalances the novel. The shy and prim little sister, gradually revealed as a blackmailer, is edged off the stage. She dissolves in a series of deaths and episodes, disturbingly well rendered but not so well organized, that dissolve in turn in too many explanations. For the first time Chandler is not drawing on *Black Mask* material, and the result combines technical uncertainty with a new creative thrust. *The Little Sister* leaves an earlier world behind because times have changed. Marlowe finds postwar Los Angeles overrun by big money and a riffraff style of living, a city with 'no more personality than a paper cup'. Neon lights and false fronts provide the window dressing for squalor and unease. The out-of-towners from their Kansas frame houses, Orrin Quest blackmailing his big sister, the actress in love with the gangster, and the greedy little sister arriving to cut herself in, are provincial imitators of the endemic fast-dollar dream. People who used to sleep in their gardens on summer nights now lock themselves inside for fear of robbery. Formerly elegant hotels have grown seedy and the suburban idea of elegance is a three-car garage.

In the beach city rooming house, smelling of gin and marijuana and stale dishes, the manager lies on a bed with an icepick stuck in the back of his neck. So does the man wearing a shirt and a toupee in room 332 of the hotel with sagging chairs and Muzak. In the silent expensive hilltop house, the blonde in a rented fur-coat has just shot the gangster, who sits in a high-backed chair with a carnation in his lapel, staring rigidly at the ceiling. Dislocated images of violence and the discovery that everyone has his price tag turns Los Angeles into the Great Wrong Place, which Auden perceived as the real background of Chandler's work. Marlowe himself echoes the feeling:

Let the telephone ring, please. Let there be somebody to call up and plug me into the human race again. Even a cop ... Nobody has to like me. I just want to get off this frozen star.

As he grew older, Chandler felt himself becoming more interested in 'moral dilemmas' than in who killed who. He even wondered whether he shouldn't 'retire and leave the field to younger and more simple men'. The feeling dates from the time that he finished the first draft of *The Long Goodbye,* begun in 1950 and published at the end of 1953. While working on the longest and most ambitious novel of his career, Chandler also woke in the middle of the night 'with dreadful thoughts', terrified at a prospect of loss and solitude, for his wife had developed the fibrosis of the lungs that was slowly weakening and killing her.

He had intended to write a novel with only one murder, but ended up with two, still far below his usual average. The result is his purest example of a mystery based on character exposition, and once more the dominant character remains largely an off-stage presence. Terry Lennox, whom Marlowe meets in the opening scene, is reported to have committed suicide in Mexico forty pages later. He doesn't reappear until the last few pages, yet controls all the intervening action, since the mystery hinges on whether he killed his rich wife or whether his confessional suicide note was a fake.

For Marlowe the most important question is whether Lennox himself is a fake. At their first meeting, an instant friendship develops. The drunk with the prematurely white hair and the scarred face seems at once young and old, dissolute and innocent. 'I'm a weak character,' he tells Marlowe. 'Mostly I just kill time, and it dies hard.' He uses ironic evasions like 'There's always a price tag' to explain the rich wife he doesn't love and his affection for a couple of Vegas gangsters. Yet while he writes himself off, he talks about honour and pride. When the wife is murdered, and all the evidence points to Lennox as the murderer, Marlowe believes in his innocence and helps him escape to Mexico. Thrown in jail for refusing to cooperate with the police, he sticks to his belief even after Lennox's suicide note closes the case. The end proves

Marlowe's instincts right and wrong. Although not a murderer, the man who talked of honour is still a fake. After using Marlowe to get himself out of a jam, he tries to buy forgiveness.

In spite of its complex and perfectly organized mystery, *The Long Goodbye* is first of all a study of Chandler's private eye as he reaches the end of his emotional tether. He not only feels a sudden desire for friendship but considers an involvement with a married woman in her late thirties, the sister of Lennox's wife. Linda Loring decides to divorce her husband and wants to marry Marlowe. In a lonely hearts scene before she leaves for Europe, she asks to be loved as well as made love to. Marlowe agrees to the second but not to the first, partly because she's too rich, partly because he's still not ready to give up the habit of independence. By the end of the novel he has said two goodbyes.

A narrator who calls himself 'one of the few honest people I have ever known' is attracted, mystified and finally saddened by a man in love with money. The narrator is Nick Carraway and the man is *The Great Gatsby,* but Chandler's narrator has the same experience with Lennox and his world. *The Long Goodbye* is equally concerned with the trap of wealth, its impact on an outsider, its connections with violence, the wreckage of promising lives. Marlowe's goodbye to Lennox, disguised as a Mexican after plastic surgery, is touched with a powerful disillusion: 'You had nice ways and nice qualities, but there was something wrong . . . You were just as happy with mugs or hoodlums as with honest men. Provided the hoodlums spoke fairly good English and had fairly acceptable table manners.' Since Lennox formerly used the name of Paul Marston. Chandler's story implies a curious subterranean link between the two men. The shared initials suggest an alter ego that reflects Marlowe's, and perhaps everybody's, potential for corruption. Throughout the novel they often echo each other, as if to show the hairbreadth separating lives of honesty and fraud.

Lennox tells Marlowe that the rich have no real fun but don't recognize it because 'they never had any'. Later, Marlowe listens open-mouthed to Lennox's father-in-law, a newspaper magnate, deliver an angry monologue on his need to buy privacy. The old man denounces the public world, newspapers included, as a huge disgusting swindle that specializes in beautifully packaged junk. 'You've got a hundred million dollars,' is Marlowe's reaction, 'and all it has brought you is a pain in the neck.' Soon after they meet, Marlowe warns Lennox that he doesn't like hoodlums, and Lennox answers: 'That's just a word . . . We have that kind of world.' Near the end of the novel, Marlowe echoes him again:

'We're a big, rough, rich, wild people and crime is the price we pay for it, and organized crime is the price we pay for organization . . . Organized crime is just the dirty side of the sharp dollar.'
'What's the clean side?'
'I never saw it . . .'

The real murderer is again a woman, but a total departure from the greedy ambitious creatures of Chandler's previous work. In the past, Eileen Wade has been briefly and violently in love with Lennox. She meets him again years later, when she's unhappily married to a successful alcoholic novelist, and he seems broken and cynical. She withdraws into a frustrated romantic fantasy of a lost and perfect love, and in an eerie psychotic moment, heightened by moonlight and sleeping pills, she even confuses Marlowe with Lennox: 'I always knew you would come back . . . All these years I have kept myself for you.'

Classifying the various types of killers he's encountered, Marlowe sees her as the killer in love with the idea of death, 'to whom murder is a remote kind of suicide'. In *The Long Goodbye* almost everyone is haunted by the idea of some kind of suicide. Its narrative excitement and wit contain an overview of aching maladjusted lives. The power-obsessed millionaire has a lonely sour intelligence. The novelist is adrift in self-pity. 'I always find what I want,' Linda Loring says. 'But when I find it, I don't want it any more.' And Lennox finally confesses to Marlowe:

'An act is all there is. There isn't anything else. In here' – he tapped his chest with the lighter – 'there isn't anything. I've had it, Marlowe. I had it long ago.'

Only cops and hoodlums remain pitiless and unpitied.

The Long Goodbye is the end of an imaginative line first charted in the thirties, and its beginning even echoes the opening paragraphs of *The Curtain* (1936). Chandler used other elements of this story for *The Big Sleep,* but not the prologue in which Carmady-Marlowe sees a drunken young man in a Rolls-Royce outside a fashionable restaurant, then encounters him again a few days later, down and out on Hollywood Boulevard. There is something 'innocent and honest' in his eyes, 'something I don't get much of in my business'. Two pages later he disappears from the story, shot by a gangster with whom he'd been involved. *The Curtain* shows how Marlowe's end was in his beginning. It also shows how far Chandler travelled, developing his most complex melodrama from this early fragment. Marlowe was always on the alert for someone 'innocent and honest'. Many false alarms later, he is still on his frozen star.

He is rescued at the end of *Playback* (1958), on which Chandler worked intermittently for three years, recasting the mechanical plot of an old unproduced movie script. After winding up the case, Marlowe receives a long-distance call from the honest though not innocent Linda Loring, and agrees to marry her. In the unfinished *Poodle Springs Story,* begun in 1959, the private eye and the millionairess have set up house together in Palm Springs. Its opening chapters are not promising, and Chandler's letters to a friend reveal his doubts: 'A fellow of Marlowe's type shouldn't get married, because he is a lonely man, a poor man, a dangerous man, and yet a sympathetic man, and somehow none of this goes with marriage.' He rightly suspected that his creative batteries were running low, and his career lost its momentum when his wife died a few months after publication of *The Long Goodbye.* The decision to marry off Marlowe is only convincing as a gesture of private loneliness. Later he foresaw Marlowe's escape from marriage – 'I don't think it will last' – but not from his battle with a world of self-perpetuating corruption. Marlowe knew that he would 'always be awakened at some inconvenient hour by some inconvenient person to do some inconvenient job'. He knew that the law was at best a very imperfect mechanism: 'If you press exactly the right buttons and are also lucky, justice may show up in the answer.' And he didn't give a damn who was elected president, because it would always be a politician.

But while he always felt something 'unbeatable' in Marlowe, Chandler no longer felt it in himself. He was sixty-seven when his wife died at the age of eighty-three, and he lost 'the light of my life, my whole ambition'. He moved his personal belongings into her bedroom and slept there. On what would have been their thirty-first wedding anniversary, he filled the empty house with red roses and drank champagne, like Marlowe in *The Long Goodbye* drinking a gimlet in memory of Terry Lennox. A few days later he threatened to kill himself. A few days after this he got very drunk, went into the bathroom, sat on the shower floor and fired two shots. Both hit the ceiling. He tried to put the gun in his mouth, then blacked out. He spent a week in a private sanatorium, then decided to sell the house in La Jolla and move to England. He lived in London for a year, drinking heavily. Back in New York, he collapsed from alcoholism and malnutrition, but after five days of treatment woke up feeling 'absolutely happy, for the first time since my wife died'. The next year he finished *Playback*, returned to England for a while, then settled in his new house in La Jolla. Before he died in 1959, aged seventy, he burned all the personal letters in his files, including those to his wife.

Brought up by two older women, his mother and his grandmother, and then marrying a third, Chandler wrote novels about people who desperately needed protection, from themselves and from 'a world gone wrong'. Part of what has gone wrong is suggested in the way Chandler equates sexuality as well as violence with danger. His novels are a notable addition to the popular mythology that represents death as a woman. The supreme example, Velma in *Farewell, my Lovely,* wants not only money but control, and reverses the usual situation by using men as sex objects. Chandler's finest grotesque scene of the woman as dominant partner in a marriage occurs when Velma commands Marlowe to kiss her. Her tongue enters his mouth just as her husband enters the room. Velma ignores him, her face half-dreamy and half-sarcastic. The elderly millionaire merely says, 'I beg your pardon, I'm sure', and goes out again. Relations between the sexes are part of the violence, and Chandler's women kill out of hatred as well as greed.

Chandler's wife was evidently the dominant partner in their marriage and a rare instance of female power that he found challenging yet benign. She could make him feel that he'd never written anything worth her attention, but that one day he might. Harder to please than a nice girl but past the age of sexual threat, she seems to have exerted an idealized romantic hold. After her death at eighty-three Chandler wrote that she'd always been 'the beat of my heart' and 'the music heard faintly at the edge of sound'. A figure beyond wife or lover, she provided a kind of magic shelter from which to contemplate streets dark with something more than night. Protected, Chandler could imagine a man who walked them without protection. Willingly tied, he could conceive a man who refused all ties. Reserved and domesticated, he could identify with the freewheeling bachelor in the provisional apartment, surviving innumerable blows on the head and the sequel of waking up in strange rooms, setting himself against gangsters and law-enforcers who behaved like gangsters. The projection of solitude is a fear from which Chandler himself escaped. Sex as aggression is a motive he never felt. Violence and greed offended a private sensibility which took revenge through anger and wit. Writing from hallucination rather than experience, he created a danger zone that has all the casual astonishing detail of dreams. Like dreams, it contains a quota of divination. Today, Chandler would find that reality has caught up with him. 'He knew it when,' as they say.

SEVEN

The Benefits of Shock

If you create the fear, you've got to relieve it.
Alfred Hitchcock

The first fear quickened in Alfred Hitchcock, he has often told interviewers, when he was five years old. Wishing to punish his son for an offence he never knew he'd committed, probably nothing more than an early habit of wandering off through the London streets alone, Mr Hitchcock sent him with a note to a family friend, the local police inspector. 'This is what we do to naughty boys,' the inspector explained as he locked the child in a prison cell. Release came after only fifteen minutes, but it came too late to release an incurable fear of the police.

The combination of Catholic and cockney is unusual in England. Hitchcock's parents formed it. As a poultry dealer in the East End the father was socially underprivileged, a member of the lower class, 'in trade' according to the merciless phrase of the time. Born in 1899, the son grows up on the wrong side of the class barrier in the early twentieth century, like D. H. Lawrence a few years before him. 'Class makes a gulf,' Lawrence wrote, 'across which all the best human flow is lost.' For the exceptional victim it also creates an image of prison and solitude.

The son recalls the father as a cunning but nervous disciplinarian, and himself as a quiet unsocial child, saying little but observing much. Enrolled in a Jesuit college, he soon begins to fear divine as well as human law. Priests become spiritual policemen who summon the spectre of evil and the terror of involvement with it. They establish a painful link between crime and punishment, the same whipping of hands with a hard rubber cane that Conan Doyle endured. For Hitchcock they also connect fear and suspense, since part of the intimidation ritual is to inform a victim that his name has been

235

entered in the punishment register, then make him spend the day waiting for execution.

At the same time he learns through the Jesuits the value of organization and control, begins to see how the habit of discipline encourages the power of analysis. For obvious reasons he doesn't share the ambition of many English children to become a policeman when he grows up. But he discovers an aptitude for engineering and moves on to a specialized school, where he studies and masters the theory of mechanics, electrical acoustics, navigation. At the age of nineteen he lands a job as technical estimator for a cable and telegraph company, and spends his evenings going to movies and art classes. All the main impacts on his life at this time are visual, art, movies, engineering. The impact of Chaplin, Griffith, Murnau and Lang become the strongest of all.

Coincidence takes him a step nearer the future when the telegraph company transfers him to its publicity department, and he begins designing advertisements. A year later he persuades an American film company in London to accept him as writer and illustrator of titles, the captions for silent movies that range from a tersely factual 'Later . . .' to 'Not by accident, they found themselves alone.' Introduced to movie techniques in general, he grows fascinated by one particular aspect. Titles can change the whole effect of a movie. They can not only make actors appear to speak lines they never uttered, but in extreme cases a drama that turns out unintentionally absurd is remade into a comedy by captions alone. Before he becomes a director, Hitchcock grasps and experiments with a technique of audience manipulation based on reversing appearances and exploiting the ambiguity in the single image. And in his early days as a director he sees a short film demonstration by the Soviet theorist Kuleshov. A close-up of the actor Mosjoukine is followed by a shot of a dead child. Kuleshov cuts back to the same close-up and Mosjoukine's face appears to be expressing compassion. Then he substitutes a bowl of soup for the dead child and cuts back to the same close-up again. Mosjoukine no longer looks compassionate, but hungry.

After writing a few scenarios, Hitchcock directs his first movie, *The Pleasure Garden*, in 1925. By this time he's become engaged to a script girl called Alma Reville, later to work on many of his films as a writer. He recalls that until they married the following year they remained 'pure', and that before he met her he'd never gone out with a girl or even taken a drink. But he'd visited a vice museum in Paris and a nightclub for homosexuals and lesbians in Berlin. Driven home by three of the girls, he accepts the offer of a cognac in their hotel room but stubbornly refuses the propositions that follow Finally two girls get into bed together and the third puts on her glasses to watch.

To the standardized trash of *The Pleasure Garden* scenario Hitchcock adds a few reminiscent touches of sexual deviation and cruelty, a masculine-feminine slant in the relationship between two showgirls, a scene in which one of them torments a rich and ancient lover. He also stages a murder in a way that outrages one of the producers, who wants it reshot, offering a foretaste of his ability to shock with a sudden and detailed outbreak of brutality. A commercial success, the film earns Hitchcock a review in a British popular newspaper headed 'Young Man with a Master Mind'.

The pattern of commercial success, with a few lapses, continues throughout Hitchcock's British career, but he immediately encounters a new form of snobbery. Provincial and stagebound, the British cinema is culturally despised, and the few critics who take movies seriously expect art only from Russia and Germany. (Apart from Chaplin, Hollywood is not favoured either.) Socially the new medium is still non-U. When Anthony Asquith, member of a privileged family, becomes a director, his peers consider it 'amusing'. When Paramount opens its new theatre in London, it sets aside a few rows of expensive seats in the mezzanine for upper-class patrons in search of amusement. While the cultural ban on British movies is lifted for documentaries in the early thirties, Hitchcock remains suspect, too popular and too anxious to entertain.

In fact, during his first ten years as a director, Hitchcock is usually working against his material. The plots of his early movies, more than half of them adapted from plays, seem impossibly old-fashioned now. But he manages to enliven them with authentic surfaces and humorous detail, and his technique never ceases to evolve, sophisticating even the creakiest moments. He learns pace and precision from American films, and absorbs expressionist devices (superimpositions, objects as symbols) from German ones. Fascinated by effects – not just in themselves, but as a means of heightening impressions – he explores every variety of process and model shot. Because of his personal background, rich characters tend to be satirized and everyday lives rendered with a keen, ironic attention. Aware of the gulf of class, and of the gulf between his own imagination and the conventions of the time, Hitchcock is already an exile at heart. The 'Britishness' of his atmosphere reflects an outsider's curiosity and ambivalence. Like most of his material, it has little emotional significance for him. Only the occasional situation engages him on a deeper level, notably in the silent *The Lodger* (1926) and the early talkie *Murder* (1930), both of which centre on an innocent person accused of a crime.

These two movies reach moments of genuine intensity, the angry crowd almost lynching the man it suspects of being a serial killer, the loneliness of the wrongly accused girl in jail. In *The Lodger* Hitchcock also explores class antagonisms from both sides. The suspect's aristocratic manner inevitably creates suspicion in a working neighbourhood, but the attitudes behind this suspicion, personified by the heroine's essentially middle-class parents, are rigid and self-righteous. In the climactic scene, Hitchcock shows the lodger handcuffed and almost impaled on a railed fence, his attitude suggesting crucifixion. The image is a striking example of the free association that Hitchcock is beginning to develop in his movies. Many years later he will say that he thinks, but is not sure, that he's outgrown religious fear. In the meantime, for more than thirty years, his movies will refer to the impact of a masochistic Christianity on his childhood.

In *Murder,* the real murderer turns out to be a trapeze artist who performs his act in flamboyant drag. In the original play this character was a half-caste who killed in order to prevent his origins being betrayed. Hitchcock retains the explanation, but it comes now from a creature decorated with sequins and ostrich plumes, and the word 'half-caste' clearly means homosexual. Since he'd have to kill the world to keep his secret, the sequence becomes absurd, but Hitchcock invests the character with a grotesque desperation. He based it on a famous circus personality of the twenties, a young Texan who called himself Barbette and was much admired by Cocteau. This souvenir of Paris dates from the same period as Hitch-

238

cock's visit to the vice museum, where he was struck by 'considerable evidence of sexual aberration through restraint'. The pressures created by sexual nonconformism and their link with violence will be developed later, especially in *Shadow of a Doubt* and *Strangers on a Train*.

An identikit of the artist as a young man emerges from the situation of an innocent accused, the images of handcuffs and crucifixion, the spectacle of a glittery female impersonator confessing to murder. Hitchcock once complained that he never overcame his fear of the police even though psychiatrists had told him that a fear could be released once its origins were understood. But as an artist he profits from this failure by making movies to release his fears and transfer them to an audience. Studying manipulation, becoming as expert as the Jesuits, he masters the technique of suggestion by image. He trains himself imaginatively by using free association within a planned dramatic structure. The idea of handcuffs as a powerful image comes from a newspaper photograph of a New Yorker handcuffed to a negro as he's taken to jail. Hitchcock stores it away and fits it later in the structures of *The Lodger, The Thirty-Nine Steps* and *The Wrong Man*. For many years he finds something mysteriously satisfying in the image of a clean bathroom. ('When I take a bath, I put everything neatly back in its place. You wouldn't even know I'd been in the bathroom.') *Psycho* shows a murderer carefully erasing bloodstains from a shower. As long as Hitchcock has to make do with stories assigned to him, dramatic structure remains an unsolved problem. But the absence of convincing material leads to another discovery: the subject of a movie is only important as a means to the kind of movie he wants to make.

When the subject is obviously flimsy, as in *Blackmail* (1929), Hitchcock seems less concerned to make it believable as a whole than to reach for moments of immediate suspense, most effectively in the scene of a family discussing a current murder, unaware of the feelings of the daughter across the breakfast table, who has committed it. When he's able to choose and develop his stories more freely, Hitchcock works within a deliberately limited repertory of characters and situations to build up a state of excitement in which wanting to know what's going to happen to someone becomes more important than liking or disliking him.

Suspense as Hitchcock conceives it is a curve of emotional crisis, originating in fear of immediate or latent danger. In its simplest terms the feeling can be traced back to his early experience of the prison cell. A child moves through a door from the everyday world into the dark unknown. The door closes, and finally opens again. What happens between the closing and the opening of the door is Hitchcock's raw material. The term in the prison cell no doubt felt more like ten days than a quarter of an hour, and Hitchcock echoes this in his control of the extremes of filmic time, stretching a moment to the breaking point or contracting a day to a few minutes. Based on narrative, his movies gradually reach a poetic intensity. In his earliest works Hitchcock reveals an allegiance to what he calls 'pure cinema', the juxtaposition of shots to create sequences of ideas and associations and also to provide sudden collisions and shocks. 'It's limitless, I would say, the power of cutting and assembly of the images . . .' In his finest American movies he uses 'pure cinema' the way a poet uses metre or cadence, and the story becomes a pretext to fill the screen – a rectangle that Hitchcock sees as *demanding* to be filled – with powerful imagery. Creating realistic backgrounds in order to lead more cunningly into the improbable, he charts a precision course into dislocation. The more familiar and ordered the world appears, the greater the impact of a fearful irrational event.

In a note on *The Thirty-Nine Steps* Buchan portrayed himself as a writer of stories in which 'the incidents defy the prob- abilities, and march just inside the borders of the possible'. Hitchcock shares with Graham Greene an admiration for Buchan's novels and has often mentioned their influence on him. It coincides with his most creative period in British films, announced by *The Man Who Knew Too Much* (1934), which borrows the idea of a terrorist group that specializes in kidnapping and political assassination from *The Three Hostages*. Although sketchy and episodic, the material allows him to create sudden and disturbing transitions as he leads a comfortable middle-class couple down the shabby back alleys of terror. Particular obsessions that will often recur include the almost paranoid sense of danger attaching to public places, with the scene of an attempted assassination at the Albert Hall,

240

and the image of vertigo, when the kidnapped child escapes across the roof of a high building.

Adapting *The Thirty-Nine Steps* itself in 1935, Hitchcock makes no attempt to reproduce Buchan's feeling for the anxiety of empty landscapes, but concentrates on its idea of the sustained chase, to which he adds a few ironic episodes. No longer a solitary figure, Hannay becomes handcuffed to a girl, and as well as being on the run from police and enemy agents has to deal with the angers, discomforts and surprises of enforced intimacy. The couple has no problem expressing antipathy under restraint, but the growth of mutual attraction proves much trickier. Unfortunately the actors are much less subtle than Hitchcock's ideas. As the first in his series of outwardly cool and inwardly passionate blondes, Madeleine Carroll at least looks right, but Robert Donat makes a dull phlegmatic Hannay. Hitchcock was often limited by the shortage of leading movie personalities in Britain – one reason perhaps for his concentration on minor characters and incidental detail. In *The Thirty-Nine Steps* the most striking episode concerns a memory artist used by enemy agents for his power of total recall to take military defence secrets out of the country. In the middle of his music hall act, Hannay calls out from the audience, 'What are the Thirty-Nine Steps?' Professional reflex obliges Mr Memory to betray his employers. A moment later violence again breaks out in a public place, but before he dies Mr Memory enjoys the relief of unloading a particularly technical secret. This weird and touching scene, like that of the trapeze artist in *Murder,* was suggested by an actual music hall figure, called Datas, whom Hitchcock had seen.

Sabotage (1936), a version of Conrad's *The Secret Agent,* brings a change of emphasis to the espionage cycle, focusing more on the inner emotions of suspense than on the kinetic drive of adventure. Although uneven and sometimes ponderous, it prefigures the domestic tensions of a later movie like *Notorious,* and builds to a final scene of chilling intensity when Mrs Verloc decides to kill her husband. Hitchcock devises an intimate visual structure to reflect the idea forming in her mind, Verloc's sudden apprehension, the confusion of the act. His movements imply a guilty acceptance of death, her cry when she stabs him suggests that she's stabbing herself.

The cycle ends with *The Lady Vanishes* (1938), a return to the mood of adventure and the first celebration of sustained virtuosity in a narrative line. A hard contemporary edge provides additional strength. (One reason *The Thirty-Nine Steps* and *Sabotage* seem dated now is that they were partially dated when they appeared, using material wrenched out of its pre-1914 period.) Hitchcock anticipated the opening of *The Birds* as he leads into a crisis situation through a rather ordinary complacent girl. Returning home from a vacation in the Balkans, she meets a charming tweedy spinsterish lady on the train. Miss Froy's disappearance is the signal for an espionage plot to unravel, and the intercontinental express becomes like Greene's *Stamboul Train*, moving in the opposite direction. A few months after Chamberlain came to terms with Hitler at Munich, the British passengers still cling to an obstinate isolationism, reluctant to take the enemy seriously. In a lightly ruthless scene, added later by Hitchcock and Alma Reville to the original script, the train moves to a siding and a gun battle breaks out like a rehearsal for the war to come. The conservative lawyer dies fluttering a white handkerchief. Cunningly, Hitchcock never identifies the enemy but suggests dictatorship in the uniforms of soldiers outside the windows. The secret agents are all ambiguously polite: a suave immaculate doctor who might be Austrian or Slav, an impassive baroness shrouded in black, a smiling Italian who vanishes into his own magician's trunk. Like the British they insist on a code of manners, which is why they almost win.

Against the neutral realistic background of the train, Hitchcock places an occasionally jolting image. Two glasses containing drugged liqueurs become magnified props, shot in close-up, anticipating the row of coffee cups in *Notorious*. When the doctor claims that Miss Froy has been found, he shoots a rear view of a woman dressed in the same clothes, then cuts to confront a false, enigmatic, disturbingly ugly face. He inserts another crucifixion image, strange and ironic, as the false nun in high-heeled shoes is shot while two men hold up her arms, trying to pull her back into the train.

Each of these movies is rooted in Buchan's idea of conspiracy and 'the thin protection' separating everyday life from the attacks of espionage and terrorism. But unlike novels by Greene and Ambler in the same period, they are not political.

Even *The Lady Vanishes* never moves beyond providing a topical frame of reference. For Hitchcock the presence of conspiracy becomes what he calls the McGuffin, a mechanism to set off a series of situations. The vital military secret is only a pretext to invent remarkable characters like Mr Memory and Miss Froy who carry it in their heads. Politics exist to allow Hitchcock to make movies, spies and assassins to create reactions of fear and shock, the bomb to go off in the wrong place.

In his American movies Hitchcock refines the idea of the McGuffin, which grows progressively simpler and more abstract as its psychological effects become more complex. Whether murderers are political or self-employed, the results of their actions are more important than their motives. Hitchcock takes the basic impulse of crime for granted in order to study its effects on other people, including thousands outside the particular story: the audience.

Going to Hollywood to make *Rebecca* for David Selznick, Hitchcock already thinks of himself as an American director. Since Hollywood movie-making now strikes him as the most advanced in the world, the great central studio becomes his natural destination. He has no immediate problem of adapting his imagination to the American scene, since his first movie there takes place in England. Ironically, the Hollywood experience begins with an opportunity to make a British film employing far greater technical resources, and a much stronger British cast, than he's ever been offered at home.

On the surface, *Rebecca* (1940) is notable for sequences in which Hitchcock relaxes his usual pace and allows the camera a greater degree of mobility than before. Beneath it, new effects parallel a new inner movement. The sentimental 'modern' variation on *Jane Eyre*, like its inflated settings, reflects Selznick's rather than Hitchcock's taste. But it introduces a new situation to the repertory, love as an emotional counterbalance to fear, and Hitchcock extends 'pure cinema' to accommodate it, elaborate and almost voluptuous camera movements as well as the juxtaposition of images. A few years later, in *Notorious,* he will bring the same style to the interactions of love and fear. The real experience of *Rebecca* is the release of a hidden romantic.

243

In the meantime, the romantic and the ironist seem slightly at odds in the first American movie over which Hitchcock was granted complete control. The credits of *Shadow of a Doubt* (1943) make a special acknowledgement to Thornton Wilder. An admirer of *Our Town,* Hitchcock sought his collaboration in developing a story about an unsuspected murderer who arrives to stay with relatives in a small California town. But since he later asked another writer to add 'comedy highlights' to the screenplay, a few minor characters (the bookish adolescent daughter, the neighbour obsessed with devising a perfect murder) are exaggerated in a way untypical of Wilder. More central to the movie is the novelist of *Heaven's My Destination,* a dark comedy about a bible salesman in the Midwest, with its lonely disoriented hero at odds with American life. He believes 'The whole world's nuts', just as Uncle Charlie in *Shadow of a Doubt* tells his niece that 'the world's a filthy sty.' The 'merry widow' murderer, looking back with nostalgia on the past, is equally a man with a mission.

The past appears under the movie credits, with an image of couples dressed in 1900 costumes dancing to Lehar's waltz. Recalled at moments throughout the story, it gradually becomes less charming and more sinister, like Uncle Charlie himself. The tune haunts young Charlie's mind, one of several mysterious affinities between them, beginning with their names. The first shot of Uncle Charlie shows him lying across a bed in a Philadelphia rooming house. The first shot of young Charlie shows her lying across her bed at home, their positions exactly reversed as in a mirror reflection. Deciding to send a telegram to invite him to stay, she arrives at the post office to learn of a telegram announcing his arrival. Outwardly she's bored with the dullness of small town life and expects her uncle to relieve it. But the discovery that he's a murderer coincides with a subtle revelation of her sexual longings. She doesn't go to the police but warns him to leave town, alternately threatening and pleading like a rejected lover.

No murder is shown, and apart from Uncle Charlie's disquieting outburst against silly rich women, and the uselessness of their lives, no motive explored. Clues are dropped, none of them final. He has remained unmarried. He takes money and jewels from his victims, but lives modestly. As a boy he suffered from concussion after a bicycle accident. He cares

244

for his niece and is touched by her innocence, yet at the same time despises her 'peaceful stupid dreams' and tries to kill her. Genial and compulsive, delicate and brutal, Joseph Cotten's performance creates a figure of troubling sympathy. And Hitchcock echoes the two-sidedness with his sketch of a flirtatious California widow, as silly and useless as Uncle Charlie claims his victims to be.

Refusing to make either protagonist black or white, Hitchcock gives the movie a suitably understated grey texture. His grasp only falters during and after an unconvincing final struggle on the train, when Uncle Charlie tries to kill his niece but falls to his death instead. Hitchcock told François Truffaut that young Charlie will be in love with her uncle for the rest of her life, but no moment occurs to clinch the point. To another interviewer he quoted Oscar Wilde's 'Each man kills the thing he loves', but the movie never dramatizes young Charlie realizing that she and her uncle have destroyed each other. 'The same blood flows in our veins,' he reminds her, and in retrospect the girl's desire for excitement seems like a false romanticism, as dangerous in its way as the murderer's. The trap of small-town life, touchingly anxious and faded mother, rather gloomy father, at least has the virtue of safety. But Uncle Charlie's death leaves all this unresolved, and while a stunning shot shows him arriving in a train that belches demonic black smoke, he leaves disappointingly on a puff of air.

During the thirties, as he sat in a train moving slowly through a French suburb, Hitchcock looked out of the window and noticed a pair of lovers standing below a high wall. While the man urinated, the girl continued to cling to him. Filed away under 'Romance must not be interrupted, even by urinating', the image is recalled many years later for a scene in *Notorious* (1946). Refusing to be separated physically, a couple continues to make love while the man answers the phone. This movie and *Vertigo* (1958) are Hitchcock's most lyrical yet disturbing melodramas, the romantic and the scabrous interlocked. The heroine of *Notorious* prostitutes or, in Hitchcock's term, 'degrades' herself for love. The hero of *Vertigo* is necrophiliac. trying to re-create the image of a dead girl in a living one. In another Hitchcock paraphrase, he really undresses her while dressing her up.

245

The origin of *Notorious* is a *Saturday Evening Post* story of which Hitchcock uses only a single anecdote: to gain secret information, a girl agrees to seduce a spy. With Ben Hecht he evolves a script about the daughter of a Nazi agent in the United States. The time is a year before Hiroshima. Alicia (Ingrid Bergman) knew nothing about her father's activities before his arrest, and after it she starts drinking and sleeping around too much. An F.B.I. agent (Cary Grant) recruits her to make contact with Sebastian (Claude Rains), one of her father's colleagues now living in Rio, and to discover the aims of his espionage group. Less out of patriotism than a desire to stop the drift of her life, Alicia agrees. Two parallel love stories develop: Alicia falls in love with Devlin the American, and Sebastian the German asks her to marry him. They create parallel elements of suspense, physical danger and emotional betrayal.

Although Devlin is attracted to Alicia, his mission obliges him in effect to sell her to Sebastian, the more passionate man, and to approve the marriage. When he learns that he's been tricked, Sebastian has to save face with his colleagues. He follows his mother's advice and starts slowly to poison Alicia. In a classic last scene, its tension derived from a complete lack of violence, one life is saved and another lost. Devlin rescues Alicia while the Germans merely watch, Sebastian pretending to his colleagues that she's being taken to hospital. But the movie ends with the implication that they've guessed his mistake and will eliminate him.

Until the last scene the nominal hero remains bitter and frustrated, almost outside the action, while the nominal villain is always sympathetic and involved. The pain of Sebastian's decision to poison Alicia seems deeper than Devlin's when he allows her to be prostituted. Caught between the enemy who loves but has to kill her, and the lover responsible for her situation, Alicia sinks into a kind of passive delirium. Rescued by Devlin, she is psychically raised from the dead. The McGuffin, hinged again on the conspiracy idea, has Sebastian working with a German scientist to develop the atomic bomb. It becomes one of Hitchcock's most ironic pretexts to create a private melodrama around a woman who almost loses her life trying to find it, a German forced to sacrifice his cause for love and an American who just escapes sacrificing his love to

246

his cause. The only other important character is Sebastian's mother, formidably autocratic, the first of several maternal predators in Hitchcock's movies.

The settings are deliberately reduced and the action in Rio centres on Sebastian's house, rich with Latin American pretentiousness and gloom. A masterly use of the fluid camera suggests both sensuality and danger. During the first love scene between Alicia and Devlin, the camera follows them slowly from the balcony across the living-room to the hallway of her apartment, as they move reluctantly towards the ringing phone but continue to express a physical hunger for each other. The ritual of Alicia's poisoning is established by a close shot of a tray containing magnified coffee cups. Sebastian's mother picks up the poisoned cup, and the camera follows it, passed politely from hand to hand until it reaches Alicia. When Sebastian throws a party, the scene opens with the camera mounted on a crane, looking down a vast staircase to the crush of guests in the hallway below. It descends very gradually, moving past chandeliers, reaching the crowd, then aiming at Alicia in the centre. It rests finally on a key clutched in her hand, the key to the wine cellars where uranium samples have been hidden in a few vintage-labelled bottles. The climactic movement combines erotic charge and extreme tension, as Devlin moves down the staircase with his arms around Alicia. The camera follows at their pace, pauses to register the reactions of Sebastian, his mother and the other Germans, follows Alicia and Devlin, stops as Sebastian weakly suggests he should come to the hospital too, indicates the growing suspicion of his colleagues, moves again as Devlin refuses, and guides Alicia to the front door. Their open physical intimacy, Alicia's body leaning against Devlin's, seems justified by her weakened state, but they are also playing a love scene at a moment of immediate danger, and Sebastian becomes humiliatingly aware of it. These subtle and elaborate patterns, like the movie as a whole, reflect Hitchcock's principle that the highest suspense rises from a deep emotional underground.

Although *Vertigo* is shot in colour and more expansively staged, in a variety of San Francisco backgrounds, it uses the same visual strategies. Scottie (James Stewart) resigns from the police force after developing a fear of heights. He takes on a private assignment to watch a woman whose husband suspects her of suicidal tendencies. In fact the woman is not Elster's wife, but his mistress and accomplice in a plot conceived to make the murder of his real wife look like a suicide. The novel from which the movie is drawn concentrates on the mechanical deceptions behind the murder. Hitchcock extracts its McGuffin as a point of departure for a study in personal deceptions, and his equation of danger and eroticism becomes even more startling than in *Notorious*. He opens with Scottie literally and metaphorically suspended above a city at night, clinging to the edge of a high roof while the cop who tried to save him pitches towards an alley below. After rapid camera movements and violent cutting have established the terrors of vertical fall, the scene fades out. Hitchcock omits the scene of Scottie's rescue because it's not important. The opening images exist to convey a state of indefinite shock and disorientation, prolonged beyond the moment of vertigo. Scottie is ready for another country, and he enters it in a long silent sequence as he follows Madeleine (Kim Novak) through different sections of the city.

He sees her enter a Spanish church and pray, then go to a cemetery where she lays flowers on the grave of a woman who died a hundred years ago. She drives to an abandoned-looking house, opens the door and seems to disappear without trace. He finds her again in an art museum, staring as if hypnotized at a portrait of the woman buried in the graveyard. By now the movie exerts its own trancelike effect, disorienting the audience as Scottie himself is disoriented, inferring the existence of some mysterious gulf between hallucination and reality and the possibility of emotional free fall. A smooth insinuating camera spies on Scottie spying on Madeleine, and a colour filter surrounds her figure with a remotely greenish aura. Scottie rescues her from a suicide attempt, the visual aura dissolves and yet she remains unreal, telling stories of dreams and reincarnations, responding with a kind of hopelessness when he makes love. The first half of the story ends when Scottie, because of his vertigo, cannot prevent her second suicide attempt. She throws herself off the tower of a mission church, and he enters a period of nervous breakdown.

Later he sees a girl in the street and follows her home. The dark hair and drugstore style suggest the opposite of Madeleine, yet the resemblance is vivid. At this point Hitchcock breaks all the rules of conventional suspense. He shows the girl alone in

248

her apartment. The setting abruptly darkens and only her figure remains. The darkness merges into the mission tower, the girl merges into Madeleine, a few quick shots establish the false suicide, the actual murder of Elster's wife, Scottie tricked into mistaking one for the other. Discarding the superficial mystery, Hichcock frees himself to lead Scottie into darker areas of hallucination. The lover now tries to make Judy into Madeleine without realizing she already *is* Madeleine; the girl tries to please him without betraying herself.

Changing the colour of Judy's hair, dressing her as Madeleine, unable to make love until the lost image is retrieved, Scottie becomes a sexual fetishist and at the same time turns one illusion into another. He embraces the perfected Judy-Madeleine, the camera circles around them, the background changes as he fantasizes himself back to a moment with the dead. Then, as if drawn too completely into his fantasy, Judy makes a mistake. She brings out a locket that Madeleine used to wear and asks Scottie to fasten it around her neck. As she moves towards him, the faint aura surrounds her figure again. It vanishes as Scottie recognizes the locket and the spell breaks. Like the key in Alicia's hand in *Notorious*, a single object seems almost magically powerful.

The agitated cutting style at the end recalls the beginning. On the edge of breakdown again, Scottie can think only of returning to the scene of a crime. He drives Judy back to the church, forces her to climb to the top of the tower. Calling her 'Madeleine', insisting that he loves her, he seizes her by the throat. As she twists away, a shadow appears at the top of the stairs and terrifies her. Losing her balance, she falls to her death. The camera reveals the intruder as a nun, then a last shot parallels the opening again. Scottie stands looking down from the tower on an empty panoramic landscape, his vertigo cured but the rest of his life achingly suspended.

No other movie of Hitchcock's is so packed with obsessive images. The credits announce an abstract pattern of vertigo that the first scene makes concrete. It recurs when Scottie notices Madeleine's hair piled spirally on the top of her head, when he witnesses the spiral fall of her false suicide on the tower, when his breakdown begins with a dream of toppling into an open grave. In realistic terms, the motif can be traced back to the 1934 *Man Who Knew Too Much*, after which it reappears in two minor films of the early 1940s. The climax of *Foreign Correspondent* is an extraordinary process shot, showing both the interior of a plane and the drop beyond the cabin windows as it dives out of control towards the ocean. The climax of *Saboteur* shows a man falling from the top of the Statue of Liberty. Hitchcock will echoe the same moment of terror at the end of *North-by-Northwest*. But in *Vertigo* he uses it as a sustained metaphor for the state of fear itself, and of falling beyond it into guilt and illusion.

Visually the climax links religion (the church, the accidental presence of the nun) with sexuality ending in death. The shot of Scottie and Judy climbing the spiral staircase to the tower even contains the link in a single image. But like all of Hitchcock's patterns, this one exists to be recognized rather than explained. Merging reality and dream, *Vertigo* sometimes recalls *The Ministry of Fear*; and Greene's 'If one loved, one feared' could be its epigraph. Yet the shared Catholic influence only points up the difference in imaginative approach. Greene superimposes morality on instinct, and Hitchcock superimposes form. His movies are ultimately and finely impartial because, as he's often emphasized, his love of making them is stronger than his love of morality. Greene transmutes original fear into original sin, but Hitchcock concentrates on refining the same emotion to its purest state. His 'pure cinema' becomes a process like alchemy, and *Vertigo* provides its supreme example.

In any interview, Hitchcock invariably brings up 'pure cinema', and in any discussion of *Shadow of a Doubt, Notorious* or *Vertigo* he can be expected to quote 'Each man kills the thing he loves.' Asked by one of his more earnest students if he doesn't find Wilde's line 'perverted', he replies: 'Everything's perverted in a different way, isn't it?' Hitchcock's way is to look at a common human assumption and find that it contains something sinister or mocking. In *Shadow of a Doubt* he jolts the cosy family idea of a 'favourite' uncle, in *Notorious* and *Vertigo* he undermines the conventions of romantic love, and in his other major cycle of American films he continues to search for an imaginative context in which to question the safe and the accepted. Their pattern of coincidence and shock becomes a metaphor for the convulsive disclosure of the unknown in the known. Psychological fear is linked to physical threat, echoing the sense of 'evil' followed by punishment inherited from a Jesuit education. In *Rear Window* the not uncommon act of spying on one's neighbours leads to confrontation with a murderer. In *North-by-Northwest* accidental involvement with an espionage plot strips the hero of all his personal defences. In *Psycho* Hitchcock structures the shocks to submit the audience itself to the attacks of a psychotic killer. In *The Birds* the heroine has to endure a sudden reversal of the laws of nature.

None of these protagonists (including the audience) is completely innocent. As the niece in *Shadow of a Doubt* and the detective in *Vertigo* become victims of their own romanticism, the hero of *North-by-Northwest* and the heroine of *The Birds* are due to have self-satisfaction challenged. The general idea of everything being perverted in a different way finally connects with the general idea planted by Catholicism, that punishment is lurking somewhere for everyone.

With *Saboteur*, soon after going to Hollywood, Hitchcock makes a fairly tentative experiment in adapting the format of his early kinetic adventure movies to the American scene. *Rear Window* (1954) is a much more ambitious attempt to graft old and new methods, and to develop parallel lines of outward and inward suspense. But in spite of some centrally alarming scenes, it remains stronger on outward movement and technical display. A broken leg confines a successful news photographer (James Stewart) to his Greenwich Village apartment, and makes him the wheelchair prisoner of a coolly aggressive blonde (Grace Kelly) who wants to marry him more than he wants to marry her. As a release from emotional pressure and physical inaction, Jeffries begins casually spying on his neighbours across the courtyard. From his window the prisoner glimpses fragments of human behaviour imprisoned behind other windows, and magnifies details that interest him with a telephoto lens. Through the peculiar actions of a dour, heavy, middle-aged man, Jeffries comes to suspect that he's murdered his wife and plans to dispose of the body.

The movie derives most of its force from Hitchcock's masterly use of visual implication to recreate a grisly murder, involving dismemberment of a body, storage of parts in the refrigerator, and a series of night-time disposal jobs. Ordinary domestic routines are interrupted by suggestive images – cleaning an axe, wrapping a saw in paper, measuring a length of rope to tie a parcel. Hitchcock assembles these details from stored memories of two English murder cases in which husbands killed and dismembered their wives. (One of them betrayed himself by not knowing what to do with the head, the other by keeping some of his wife's jewellery.) By concentrating on the dilemmas of mutilation, he makes the act of murder seem at once brutal and absurd. In an equally original way he portrays the murderer as diabolic yet persecuted. After realizing that he's been watched, he confronts Jeffries to protest an invasion of privacy, and as the criminal forgets his guilt and stands on his human rights he changes into an accusing, almost despairing figure.

Only the surrounding texture dissipates the total effect. It grows progressively thinner as life behind the other windows dissolves into stereotype: lonely spinster, young honeymooners, childless couple fixated on dog. Figures preoccupied in different ways with love or marriage, they are conceived to reflect Jeffries's ambivalence towards both, and a slick idea excites technical virtuosity rather than authentic observation. Apart from one brief episode near the end, all the action across the courtyard is registered through the photographer's eye. The device creates a dynamic visual tension between peeper and murderer, but makes the other windows seem more like television sets with different series programmed on each screen.

In *North-by-Northwest* (1959) Hitchcock returns to the Buchan approach of his later British movies, but uses the chase story as a pretext for a fable: Establishment man suddenly forced to live for a few weeks as an outsider. The script, on which he collaborated with Ernest Lehmann, found its point of departure in a newspaper anecdote about a man mistaken for someone who never existed. Its protagonist becomes a more fully developed version of Jeffries in *Rear Window,* a merchant of images and an escape-artist in private life. Roger Thornhill (Cary Grant), a New York advertising executive, is kidnapped by members of an unnamed espionage group who believe him to be an F.B.I. agent. He escapes, then has to escape from the police, who believe that he assassinated a diplomat in the United Nations building. Leaving New York by train, he meets a girl (Eva Marie Saint) who pretends to help him but is really a member of the group and the mistress of its leader (James Mason). He survives a series of further attacks on his life and finally discovers that American intelligence has exploited his situation: the Professor, one of its most immaculate decision-makers, knows that Thornhill has been mistaken for a non-existent decoy and allows the misunderstanding to continue in order to trap the enemy. The girl herself turns out to be a double agent; she and Thornhill complete the mission together, then set out on the next adventure of marriage.

The lightest in tone of Hitchcock's major films, *North-by-Northwest* is also the most freely inventive. Landmarks of a private territory flash by as the hunted man moves through cycloramic American landscapes and dodges out of a succession of tight corner. They include a love relationship that echoes *Notorious*, an assassination in a public place, a charming criminal (Van Damm, the enemy agent), a key object (the Chinese statue containing microfilmed secrets), a possessive mother, a sexual nonconformist (the spy, jealous of Van Damm and the girl), a touch of vertigo and a classic experience of terror in broad daylight. The motifs unfold with a casual air, just as the suspense conventions exist to be subverted. Hitchcock has described the McGuffin as 'the emptiest, the most non-existent and the most absurd' of his career. In a story about spies, nobody mentions the word. The Professor refers to Van Damm only as 'an importer and exporter', reducing espionage to a perfect (though sinister) abstraction. In their urbanity and complete lack of scruples, the intelligence antagonists complement each other.

With plot explanation at a new minimum, the movie concentrates on the flight and pursuit of a man already on the run from himself. It becomes sardonically apt for Thornhill to be mistaken for a man who doesn't exist, since he lives in a Madison Avenue vacuum of success. Not unaware of it, he jokes about the initials R.O.T. on his personalized bookmatches. Across two failed marriages lies the shadow of a giddy but devouring mother, the kind of woman Uncle Charlie would have felt compelled to destroy. It becomes equally apt for Thornhill to be wrenched from comfortable familiar surroundings and left to fight for survival in open country. Exposure leads to self-exposure. When they first meet on the train, Eve seems merely available for seduction and therefore exciting. Revealed as an enemy agent she becomes dangerous and therefore more exciting. Revealed as a double agent whose affair with Van Damm is a trick to get information out of him, she puts Thornhill immediately on the defensive. He suspects that he's falling in love with her, and finds the possibility much less exciting than mistrust. The fear of emotional involvement emerges in a subtly offhand and deviously romantic scene.

The most drastic and cunning public assassination in Hitchcock's movies occurs when a U.N. delegate is knifed in a building dedicated to the establishment of world peace. Rapid cutting speeds up the impact, but stretched-out time delays it in the almost hallucinatory sequence of the crop-dusting plane that attacks Thornhill in the Midwest cornfield. This episode comes from an image in the novel of *The Thirty-Nine Steps* that Hitchcock never used for his movie but obviously stored away. Alone on the moors, Hannay surveys an empty and silent landscape, then sees a monoplane in the sky. As it dives towards him, he runs for cover to avoid 'espionage from the air'. Hitchcock extends this scene at both ends. A deliberately paced pattern of shots establishes Thornhill's isolation in a flat unprotected setting. Then the pace intensifies as Thornhill runs for cover, not from espionage but from a volley of machine-gun bullets. The sequence not only epitomizes Thornhill's total dislocation. It grows into one of those scenes, like the shower murder in *Psycho* or the massed attacks of *The Birds*, when Hitchcock touches a raw collective nerve, projecting a paranoid dream of punishment arriving out of the air or from the sky.

The image of Thornhill machine-gunned from the air leads directly to Hitchcock's two following movies, *Psycho* (1960) and *The Birds* (1963). In each the most spectacular effect is the same, an orgasm of violence that occurs long before the dramatic climax. The plane attacks Thornhill about halfway through *North-by-Northwest*. The first and most savage murder in *Psycho* and the first massed assault of *The Birds* take place about forty-five minutes after the story opens. Like Thornhill, the characters seem arbitrarily chosen and completely unprepared for sudden danger and death. As a motive behind the punishment gradually emerges, it forms the innermost pattern of each movie.

The first third of *Psycho* concentrates on a girl who works for a real estate agent in Arizona and steals $40,000 that her employer hands her to deposit in the bank. She drives out of Phoenix in a state of panic, uncertain where she means to go. For some time Hitchcock leads the audience to expect a story about the girl's predicament, whether she'll be caught, or have a crisis of conscience, or offer the money to her penniless lover. She stops for the night at an empty isolated motel. Its manager is Norman Bates (Tony Perkins), a shy but friendly young man who engages her in a long, curious conversation about his hobby of taxidermy (stuffed owls look down from the office walls) and his feeling that life is a series of 'private traps'. Norman's most serious trap appears to be his invalid mother, of whom he's obviously afraid and who lives in a California Gothic mansion above the motel. The girl says good night to Norman, then takes a shower before going to bed. Time is stretched out as the girl turns her face to the jet. She seems to derive sensual pleasure from it, and also perhaps to express an unconscious need to cleanse herself. The stream of water carries and diffuses light like a stained-glass window. A blurred female figure appears on the other side of the shower curtain, and Hitchcock compresses a murder into seventy close-ups and forty-five seconds of film – 'pure cinema' in the cause of pure brutality, repeated thrusts of a knife and spurts of blood, a screaming mouth, a huge glazed single eye, a hand sliding down a wall, a face hitting the floor. A quiet but equally astonishing sequence follows. Norman Bates enters the shower carrying a pail and mop. Like an obedient son trained to clean up after his untidy mother, he erases all the bloodstains, wipes the floor, flushes the toilet, drags out the naked body and leaves the little bathroom impeccably pure and white. Putting the girl's body in the trunk of her car and driving it to a nearby pond, he seems more childlike than ever, greedily munching candy as he watches the car sink into the muddy water.

With his massacre of a girl who appeared to be the movie's leading character, Hitchcock leaves the audience dazed and

255

completely on its own. Three other characters appear or re-appear: the girl's lover, her sister, and an insurance agent assigned to trace the stolen money. The same briefly glimpsed figure of Mrs Bates soon stabs the agent; the lover and sister remain sketchy and at an emotional distance, so the audience has no one to identify with – except Norman.

Hitchcock later compared the audience of *Psycho* to people entering the haunted house in a fairground and demanding to be scared. The real purpose behind his movie is to analyse the mass mind, not Norman's. After an extended period of false alarm, he manoeuvres a victim-audience into total shock and locks it in the same room with a dangerously disturbed young man, the proven accomplice of his mother's crimes. By imply-ing that Norman is also a victim, he excites sympathetic cross-currents and a degree of mass identification. The next step is even more cunning. Without alienating the audience's affec-tion for Norman, Hitchcock reveals him as the actual murderer.

Years ago the boy killed his widowed mother because he believed she'd taken a lover. Since then he's inhabited a secret twilight zone, talking to a fully dressed skeleton stuffed with sawdust and 'becoming' his mother when sexual tensions com-pel him to murder again. Yet the final image of Norman, huddled inside a blanket under a bare police station wall, makes him pitiable rather than obscene. As he notices a fly settle on his hand, Hitchcock briefly superimposes the mother's face on the son's. Then Norman decides not to kill the fly because Mother never like violence. Lapsing into a terminal confusion of identities, he is still a victim – not of his mother, as Hitchcock first led the audience to believe, but of a psychosis. It places him beyond moral judgement, and his persisting childishness seems like a reminder of the fact.

The subject is horrible, as Hitchcock has said; unrelieved by a single admirable character; yet it arouses a strong mass emotion. He attributes this to the power of film-making. The deceptively modest black-and-white style conceals a subtle and barbed skill, but the mass reaction it generates is not abstract. Hitchcock begins his play on audience fears with the relatively easy ploy of establishing emotional complicity with a thief. He ends by cementing it with a deranged killer. To elicit such a powerful response is to touch another collective nerve.

Norman's act of mass hypnosis shows that instinctual fears and fascination with violence are more conclusive than acquired morality.

The Birds shifts the phobias of a solitary individual to some traditional feathered friends. It derives from a story by Daphne du Maurier, itself derived from a short novel by Arthur Machen, *The Terror*, in which people are also attacked by moths and farm animals. Machen's fable, against a background of the First World War, implies that the animal kingdom has lost respect for the human empire: 'Hence, I think, the Terror. They have risen once – they may rise again.' Although Hitchcock's movie withholds any specific explanation, its human characters are uncertain and conflicted, and the end suggests the birds only pausing before their next assault. Hitchcock once said that he conceived his films as 'beneficial shocks', aimed to disturb the false equilibrium of civilized manners and to jolt emotional numbness. The intent certainly appears strongest in his extraordinary series of movies made in the late fifties and early sixties, *Vertigo, North-by-Northwest, Psycho* and finally *The Birds*.

Although an early shot of birds against a darkly clouded sky strikes a throwaway warning note, the movie develops at first like a romantic comedy of manners. As in *Psycho*, Hitchcock approaches the central situation by way of a detour. A rich San Francisco girl (Tippi Hedren) begins a flirtation with a handsome but stolid lawyer (Rod Taylor) who lives in Bodega Bay, an oceanside community farther up the coast. When she buys a pair of love birds as a birthday present for his young sister, Hitchcock lightly extracts two metaphors from the scene: Melanie's own life in a gilded cage, and the conventional association of birds with love and friendship. When the attacks begin, a third and contradictory metaphor emerges. The birds swoop down on the centre of town, and as Melanie takes refuge in a glass-walled phone booth, the usual roles are reversed. Birds become masters, the human being is trapped in a cage. By the end, while the connection between birds and love has not been entirely broken, it seems very insecure. As Melanie and the lawyer's family escape from Bodega Bay, the young sister asks if she can bring her love birds along. Hundreds of gulls and crows respond to this innocent act of faith with an ambiguous stillness, watching and muttering as the car drives away.

The birds always pause and regroup between attacks, their plan of campaign as enigmatic as their motives. Like the schoolboy registered for punishment by the Jesuits, each character in the movie suspects his name has been entered for corrective shock, then has to wait for it. The atmosphere of delayed judgement creates the most disturbing suspense, epitomized in the scene of Melanie sitting outside the schoolhouse unaware of crows massing on telegraph wires behind her. Since her brittle self-satisfaction is Hitchcock's chief target, she has to wait longer than anyone else. Alone in an attic room, she endures the climactic attack. Bloodied and gangbeaked, she revives from a stupor and begins to beat the empty air with her hands, a strange and intense gesture that betrays more than the reflex of panic. The preceding scene has shown the family sitting in the barricaded house at night, a complete human unit now in a cage. Outside the windows, birds start to peck at the slats of wood. Beaks jab and splinter their way through like atavistic fears conjured up from the darkness. Long after they've finished with her, Melanie seems unaware that she's woken up from a nightmare and still strikes out at apparitions. Impartial as ever, Hitchcock never tips the point, but the frenzy and manic strength of normally domestic creatures suggests a form of supernatural possession.

The final image is of indefinite suspense: tribes of birds perched on the ground, on fences and trees, in a violent early morning light. The soundtrack accompanies it with an electronic murmur just above the level of silence. Extremely ominous, its effect is less annihilating than the shot of Norman Bates huddled against a vacant wall, since fear unites rather than disrupts the family in *The Birds*. As uneasy relationships shift into closeness, Hitchcock finds some of his subtlest human patterns. The lawyer's widowed mother begins as a predator no less potentially dangerous than the birds, but ends by recognizing her terror of loneliness, as if the greater terror exorcizes it. Making an effort to understand her, Melanie moves beyond playing games and shows her vulnerability. The lawyer realizes that he underestimated her and depended too much on his mother. *Maybe* there is something in the idea of love birds after all.

At moments the images of violence arriving from the sky are technically unconvincing, most of all when the birds attack the children outside the schoolhouse. But there are two stunning sequences of assault on an individual and on a whole community: the birds closing in on Melanie and swooping down from above the bay on the town itself. Here an aerial shot emphasizes the isolated surround of farmland and ocean, and compels the eye to a few details at the centre, the gas pump on fire, the horse and cart overturning, the abandoned hose spouting water. Most haunting of all is the aftermath of an attack not shown, as the mother drives over to the house of a neighbouring chicken farmer to find him eyeless and mutilated in the wreckage of his bedroom, a dead gull embedded like a signature in a shattered windowpane. Like the shot of Norman's bedroom in *Psycho,* with its chastely rumpled bed and weird clutter of childhood toys and Beethoven recordings, it invades the subconscious by suggesting a mysterious psychic upheaval behind the physical disorder.

Coincidence, so often used by Hitchcock as a dramatic hinge, also haunted the beginning of his American career. The subject of his first Hollywood film was offered, not chosen, yet it released one of the vital patterns in his subsequent work. In *Rebecca,* underlying the gloss of a conventional best-selling novel and production, is the situation of ordeal by riddle and warning that so many of Hitchcock's later characters will endure. Almost a quarter of a century later it is still there in *Marnie* (1964). This movie, like *The Wrong Man* (1957) and *Strangers on a Train* (1951), is spasmodic and rather disjointed, but contains sequences on a high imaginative level. Together they complete an indirect self-portrait that emerges almost subliminally, like Hitchcock's own brief superimpositions, from his work as a whole.

A childhood trauma has left Marnie (Tippi Hedren) with a sexual fear of men and turned her into a compulsive thief. For a rich and highly sexed publisher (Sean Connery), a beautiful safecracker is an aphrodisiac, and he falls in love with her. The fetishistic love story recalls *Vertigo,* but its tone is more literal and restricted by case-history dialogue. Hitchcock finds a much stronger tension in the scenes of Marnie trying to overcome the past by blocking it from memory. Like the birds

259

hurling themselves against boarded-up windows, it forces itself back into the present. Anger and shame and blood have the same colour association for Marnie, and Hitchcock saturates the screen with a violent red to convey her subjective reaction to a spill of red ink on a white shirt, a bunch of gladioli, a scarlet hunting jacket. Expressionist touches recur in the final scene when Marnie relives the trauma with her harsh and embittered mother. A slum street in a harbour city leads to the unexpected dead end of a huge towering ship. The deliberately artificial set and painted backdrop evoke a private place somewhere between the actual and the remembered, and the sense of confinement and menace suggests a parallel with Hitchcock's own childhood.

In *The Wrong Man* a New York jazz musician is arrested for a murder he didn't commit. The first hour provides a hypnotic summary of Hitchcock's fear of the police. Confinement is again the keynote as reiterated images of handcuffs, finger-printing devices and prison bars insist on the humiliating ritual of arrest and accusation, and Balestrero is gradually reduced to an impassive cipher. The tension drops when the emphasis moves to Balestrero's wife and her breakdown under stress, but the climax is again very personal in its ambiguous attitude towards the Catholic faith. Encouraged by his mother, Balestrero prays for a 'miracle'. As he does so, the real murderer is discovered and Hitchcock slowly superimposes his face on Balestrero's, revealing their strong physical resemblance as one merges into the other. Then Balestrero offers another prayer, this time for the wife's recovery. But there is no sign that it will be answered, and Hitchcock leaves his protagonist on the frontier between miracle and coincidence.

In *Strangers on a Train* a dangerously intelligent lunatic proposes an exchange of murders to a famous tennis player whom he meets for the first time on a train. Bruno offers to kill Guy's wife, who stands in the way of his marriage to a senator's daughter by refusing to agree to a divorce, if Guy will kill Bruno's rich tyrannical father. The police, he's convinced, will never be able to solve two murders without traceable motives. Although Guy rejects the proposal, his unconscious reacts with a stab of interest. He leaves his cigarette lighter behind and Bruno pockets it. As an object once again becomes a psychological clue, and its slant recalls young Charlie finding the dead woman's ring in her uncle's bedroom, the human pattern of Guy and Bruno promises a variation of *Shadow of a Doubt*. But this time the innocent attracted by the damned is a blurred passive character whose dilemma (how to free himself from a slut and deliver himself to a frigid Washington socialite) too obviously suggests the victim type. Unhappy with Raymond Chandler's first script, Hitchcock apparently never found a satisfactory writer for the project. He salvages from it an electrifying sequence of a fairground killing and a portrait of an engaging maniac for whom murder is the ultimate adventure. In a movie curiously peopled with unattractive women, Bruno's dazed and doting mother emerges as the only sympathetic female character and at the same time provides a key to his homosexuality. Although film censorship still imposed an almost total reticence on the subject, Hitchcock and a talented actor (Robert Walker) found subtle accents to imply it. Following the classic pattern of sexual tensions that lead to imaginative derangement, Bruno joins Uncle Charlie and Norman Bates in the pantheon of murderers who fascinate by being extreme. Insane people interpreting reality in their own way, they live beyond moral boundaries.

Observing that in real life people's faces seldom express violent emotions, and remembering Kuleshov's experiment in which 'pure cinema' imposed different feelings on an unchanging face, Hitchcock demands a kind of emotional neutrality from his actors. They become masks that disguise and reveal at the same time. Over the years he has created a similar mask for himself – the pokerfaced master of criminal ceremonies. This remarkably calculated act even exploits his physical appearance. The first great criminal endomorph of fiction, Count Fosco in *The Woman in White*, exploited his soothing curves and protuberances in the same way. When Sydney Greenstreet played not only Fosco but Peters and Gutman in filmed versions of *The Mask of Dimitrios* and *The Maltese Falcon*, the secret ruthlessness of obesity became movie folklore. Hitchcock's television persona, the gourmet whose taste extends to crime, seems to make an ironic reference to the type. The defiant traces of a cockney accent and the grotesque effects – he once appeared as an angel, with wings and halo – are all part of a deliberate mystification technique. Reserved by

261

nature like most public showmen, he devises an image both to promote and protect himself. In this kind of absurdism he echoes Dali, whose private and disturbing imagination also finds notoriety and release in clowning.

With their use of photographic realism to convey unreality, Dali's paintings often suggest a single frame from a movie, and a single frame from a Hitchcock film could sometimes be a surrealist painting. Both artists compose in a similar way, using vertical lines to suggest fear and tension, and a horizontal line for space and solitude. Like one of Dali's elongated figures or processions in a desert, *Vertigo*'s final image concentrates its shock on a man looking down from a high tower, the flat receding landscape emphasizing his isolation. Near the end of *North-by-Northwest* Hitchcock creates an extraordinary juxtaposition when two people cling to a high ledge on Mount Rushmore, overlooked by the huge stone faces of American presidents, beyond astonishment and literally stable as rock. Many scenes and details from his movies could be titled like surrealist paintings: Human Being Caged by Bird, Cigarette Extinguished in Fried Egg (*To Catch a Thief*), and as a presentation of the extreme not even Dali has gone further than Young Man Dressed As His Dead Mother Knifing a Naked Girl Under a Shower.

'The sexual instinct, the sentiment of death, and the anguish of space-time' – Dali's inventory of his own obsessions applies equally to Hitchcock. They have further affinities as born Catholics later strongly influenced by psychoanalysis. When Hitchcock was planning a dream sequence for *Spellbound* (1945) he asked the painter to collaborate with him. The producer vetoed many of their ideas as too costly and both were disappointed with the result; the movie itself is disabled by an impossible script, about a lady psychiatrist who falls in love with an amnesiac patient suspected of murder; and yet Hitchcock extracts from the asylum setting some of his most revealing moments of free association. Over a shot of lovers embracing he superimposes a series of doors opening on a perspective of infinite distance. To retrace an early traumatic memory he begins with fork prongs indenting a white table-cloth, which lead to a shot of ski trails and then to the key moment of a child sliding on to the spikes of an iron fence. There is also an image that anticipated *Psycho* as the camera discovers an aura of fear in an empty bathroom, and its fixtures become like menacing alienated objects.

A man who locates fear in a toilet seat, or a bunch of red gladioli, or a piece of rope, obviously finds nothing safe in the ordinary. His mistrust of the everyday article naturally extends to the everyday world, where innocent men are accused of murder but the most apparently innocent also commit it. Describing himself as full of fears, Hitchcock also confesses a need to be surrounded by order: 'I get a feeling of inner peace from a well organized desk.' His movies reflect the same emotional symmetry, their tensions created by his unconscious and resolved by his sense of form. On the most extreme situation Hitchcock imposes an ultimate restraint. His early life submitted him to the polarities of restraint: the repression that excites fear and the discipline that supplies release. For the child in the prison cell, the same door closed and opened. Later a stable and fulfilling marriage helped to appease his in-securities, another pattern that the movies explore when they emphasize parental relationships as destructive and love as one of the coincidences of danger.

The most ironic pattern in Hitchcock's art lies in its relation to commercial pressures, another form of restraint that proves finally stimulating. His temperament demands commercial as well as creative success, since the more popular his movies, the more powerful his ability to manipulate an audience and to reach an area of the collective unconscious. Connecting with millions of people becomes a method of self-defence. Hitchcock has said that whenever he conceives a threatening dramatic situation, he instinctively puts himself in the victim's place. With each successful film he restores equilibrium by putting his audience in the same place. The last polarity emerges as the sound of applause dissolves into the mass echo of his own most extreme fears.

Epilogue

The situation of our time
Surrounds us like a baffling crime.

W. H. Auden,
New Year Letter

As a Jew in Paris during the German occupation, Sartre found himself enjoying the constant threat of arrest. It alerted his imagination and proved an antidote to habit. The potential victim entered into the same relation to danger as the potential murderer, prepared to accept the challenge of the extreme and the unknown.

Murder as an expression of individuality is implicit in the novels of the first crime-artist, Wilkie Collins, above all in his portrait of Fosco in *The Woman in White*. The expanded criminal mind has an imagination of the extreme, going beyond the act of killing to espionage, hypnotism, the use of drugs to control human behaviour, even the preservation of the body after death by a method of freezing it. Bordering on the magical, referred to as a magician by several other characters in the novel, he combines the criminal and the occult at a time when interest in both happened to synchronize. As Collins develops the art of the crime novel, Frederic Myers begins his research into psychic phenomena in England, the Fox sisters excite America with the possibilities of spiritualism, and Madame Blavatsky records her transcendental exploits in the Far East. The public responds to both experiences, partly to escape the routines of increasingly mechanized life, but partly because the exploration of criminal reality has a natural link with the pursuit of the irrational.

In *The Woman in White* disturbing and apparently inexplicable things happen, then rational forces undertake to detect and explain them. But when the irrational events have been accounted for, real fears arise to replace imaginary ones. Although Fosco dies, he leaves behind an aura of dangerous

265

ideas, notably that solved crimes are only the tip of the iceberg, crime itself is more exciting and often more rewarding than honesty, and good and evil will become meaningless when the chemist-magician learns to stimulate or tranquillize anyone to behave out of character. Like all subversives, he has a touch of the prophet. With later events already authenticating his first two claims, psychoanalysis and chemotherapy are now engaged in trying to establish the third.

The Moonstone carries Collins's other delayed charge, as the psychic steps in to help the logician solve a crime. By the early twentieth century Sherlock Holmes has begun to doubt the omnipotence of reason, even when fortified by cocaine, and Conan Doyle himself embarks on a journey to the occult. A few years later Chesterton suggests that while the criminal is a creative artist, the detective is only a critic. To overcome the threat of a powerful imagination, he proposes the marriage of reason and religion. Detective and priest merge in the roles of inquisitor and confessor as Father Brown confronts the criminal with an ultimate Father Figure. Then Simenon confronts him with a more professional antagonist who aims to enter his mind rather then save his soul. Still, Maigret shocks his rationalist colleagues by placing intuition above method and empathy above evidence, once again meeting the murderer on his own imaginative terms.

The first discovery of the crime-artists is that reason cannot explain a departure from law and order since the motives behind it are irrational. Even Holmes, for whom reason is a priesthood, begins to grope for biological and religious explanations of 'the circle of misery and violence and fear'. For all his ingenuity in exposing the criminal, he remains unsure that he understands him. Father Brown claims to reach him as a sinner, but this assumes that all criminals have a sense of sin. While Maigret comes much closer than either, he still represents authority and is not a free agent. The nature of great detective figures is that they can only approach the hunted from the hunter's point of view.

Buchan revises the balance. Bored by 'suburbanism' and all the safe routines of life, Hannay responds to the criminal as a destructive creator and recognizes the part of himself that finds release in danger. But the Hannay novels suggest more than the emotional hold of crime on the ordinary impatient man. They raise the fear that it has secretly penetrated many levels of society, including the most respectable. With their paranormal techniques of disguise, Hannay's opponents reassert the links between crime and magic. (Forty years later, Kim Philby provides an odd confirmation of this view: 'The first duty of an underground worker is to perfect not only his cover story but also his *cover personality*.') They are also powerfully organized. The central idea behind *The Thirty-Nine Steps* and *The Three Hostages* is that nihilists have formed syndicates not to rule the world but to destroy it. In spite of Buchan's naive political views, it serves as an effective metaphor for crime as an active force in societies so 'accustomed to death and pain' that they risk being absorbed by it.

More realistically identified, syndicates recur during the thirties in the novels of Greene and Ambler. In *A Gun for Sale* and *The Mask of Dimitrios* governments conspire with armament manufacturers to produce a climate of violence. Moving beyond the political issues, Greene and Ambler agree that violence is also part of the climate of human nature, but moving beyond the current symptoms to the unending cause, they diverge. Ambler perceives the naked ape disguised in velvet, and Greene a spiritual battlefield lying 'under the shadow of religion – of God and the Devil'. Simenon in his non-Maigret novels rejects both points of view and believes only what he sees in the present, a period that spotlights the murderer as a solitary individual somewhat more desperate than other people. After seeing a documentary film about naked apes, he finds them less disturbed and more peaceful than naked men, untouched by the idea of original sin or the problems of material evolution, and suggests that the only valid nostalgia is for prehistory.

Writing like Simenon as a field naturalist and confining his vision to immediate experience, Chandler stays close to him when he interprets murder as 'a frustration of the individual', but moves away when he adds 'and hence of the race', since this warns of a collective rather than an isolated gesture. His restless expanding southern California community interacts with the sexual and success fantasies of the movies, creating a pre-Watergate movement towards profit and power as politicians and lawyers and police chiefs combine with gangsters in the organization of crime. Hitchcock's movies,

267

touching nerves of both aggression and guilt, complete the pattern. They imply that if audiences could dream collectively, they would dream of *Psycho* and *The Birds*.

Whatever the route, it leads to the same existential moment, violence as compulsive overflow, orgasm and excrement. In 1948, wondering why critics kept the crime novel in a literary ghetto and never discussed it alongside 'serious' fiction, Chandler claimed that 'far more art goes into these books at their best than into any number of fat volumes of goosed history or social-significance rubbish'. Far more matter as well, he would have added today, when so many volumes that analyse murderers' minds and the springs of violence arrive at the essential points made by crime-artists years ago. As violence grows at once more extreme and more commonplace, of course, there is more room for analysis after the fact than for intuition before it. It becomes difficult to see any area left for Greene and Ambler to anticipate; Hitchcock's most recent movies lack his usual strong pretext; Simenon has retired. *In Cold Blood* reflects the problem as a whole. Like the artists I've examined, Capote sensed the relation between a particular act of violence and his own life. This, rather than the case itself, gives his book its extraordinary tension, for the so-called motiveless murder – which is only a murder for which the motive remains unconscious, a gesture of personal revenge on childhood – had been 'invented' and explored many years earlier in *A Gun for Sale* and *La Neige était Sale*. So Capote's book is at once a compelling personal adventure and an example of how news itself becomes a novel with the names changed. In the same way *The Confidential Agent*, with its view of the spy as a divided man by no means uncritically loyal to the authorities who employ him, upstages the revelations of Soviet agents coming in from the cold twenty years later. And the recent exposures of C.I.A. activities are only an echo of *The Quiet American* and *The Intercom Conspiracy*, which already showed how the undercover worker could also be an extension of government and even dictate policy.

Apart from the social intelligence of melodrama, of which many other examples occur in this book, there remains the question of the kind of art that Chandler believed he and a few

268

others had created. It began for him with the challenge of finding art where it might be least expected, in a form so often attacked as crude and improbable: 'only a thriller . . .'. This seems to me crucial, since all crime-artists renounce established notions of crudity and improbability, and undertake to prove them complacent. Collins analyses the power of accident, Conan Doyle identifies truth with the long odds, Greene feels his imagination respond to the warning of 'hairbreadth escapes in a real world' and 'the death that may come to all of us' in Buchan's novels, Simenon shows the most ordinary person haunted by expectation of violent disaster. Melodrama projects the same kind of fear that Kafka abstracted into the fable of *The Burrow,* where an unspecified animal lives in constant terror of pursuit and attack from anonymous and disguised enemies, some of them even invisible, menacing sounds that he hears burrowing their way towards his underground shelter. The point of the fable is not the reason for the animal's fear, but the fact that it dominates his life, which he views entirely in terms of danger and safety. The same polarities exist in the world of melodrama, which creates a level of unexpected happening so intense and compressed that there is no time to choose, only to guess. On this level, where coincidence becomes a universal law, there is always the next danger but no perfect burrow. The moment is all.

In an atmosphere controlled by real and imaginary fears, murder no longer seems the great unpardonable act, only the mechanism of the last resort. The best melodrama finds subtlety on the far side of shock by creating complex patterns of identification for the reader (and in Hitchcock's case the audience), forcing him to reconcile the experiences of criminal and victim and to perceive elements of both in himself. He is reminded that the destructive act, in its rejection of conventional limits, has a strong primitive appeal. His sympathy with a victim is undermined by other feelings, that victims as a class are too stupid, or too clever, and somehow deserve their fate. 'The world beyond the door', as Ambler called it, touches off a sense of latent boredom as well as reinforcing latent fear. The detective or protagonist, from Holmes to Marlowe, from Hartright in *The Woman in White* to the heroes of Greene's later novels, acts as interpreter of coincidence and violence. According to his belief in justice or destiny or

269

divine will, he tries to resolve them into an emotional or moral symmetry.

The form is debased when it only creates identification with the assassin, a mark of rather bad writers like Ian Fleming or Mickey Spillane. Apart from exploiting the limited sadistic thrills of violence, they miss a basic imaginative point: the victim as a focus of human accident, an offstage presence who continues to dominate the action, interrelating past and present. The murder of a frightened racetrack gangster, unimportant in himself, becomes the key to everything that happens in *Brighton Rock* and affects all its relationships. The secretary who steals from her employer unintentionally sets off the central action of *Psycho*. At a trial, the murdered wife of *Les Témoins* influences the lives of people who never knew her. A wrongly identified body is the crucial point of departure in *The Mask of Dimitrios* and *The Lady in the Lake*.

In this way melodrama offers a rite of passage, like ceremonial mysteries in ancient Greece, revelation through initiation and sacrifice, knowledge acquired by secret and violent experience. It returns to myth, and even stretches reality to accommodate the occult element of myth, echoed in the idea of the dead continuing to operate among the living, and in the level of unexpected mysterious happening – the unconscious processes of memory explored in *The Moonstone,* the magic possibilities in trained perception of the visible world suggested by Conan Doyle, Greene's hired killer whose actions coincidentally prevent a war, Chandler's Velma who defies the law of probabilities to the end by shooting herself twice through the heart, Simenon's doctor who improvises murder as a last-minute substitute for suicide, Hitchcock's domestic birds powerful enough to peck their way through boarded windows. Here the dangerous edge becomes an extreme limit of the possible and melodrama the art in which, as Gertrude Stein wrote, 'another mystery crops up during the crime and that mystery remains'.

Bibliography

Wilkie Collins

Nuel Pharr Davis, *The Life of Wilkie Collins* (Urbana, London, 1956)

T. S. Eliot, *Dickens and Collins* (in *Selected Essays*, Faber and Faber, 1932)

A. C. Swinburne, *Wilkie Collins* (in *Studies in Prose and Poetry*, London, 1894)

Conan Doyle

John Dickson Carr, *The Life of Sir Arthur Conan Doyle* (John Murray, London, 1949)

Pierre Nordon, *Conan Doyle* (John Murray, London, 1966)

G. K. Chesterton

Dudley Barker, *G. K. Chesterton* (Constable, London 1973)

Jorge Luis Borges, *On Chesterton* (in *Other Inquisitions*, University of Texas Press, 1965)

John Buchan

John Buchan, by his Wife and Friends (Hodder and Stoughton, London, 1947)

Graham Greene, *The Last Buchan* (in *Collected Essays*, The Bodley Head, London, 1969)

Graham Greene

Kim Philby, *My Silent War* (Introduction by Greene; McGibbon and Kee, London, 1968)

Simon Raven and Martin Shuttleworth, *Interview* (in *The Paris Review*, 1953)

Peter Wolfe, *Graham Greene, The Entertainer* (Southern Illinois University Press, 1972)

271

Georges Simenon

Carvel Collins, *Interview* (in *Writers at Work, the Paris Review Interviews*, The Viking Press, New York, 1958)

John Raymond, *Simenon in Court* (Hamish Hamilton, London, 1968)

Roger Stephane, *Le Dossier Simenon* (Robert Laffont, Paris, 1961)

Raymond Chandler

Dorothy Gardiner and Kathrine Sorley Walker (editors), *Raymond Chandler Speaking* (Hamish Hamilton, London, 1962)

Ron Gouelaert (editor), *The Hard-Boiled Dicks* (Pocket Books, New York, 1967)

Thomas Sturvak, *Horace McCoy and The Black Mask* (in *The Mystery and Detection Annual*, Donald Adams, Beverley Hills, 1972)

Alfred Hitchcock

Peter Bogdanovich, *The Cinema of Alfred Hitchcock* (Museum of Modern Art Film Library, New York, 1963)

Raymond Durgnat, *The Strange Case of Alfred Hitchcock* (Faber and Faber, London, 1974)

François Fruffaut, *Hitchcock* (Secker and Warburg, London, 1968)

General

W. H. Auden, *The Guilty Vicarage* (in *The Dyer's Hand*, Faber and Faber, London, 1963)

Lawrence D. Stewart, *Gertrude Stein and The Vital Dead* (in *The Mystery and Detection Annual*, 1972)

Julian Symons, *Bloody Murder* (Faber and Faber, London, 1972)